From the Inside Out

Memoirs and Occasional Papers
Association for Diplomatic Studies and Training

In 2003, the Association for Diplomatic Studies and Training (ADST) created the Memoirs and Occasional Papers Series to preserve firsthand accounts and other informed observations on foreign affairs for scholars, journalists, and the general public. Sponsoring publication of three book series is one of numerous ways in which ADST, a nonprofit organization founded in 1986, seeks to promote understanding of American diplomacy and those who conduct it. Together with the Foreign Affairs Oral History program and ADST's support for the training of foreign affairs personnel at the State Department's Foreign Service Institute, these efforts constitute the Association's fundamental purposes. John Tinny's *From the Inside Out* is the twenty-fourth volume in the series.

Claudia Anyaso, ed., *FIFTY YEARS OF U.S. AFRICA POLICY*
Janet C. Ballantyne and Maureen Dugan, *FIFTY YEARS IN USAID*
    Stories from the Front Lines
Thompson Buchanan, *MOSSY MEMOIR OF A ROLLING STONE*
J. Chapman Chester, *FROM FOGGY BOTTOM TO CAPITOL HILL*
    Exploits of a G.I., Diplomat, and Congressional Aide
John Gunther Dean, *DANGER ZONES*
    A Diplomat's Fight for America's Interests
Robert E. Gribbin, *IN THE AFTERMATH OF GENOCIDE*
    The U.S. Role in Rwanda
Allen C. Hansen, *NINE LIVES, A FOREIGN SERVICE ODYSSEY*
David Jones, ed., *THE REAGAN-GORBACHEV ARMS CONTROL*
    BREAKTHROUGH: The Treaty Eliminating Intermediate-Range Nuclear Force
    (INF) Missiles
John G. Kormann, *ECHOES OF A DISTANT CLARION*
    Recollections of a Diplomat and Soldier
Nicole Prévost Logan, *FOREVER ON THE ROAD*
    A Franco-American Family's Thirty Years in the Foreign Service
Armin Meyer, *QUIET DIPLOMACY*
    From Cairo to Tokyo in the Twilight of Imperialism
William Morgan and Charles Stuart Kennedy, eds.,
    AMERICAN DIPLOMATS: The Foreign Service at Work
Theresa A. Tull, *A LONG WAY FROM RUNNEMEDE*
    One Woman's Foreign Service Journey
Daniel Whitman, *A HAITI CHRONICLE*
    The Undoing of a Latent Democracy
Virginia Carson Young, *PEREGRINA*
    Unexpected Adventures of an American Consul

For a complete list of series titles, visit www.adst.org/publications

From the Inside Out

John D. Tinny

MEMOIRS AND OCCASIONAL PAPERS SERIES
ASSOCIATION FOR DIPLOMATIC STUDIES AND TRAINING

NEW ACADEMIA PUBLISHING · VELLUM
Washington, DC

VELLUM/New Academia Publishing 2013

The views and opinions in this book are solely those of the author and not necessarily those of the Association for Diplomatic Studies and Training or the Government of the United States.

Printed in the United States of America

Library of Congress Control Number: 2013937401
ISBN 978-0-9886376-2-7 paperback (alk. paper)

VELLUM   An imprint of New Academia Publishing

NEW ACADEMIA   New Academia Publishing
PUBLISHING   PO Box 27420, Washington, DC 20038-7420
info@newacademia.com - www.newacademia.com

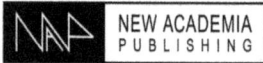

Notice

Dear Reader,

These memoirs are the dim memories of an agèd, failing mind as if reflected in the shards of a shattered mirror. No one can in truth make more out of them. If words, images, and other manifestations have given offense, the author apologizes and begs forgiveness. However, such persons should be flattered and pleased that their existence has been noted, recorded, and identified to their glory and fame. No venal, derogatory motive was contemplated, no greed, avarice, or hope of unholy gain stained the grace and beauty of their remembered words, images, and dreams. Legatees of the words, images, actions, and history of all that has gone before, they are part and parcel of the author's consciousness, psyche, and thus his memoirs.

—*The Author*

Postscript: The author has changed some names; and the manuscript has been edited to conform to the publisher's requirements, for which the author wishes to disclaim responsibility.

Contents

Prologue

For lust of knowing what should not be known
We take the Golden Road to Samarkand.
  – *James Elroy Flecker*

From the crest of the highest dune I have a clear view of the sweep of the entire horizon, an unrelieved landscape of light and shadow. The scene is seductively feminine with sensuous dips and hollows, swelling then falling as if alive, fading into a distant golden haze. It is a horizontal, circular world, immobile in time and space, and I stand dead center. Constant winds whip a feathery pennant of sand from each knife-edge crest. The sand is in motion, yet the dunes are immutable. The silence grows thicker as flying grains of sand sing a solemn, deep-throated dirge of peace and tranquility.

Underfoot the sand is yielding, almost liquid. With each step my foot sinks deep into a palpable softness and starts rivulets of sand running down, down until I lose track of them. So I stand motionless, caught in contemplation of the serene beauty around me.

The unblemished dome of the cloudless sky augments the rise and fall of the dunes. Unmarred by signs of man or beast, the scene satisfies the eye with seeing. It is like a wide, wide ocean reaching out forever yet different. This is an ocean of sand, the Great Sand Sea of Calanscio, heart of the great deserts of North Africa. Here the singing of the sand stills the tumult of thoughts raging in my head and satisfies the ear with hearing. It is hot, but I sweat without moisture, and, beyond thirst, feel nothing in the dry air. I drop to my knees, embrace the warm, comforting sand. Finite grains of sand run through my cupped hands—an hourglass of infinity.

As do human lives, they run their course and disappear into the infinity from whence they came. It is no surprise that desert dwellers facing the unknowable submit. "*In sha'allah,*" they say, "as God wills." The calm and peace are unearthly. Is this heaven?

Alien and unreal, it is not heaven but a vast and little known part of the earth. This great expanse of blown sand is bounded on the east and north by Mother Nile and the Mediterranean Sea; on the south by the jagged, black Tibesti Mountains framing the wastelands of Chad. Westward, it stretches a thousand miles to the Pillars of Hercules. From my vantage point the Sand Sea seems infinite— borders meaningless. Devoid of any other living thing, I claim it as mine, all mine.

For me it is not alien but real, and I am not a true desert dweller. I do not accept the unknowable. I do not know what God wills. The Sand Sea brings together the finite and the infinite. Flecker's Golden Road ends at a mythical Samarkand—the lofty pinnacle of a glorious Foreign Service life. Alas—this dune, not Samarkand—is the last milestone in my journey on the golden road.

To travel that road was my dream of glory begun at the end of World War II in the waters of the Gulf of Panama off the Isthmus of Darien. There, I gazed, not upon the Pacific, but on the heights of the life of a Department of State Foreign Service officer in a glamorous world of diplomats and embassies. Seduced by a beautiful woman, I renounced years of wartime duty in the navy and the seas I knew. With brave abandon, a smile of hope and giddy with expectations, I set sail on unknown waters.

The all-knowing director general, the DG, of the Foreign Service set the tone for my career, my quest, and indeed my life with one direct, haunting, and provocative question. What did he know I could not have known? For half a lifetime and more have I pondered his question.

Godforsaken San Pedro Sula was the beginning of the end, so I start there. Other consulates and embassies took a dozen years of my life; there are chapters on them. Those years were lovely, exciting, my best. The climax came here at the Great Sand Sea. However tightly I clutched at the dune, like the sand, the road escaped my fingers. I clawed frantically at my vision of Samarkand, but it vanished into a golden haze.

An anticlimactic life has continued for decades seemingly without end. The desert revisited is joyless. Years with the taste of disappointment in my mouth were not all bad. Golden years have replaced a golden road. In failing light it is time to set down fading memories of my quest.

These pages in your hand are like the shards of a mirror that once reflected the grim faces with their bitter truths and the sad lies of those who peered into it. My mirror, like a Mobius strip, had two sides, the real and the dream, but only one surface. Shattered, it may not reflect the picture truly. I only hope these fragments will reflect well enough events and passions on the golden road to Samarkand to at last give me, and you, the answer to: "Just where is San Pedro Sula—Mr. Tinny?"

1

Summer 1956, First Post, First Week

"San Pedro Sula!"
"San Pedro Sula?"

Until this moment amid surprised oohs and aahs, some pleased and some not, and with appropriate dramatic pauses, the director general (DG) of the Foreign Service had been revealing our first posts to the nineteen members of my June 1956 A-100 Orientation Class of new Department of State Foreign Service officers. My fellow fledgling FSOs, starting alphabetically with Fred Beattie, had gotten such desirable posts as Munich, Paris, Strasbourg, and other embassies or consulates general. To top it off one man had actually been assigned to the secretariat, the secretary of state's office. The DG came at last to the Ts. "Bogotá," a large and important embassy, he called out for Frank Thomas, who would serve with Donald Ferguson there. Now it was my turn. He called out those three words—San Pedro Sula—and then came the pause, not too short, not too long. He repeated the name, this time as a question—silence.

The director general, redoubtable, revered Ambassador Raymond A. Hare, a thirty-year veteran diplomat and ambassador many times over, pinpointed me with his characteristic quizzical gaze and asked, "Just where is San Pedro Sula—Mr. Tinny?"

Neck muscles tensed, curious new FSO eyes and those of our instructors, suave Jan Nadelman and ebullient Joseph Montillor, swiveled as one and locked onto me. Was this a gap in the curriculum at FSI, the Foreign Service Institute? Surely, the DG would have made it his business to know, at least, the location of each of our posts around the world. Worse yet, was this a test?

After ten stressful years of tests, dashed hopes, failures, and finally one success, just when I thought the agonizing was over, another test? The real question was not the geographic location of San Pedro Sula. Disclosure of our first assignments were kept secret from us until revealed by the DG—his traditional prerogative. It was a playful game to relax us after many weeks of intensive study and scrutiny. The real question was what should I say without looking too dumb or too smart. Too dumb is bad, too smart may be misconstrued. Start off humble.

My struggle to become a Foreign Service officer had begun at the U.S. Submarine Base, Coco Solo, Panama, soon after the end of World War II, in September 1945, and stretched over the next ten years. After May 1945, when war in Europe ended, my ship, PC 1181, had been assigned convoy duty in the south Atlantic and Caribbean, based in Panama. After August 1945 and war in the Pacific ended, a period of hectic demobilization followed, and the PC 1181 was ordered back to the States. While pondering my future and a naval career, I was ordered to take command of the USS PC 586 and keep her in Panama.

During the final months of the war I had met and afterward dated Ruth Beard, a beautiful woman, ten years my senior, and secretary to Captain Hill, the readiness officer in the navy's Panama Sea Frontier Readiness office. Ruth had been in the Foreign Service before the war and although not an officer had reached high staff level. During the war she had worked for the navy. When the war ended, she returned to the State Department as secretary to Frank T. Hines, U.S. ambassador to the Republic of Panama. Ruth led me by the hand into an arcane, unfamiliar, but glamorous world of diplomats and consuls, embassies and consulates, in other words Foreign Service officers and their habitats.

She pinned me down when she asked: "Why the navy when you could be an ambassador?"

Heady words for a twenty-one-year-old lieutenant, junior grade, even if I was the proud captain of my own, albeit small, ship. My ship was a nameless 173-foot, steel-hulled patrol craft, armed to the teeth with depth charges, rockets, a hard-hitting cannon, and sonar and radar gear, designed for antisubmarine warfare and oceangoing convoy duty. Now, as the only active warship assigned to the Panama Sea Frontier and Fifteenth Naval District, she and I were busy with routine jobs such as "friendship" visits to neighboring countries. After the war she was named the USS *Patchogue*.

Propitiously, as Ruth led me down a primrose path toward the world of diplomacy, a notice on the base bulletin board announced written examinations for the State Department's Foreign Service. It said: "just write" to the Board of Examiners, BEX, Department of State, Washington, D.C., and ask to take the exam, and so I did. It was Ruth who called it "so simple."

I heeded Ruth's siren call and abandoned the high seas for high diplomacy and, after bureaucratic foot dragging, went on inactive reserve duty with the navy. To keep my options open while waiting after "just writing" to the Board of Examiners, I took reserve cruises in the next three years to the Pacific, South Atlantic, and Mediterranean.[1] I also earned my bachelor of arts degree in world history from the University of Miami, begun in the navy's V-12 program in February 1943.

The BEX invitation to "just write" was a euphemism for an autobiography, an essay on why you wanted to join the Foreign Service, photographs, and a long application to take the Foreign Service exam. In September 1948 I was invited to take the exam, a once-a-year, three-day intellectual marathon at the nearest Federal Reserve District office, for me, Atlanta. This exam was not so simple—strike one.

Invited back, the next September I returned to Atlanta with Robert Miller, whom I had met the previous September in Atlanta. He too had not gotten a hit. In the intervening year, he and I had rented a small apartment in Coral Gables. The "BEX monster" had improved the exam and what once had seemed so simple again was not. Bob and I again fanned the ball—strike two.[2]

Later that fall, doing graduate work in Political Science at the University of Florida, I met at our Navy Reserve Unit in Gainesville, and married the following summer—on September 9, 1950—Harriette Josephine Hicks, a long-legged, dark-eyed beauty. I thought she looked like the movie actress Jane Wyman, first wife of Ronald Reagan. Josephine had been a WAVE, a member of the women's division of the U.S. Navy, in World War II, stationed at Correy Field in Pensacola and the commanding officer's yeoman. While I tried new tactics to better my chances in a third tilt with the "BEX Monster," Josephine got her Bachelor's degree in Business Administration.

In June 1950, before September rolled around with its invitation to Atlanta, we had a down and dirty shooting war in Korea. The navy promptly recalled me to active duty, and for most of the next few years I swept mines off Korea on a fleet minesweeper, the USS *Dextrous*, Ian Laird, commanding. Mines are treacherous, insidious weapons, and minesweepers are logical casualties.

We steered carefully and swept gingerly that first winter, while sweepers *Magpie, Pirate, Pledge,* and *Partridge* were blown sky high and took heavy casualties. Bodies of most casualties in the center of a minefield were never recovered. One thing smart minesweepers do is stay out of unswept waters. Bravely but foolishly rushing to help a stricken sweeper can be fatal. Mines took their toll on three overly self-important destroyers. *Brush* and *Mansfield* took heavy casualties. *Walke* hit a mine, with 66 killed or wounded, the Navy's single greatest loss of life in Korea. A battleship once brusquely ordered us out of her way while we were sweeping. Our skipper politely mentioned to that haughty and beautiful ship that she was in unswept water. Silent, not brusque now but with a quick puff of black smoke, the "battlewagon" made a hard turn at full speed and in minutes was over the horizon.

Minesweepers are named for birds and appropriate and euphonious words, e.g. *Dextrous,* my ship. I liked our voice call sign, "Expert Easy."

These were tense, traumatic days, the casualties and the war were personal. It was cold on the beach and even colder on the Yellow Sea in the west and the Sea of Japan, off the east coast of Korea. One bright spot in our lives was that we had good Navy chow, well prepared and seasoned thanks to an electrician's mate, Jerry Swan who had served in World War II and had been recalled. Cooking was his hobby. The crew knew when Swan had helped in the galley because everything tasted better.

We were lucky. Most of our crew were downy-cheeked college freshmen, but we had a few key experienced minesweeper sailors. Our most experienced sweeper was Chief Warrant Officer Maurice Rider, a boatswain's mate. "Boats" won his first Navy Cross, the navy's highest award, after eleven years on the Yangtze River Patrol. He manned his antiaircraft gun on the gunboat, USS *Panay,* sunk December 11, 1937, by the Japanese, until the water was up to his knees on the boat deck. He won his second Navy Cross on December 7, 1941, again manning an antiaircraft gun on the USS *Arizona* until she went down, sunk by the Japanese at Pearl Harbor. A World War II destroyer escort was named for him. A man of many talents, his tales of life on the China station must have been true. No one laughed while he rolled Bull Durham cigarettes with one hand and told his stories. He had met and married a White Russian refugee from Shanghai's Russian colony. She didn't claim to be Anastasia or royalty, but she had style. She and salty Boats were a truly picturesque couple.

Boats also knew how to sweep hard to find mines and survive. My ship and our squadron as a whole found many of the 3,000 mines the Koreans claimed they planted in the most concentrated mine fields ever. He would have won a third Navy Cross had we been sunk by the Koreans, or the Chinese. Both tried, but it wasn't to be. Just as well, and not just because I am here to tell the tale.

Koreans planted mines by hanging three or four under their picturesque little fishing boats then dropping them, strategically placed, before we shot up them and their boats. The gun crew on our main battery, a 3" 50, were like Deadeye Dick and didn't need many shots to range in on a fishing boat. Fewer fishermen in cute boats meant fewer mines. We took prisoners, once, a surly lot. After the war the gun captain, whose name was Smith, drowned swimming while on rest and recreation leave.

Other targets of opportunity included the trains and railroads running up Korea's east coast. On clear nights at 19,000 yards offshore, when white steam billowed from a tunnel entrance, we knew a train was on its way. We fired away until there was no more steam, or train.

After thirteen months sweeping mines, Chinese or Korean gunners got our range one day up near the Siberian border. A couple of their 90mm cannons crippled us, but we could still sweep. They killed or wounded four crewmen. Electrician's Mate Gerald Swan died at general quarters manning his 20mm machine gun, and I closed his eyes. Our chow was never quite as good as before; now it had a bitter taste. *Dextrous* earned five Battle Stars in the Korean War, same as in World War II.

Months later we brought the crippled *Dextrous* home to San Diego for overhaul. It was a heavy weather trip with one more memorable typhoon. In mid Pacific a young, inexperienced mess cook on an accompanying sweeper, who had gone to the boat deck to clean his mop, was washed overboard. We searched for hours but didn't find him. His mop was found leaning against the railing. After a short stint in Coronado training for under water demolition (UDT), team five, I was assigned to a harbor defense unit in Norfolk, Virginia. Hauling in a mile-long string of anti-torpedo nets in September 1952, I broke my right wrist. My injury was not combat related, so no medal. The wrist still hurts.

When the armistice stopped the shooting in Korea, the navy relegated me to inactive duty. In the aftermath of a second war, once again I pondered a future up for grabs. Meanwhile, Josephine and I with two sons, Clayton Murrell and David Austin, were in Jacksonville, Florida and had to make a living. We both got jobs. My first job was with a steamship agency, then I took an offer from the Barnett National Bank, aiming for the international department. These were stopgap measures, because Josephine and I agreed I should take my third swing at the written exam in September 1955, exactly ten years after first "just writing" to the Board of Examiners. It would be my final swing at the "Monster," because the next year I would be over the exam's age limit. Like *Casey at the Bat,* a strike would mean that Ruth's efforts and mine, and ten long years, would be down the drain. There would be no joy in my personal "Mudville."

Glory be! There was joy in Mudville. A third swing was enough—I passed the written exam. The next hurdle was a security background check. With my navy history still fresh, although I had no medals, this was not a problem. Security officers did interrogate our neighbors. The third and final hurdle was the dreaded oral exam, cloaked with a great deal of rumor and misleading information.

The time honored procedure was that two or three highly respected senior Foreign Service officers, usually of ambassadorial rank, would visit the candidate on his home turf and give him a visual going over. At the same time for several hours they would throw out pertinent, and perhaps, impertinent questions. At the end of the day the candidate would pass and be accepted or, in so many words, be told to seek an alternative career. There was no argument and no appeal to their decision.

For a change the gods were with me. My examiners, courtly retired Ambassador William DeCourcey and debonair Consul General (CG) Lewis could not have been nicer. CG Lewis, posted to Monaco, had just come from officially witnessing the wedding of Grace Kelly and Prince Rainier III. Later, I encountered Mr. Lewis in Washington and he ruefully told me his son had failed his oral exam.

A Foreign Service officer's first responsibility is to present and represent the United States abroad so we must know our own country. Their main question to me was to explain the process of electing the president set forth in Article II of the Constitution. I was able to satisfy them.

Instead of a grueling exam, although I was aware of their scrutiny, we had a pleasant visit and I got a glimpse of Foreign Service life in Monaco. The two made some encouraging, noteworthy suggestions. They didn't like my necktie, a light colored one identical to one I had seen former Florida governor Fuller Warren wearing. They officially invited me to Washington by Memorial Day, 1956. I asked why not tomorrow? Their secretary took care of the paperwork. My starting salary as a beginning FSO-8 would be a handsome, to me, $5475, *per annum*. At our swearing in I, and other FSO-8s, would be promoted to FSO-6. I immediately telephoned Josephine with the good news and we celebrated with lunch at Jacksonville's modest, old fashioned but much loved Seminole Hotel.

At last my struggle to join the Foreign Service was over, or so it seemed. Now, was my barely begun journey on the Golden Road to

Samarkand, to be derailed by: "Just where is San Pedro Sula—Mr. Tinny?"

Ambassador Hare waited patiently for my answer. Was it possible he really did not know? If so, it was brave of him to admit it. Who would have thought the director general of the Foreign Service did not have basic knowledge of our worldwide 275 embassies, legations, missions, consulate generals, consulates, and special offices, however insignificant they might be?

This challenge, whether an honest question or a test, must be faced squarely. With my heart and my future in my mouth I stood up, faced the director general and my classmates. Sweating from every pore, I dared not reach for my handkerchief. My classmates and instructors, friends now but soon to be competitors in a worldwide battleground for posts, also ignorant of San Pedro Sula and what I knew, were anguished over my dilemma. There was a low susurration of relief that it was me, not them. Please pardon the cliché, but you could have heard a pin drop had anyone dared.

Luck and the gods were with me and I knew much about San Pedro Sula. Yesterday a bright, new, overzealous personnel officer, on almost her first day on the job, eager to show off how much she knew, but not privy to the tradition that first posts were to be revealed by the director general, had divulged mine to me. When I told this horrified, frightened young lady what she had done we agreed to keep it our secret. As I scurried down to the Foreign Service lounge, it seemed "so simple."

The lounge was our home away from home. Our mail went there, telephones, typewriters, stationery, carbon paper, and anything else we might need was there. We gathered and rendezvoused there, although we did have to go to the cafeteria for coffee. People returning from posts overseas made it their first stop. Most important, all the post reports—the lengthy descriptive reports from every post, designed to prepare newly assigned FSOs and staff with information and advice they needed before heading out—were kept there. Updated periodically, the report for San Pedro Sula was only six months old and I read and reread it hungrily.

"Ambassador Hare," I said, "San Pedro Sula is, I recall reading somewhere, a town in Honduras, on the Caribbean side, with probably a very small consulate."

"Thank you," the quizzical gaze never wavered, "Mr. Tinny— please, sit down." I did.

This was worse than the official oral exam, had I passed or somehow revealed too much? Why did I say "very small"? I hadn't lied but was not completely honest. Had the personnel officer broken down and confessed so that Ambassador Hare knew the truth? Was it a test? Maybe he didn't know after all. Would what I didn't know hurt me? That was the heart of the matter.

The latitude and longitude of San Pedro Sula were not the question. The question was where did my crucial first post and I fit into the Foreign Service. Was I on that narrow, uneven golden road so longed for, or was this a bumpy detour to God knows where? The answer to that question remained to be discovered, at a time equally unknown, years down the road.

While our days at FSI on C Street behind "old state" dwindled down to a precious few, San Pedro Sula became a butt of jokes and jibes as details of its post report became known. Honduras it said, is the original and still the quintessential "Banana Republic." The Post is only a "Tin(n)y," (play on my name) two man consulate. The post report urged: "bring a household (underlined) automatic or revolver, suitable for use by a man or a woman for personal defense, with ammunition...potassium permanganate to sanitize vegetables...a strong short wave radio for news... and a spring, or battery operated phonograph for playing Victrola records (in the dark when the power goes off) for dancing, or whatever."

For Josephine, I had a ladies .32 Smith & Wesson revolver my father had customized for my mother, adding a hand carved wooden grip. For myself I had a Colt .45, A1911 automatic my father had carried in World War I and I carried in World War II and Korea. I had a Hallicrafters short-wave radio, a gift from one of my father's rich employers, Peter O. Knight, Jr. an RCA phonograph with a 12-inch speaker and Josephine had a portable record player from college days. I forget where we got the potassium permanganate, but we did. I also had a box full of transformers for converting 220 volts to our 110 volts.

Health controls were not funny; diseases such as polio, tuberculosis, typhoid, and smallpox were endemic, and the dust in the dry season caused asthma. Our two boys suffered from asthma, especially Clayton, the older one. The keynote of the post report, borne out by the frequency of the phrase "lack of" was that the post was "outstandingly boring, frustrating and monotonous." The report ended with the admonition to "count the days."

My colleagues, impressed I had known where it was, and only now will they know the truth, sympathized but were glad it was me, not them. They laughed good naturedly at my expense. They didn't joke about their glamorous posts and were smugly pleased with themselves.

New FSOs had a choice of a departmental assignment or a field post. Ten had elected the former; nine, of our nineteen, a field post. Those who had graduate degrees from either Georgetown University School of Foreign Service, or Johns Hopkins School of Advanced International Studies were assigned to important embassies and consulate generals. Our two Annapolis and West Point graduates, one each, got prestigious departmental assignments. Two Princeton men got top departmental assignments, one to the secretariat and the other to the office of the executive director for near eastern affairs. The former, J. Harden Rose resigned soon after his appointment to marry Georgia Rockefeller. I asked her why she was named "Georgia." She said it was because her family owned so much land in that state. When last I heard they were living on Cumberland Island. A third Princetonian got the choice consulate general Bombay. Our only former marine, and only Harvard man, went where he had requested in the department. Although it seemed random, the five of us who had served in the navy in World War II, excepting me, did better than the five WWII army veterans including one army air corps veteran. Six of the nineteen were from New York, thirteen called ten various states—and one foreign country, Germany—home. Whether married, with or without children, or single, seemed irrelevant.

One of our two women, Winifred Hall, a divorced single mother was assigned to Paris, a contender for best post. The other, Catherine Frank, got Seoul, a political hot spot simmering from the Korean War, therefore a choice assignment. The debate as to who got the best assignment was ongoing and indecisive. Of the five of us who did not have advanced degrees, one got Port au Prince, a poor prospect, three got routine departmental assignments and finally there was me.

All, except me, agreed, their patronizing aside, that the worst post was San Pedro Sula. It was, of course a "hardship" post meaning some aspects of life and duty there were measurably dangerous. It had a 15 percent differential, 25 percent is the maximum, which meant a 15 percent increase in salary or a 15 percent increase in time served. Duty at a "hardship" post had to be requested and I had requested one. That was rather like volunteering for a suicide mission. With its medical hazards, political instability, Cold War tensions and lack of most basic amenities I don't see what post could have been worse. Perhaps 25 percent hardship posts were a myth. San Pedro Sula was the only "hardship" post our class received.

Secretly, I was pleased with a post so unique and obscure as to be unknown at the service's top level, but what did that imply? Was it a suicide post, a graveyard for Foreign Service officers? My future, indeed, my life would depend on the answer, my answer, to Ambassador Hare's question.

San Pedro Sula was founded in 1536 by conquistador Don Pedro de Alvarado from Badajoz. The Mayans called him "Tonatiuh," which means "sun" in the Nahuatl language. A favorite lieutenant of Hernan Cortes, whom he had accompanied into the area two years earlier, De Alvarado was a sturdy man with the thick auburn or chestnut, *castaño*-colored hair and beard and blue or hazel eyes, characteristics of Andalusians. That description would have fitted many of my hundreds of Honduran visa applicants. Some, with the blackest hair, would claim it was *castaño*. In sunlight their black hair sometimes did have chestnut highlights. Don Pedro was good mannered and wore rich clothes, gold chains around his neck and rings on his fingers. He was brave, impetuous and had a "ruthless, brutal unconcern for human life." In short, he was bloodthirsty and cruel to the bone.

Protected by his burnished steel *cuirass* (breastplate), Don Pedro pointed with the fine Toledo blade of his sword glinting in the sun, how his namesake town was to be laid out. To the Indians he was truly a being from another world. His prancing, lavishly caparisoned warhorse was a marvel to them and a beauty, as I found its descendants to be. He founded other towns and governed Guatemala. At age fifty-six in 1541, he and his horse went down fighting in a bloody pitched battle near Guadalajara.

San Pedro Sula is situated thirty miles inland from the Caribbean, on the northwestern slopes of Cordillera Nombre de Dios (Name of God Mountains), the first range of many. The peaks and valleys of these *cordilleras* create vistas of great beauty, conceal possibilities of great wealth, and make travel difficult. Now, 430 years later, Don Pedro, the first Sanpedrano, would have felt at home here in this benighted town founded, not with a prayer or blessing but with his curse of enduring cruelty.

In Spain *hidalgo* is a Spanish word for presumptuous, minor, even insignificant, nobility. In San Pedro Sula the word referred to presumptuous, scurrilous, and even violent rough necks, often teenagers, who paraded around town wearing pistols on both hips in ostentatious locally crafted leather holsters. On some holsters the work was good and I bought a holster for my Colt .45 and one for a machete. After wearing guns was outlawed, the roughnecks were still around but used machetes. There were many armless and handless *sanpedranos*, citizens of San Pedro Sula.

The *peons*, farmers and manual workers, were mostly *mestizos* (half breeds), but not always. Many with the *castaño* (chestnut-colored hair) of both sexes from age five up carried long, sharp and truthfully more dangerous Connecticut made machetes. These accounted for the many one-armed and otherwise maimed Hondurans. Blatant, unnecessary roughness, unwarranted, universal brutality to animals and humans alike, murder, and robbery were endemic. To Don Pedro the unpaved dirt streets (original cobblestones had long since been dug up as old fashioned), grass shacks, adobe huts, the central plaza, the *quartel*, the Army's fortified barracks, and the Cathedral would have been familiar.

Cinder block houses and buildings, the flyblown *Hotel Bolivar*, garish in design and color, would be unfamiliar. A long, narrow cow pasture in town called the airport, with an open sided , thatch roofed hut for a terminal, would have been a mystery to *Don Pedro*. However, San Pedro Sula, close to the important fruit growing and lumbering industries, the main seaport of Puerto Cortes and with basic manufacturing enterprises had become the commercial/ industrial hub of Honduras.

The post report and other descriptions were music to my ears. I was mesmerized by the potential, hidden prospects as had been Don Pedro. Three hundred years after Don Pedro, John Lloyd Stephens, sent by John Quincy Adams as ambassador to the Federation of Central America was enthralled. Stephens searched fruitlessly for the government of Francisco Morazon, a Honduran and only president of the short lived federation. An artist and writer, Stephens revealed the richness, glories, and beauty of the lands from Chiapas in Mexico to Costa Rica. He uncovered Copan, the sophisticated "Athens" of the Mayas. Surely, San Pedro Sula cannot be Flecker's Samarkand, or can it? One thing I know, here I will be the American vice consul; better that than the King of England.

The passengers on the Transportes Aeroes Nacional (TAN) flight from Miami to San Pedro Sula, via Havana, Jamaica, and Belize, displayed more faith in the church than in the national airline of Honduras. They crossed themselves with feeling each time our fat bodied Curtis C-46 commando transport waddled out to take off or circled to land, then clutched the arm or leg of their neighbor, especially if of the opposite sex. Carrying a full load, my wife sat with our two boys who had to share a seat. I was between the window and a nervous Honduran woman with long, sharp fingernails.

The ungainly C-46s designed to be luxury passenger carriers in 1937 became World War II workhorses. They carried tons of war matériel from India to China over the "hump," and in Europe thousands of paratroopers. Despite its virtues many crashed because of inherent design flaws. As we took off I wondered about those flaws and whether this particular aircraft was a veteran of the Pacific or European wars. The décor was austere, a lot of bare metal showed but bullet holes had been patched. On takeoff, with both 2,000 horsepower Pratt & Whitney engines at full bore, pulling with every ounce of power they had, the plane rattled and banged as if it were coming apart at the seams.

Day one. The arrival of the weekly TAN flight was signaled by the plane gunning its engines as it roared over town, to send the people running to the airport, and over the landing strip, to send the cows, prodded by rifle toting soldiers, scurrying the other way. Clearing formalities such as Customs and Immigration were accomplished with a flourish of the consul's hand, who was a stickler for such formalities, and a smile. My wife and I waved our handsome black diplomatic passports for the first time in a foreign land to the glee of all officials there assembled. Clearly, it was no small thing to be the American vice consul in San Pedro Sula.

Charles E. Paine, "Charlie," a direct descendant of Robert Treat Paine, a signer of the Declaration of Independence, was consul and principal officer and our reception committee along with Jay Max Maisel, director of the Bi-National (Honduran and American) Sanpedrano Cultural Center. They were busy introducing us to the people I would know and work with in the coming years. Most everyone who was anyone, Honduran and expatriate, came to meet the TAN plane if only to see who was arriving or leaving. This flight continued to the capital Tegucigalpa, referred to as "Teguc." Notable exceptions were Aida Trau and Lucy Briscoe, the consulate's clerks who had stayed at the office, and Lucy's father, Jack.

Jack Briscoe, a British subject, was the longtime honorary British vice consul and took that role seriously, never mind the honorary. His day job was general manager of the Tabacalera, S.A., a subsidiary of British-American Tobacco (BAT), in the United States: Brown & Williamson. Tabacalera was the largest employer and most important company in San Pedro Sula. Jack was a power in both expatriate and Honduran communities. Diplomatic niceties required that Jack, as the other half of the consular corps, greet the new American vice consul. His absence, and Jack himself, were the subject of much comment. He was, I gathered, handsome, personable, and especially popular with the ladies. Pretty, fresh-faced young European and American matrons—Jack valued experience—were fair game and pursued, with rejection not an option. A measure of his charisma, as a man and his abilities as an all around athlete and expert game hunter, he was liked, admired, and often emulated by their husbands.

The Cold War theater in Honduras was "hot" with ongoing guerrilla attacks on the U.S. owned Honduran banana raising companies and threats by Communist agitators to attack Tabacalera.

Company employees said Jack sent greetings but ongoing "nego-tiations" demanded his presence. He was said to be either at the fortress-like cigarette factory in the center of town, or at his home in the Tabacalera employees' residential compound, which also served under the lion and unicorn as the British consulate. As we left the airport he was in fact in his den at home, cleaning one of his beautiful high powered British hunting rifles; a strange tool for "negotiations." What happened next in that room no one knows for certain, except at least one other person.

Charlie, twice divorced and now single, had graciously insisted that we stay with him in the roomy new consulate residence for a few days until our almost ready house was ready. We all, except Max, piled into the consulate Jeep with our luggage and Charlie drove us through town. In the rainy season the four-wheel drive would be needed, there was not a single paved street. Today was hot, dry, and dusty and with all windows open so was the inside of the Jeep. We were happy and excited as we passed the *quartel* (Army barracks), *ayuntamiento* (City Hall), Cathedral with towers, and the *supermercado* (supermarket). It was thrilling except the last, which was a disappointment, especially to Josephine.

"Ven, rápido! El Consul, Señor Briscoe esta muerto, asecinado!" ("Come quickly, the consul, Mr. Briscoe, is dead, murdered!") We were greeted by this news shouted out as we drove through the consulate compound gates, and the euphoria of our arrival evapo-rated. Automatically assumed, assassination exemplified the life-style of San Pedro Sula and its paranoia. He had been found by his Honduran wife on the floor of his den, shot dead by a two-dollar bullet from his nickel-plated two-thousand-dollar rifle.

While Josephine and the boys unpacked and got us settled in, Charlie and I spent the rest of day one in the office. While I worked on getting a telephone call to the embassy in Tegucigalpa over 150 miles of dangling wire to give them the news, Charlie drafted a classified telegram to the embassy and department giving more specifics. He outlined the dangers of Jack's death on the explosive political and labor situation in San Pedro Sula, the banana industry, Honduras in general, and even all of Central America. I encrypt-ed Charlie's message using a one-time pad, our only encryption system, and familiar to me from my navy days. We were getting news from Hondurans and expatriates worried at the implications reverberating from the crack of that rifle shot. In this commercial center many local businesses relied heavily on British and American connections while these and other foreign interests relied on stability here. Would British-American pull out bring unemployment, recession, and chaos? Commerce defined the two worlds of Sanpedranos. We, the foreign "imperial colonialists," were greedy interlopers. Proud, haughty sons and daughters of Don Pedro de Alvarado, the descendants of the Mayans, and last Jamaican blacks were our downtrodden victims. Was the expansion of militant Cold War Soviet Communism to be their answer?

Rumors about Jack's death abounded even before he was cold. First impressions were that it was an unloaded gun that was loaded type accident. However, that theory seemed so implausible in the light of Jack's reputed competence with his guns that it quickly gave way to the notion of suicide. That too seemed out of character and was about to be rejected, except, that left what? Murder by someone known was too insidious and complicated, too personal, too incestuous, to contemplate. Political assassination by an anonymous *agent provocateur* was more palatable locally, more objective and seemed so natural. Either way de Alvarado would have understood and have been pleased.

Day two. The Tabacalera senior staff, about half and half "Brits," British, and "Yanks," Americans, did what had to be done with British tight lipped, chin up aplomb. Jack's deputy, a Brit named Pell, took charge as general manager and as Her Majesty's honorary vice consul. Charlie and I sent more telegrams, made telephone calls and handled some of the urgent non-immigrant visas and American citizen problems. Lucy and her mother were not to be seen.

According to Tabacalera's American plant manager labor relations were tense, perhaps to the point of premeditated assassination, by an outside hired killer. The chief accountant, also an American, confirmed that Briscoe's books and accounts were in good order eliminating malfeasance. The recent six month Communist-led strike of Boston's United Fruit Company, headquartered in La Lima, ten miles southeast of San Pedro Sula, had missed by one day driving that company out of the first "Banana Republic." East in La Ceiba, smaller Standard Fruit, founded by the Vaccarro Brothers of New Orleans would not have survived alone for long. Professional union organizers fanned the flames. Demonstrations became deadly riots. Machetes, the *peons'* weapons of choice, became political tools. Trees in the banana plantations, or *fincas*, were poisoned, warehouses ransacked, and workers' quarters burned. Threats became killings and stolen dynamite became bombs. As always, it was the workers and their families who suffered and died. The day before United Fruit planned to abandon its holdings the workers had rallied to the company and foiled the communists' takeover offensive.

Furious now, the Soviet organizers gathered local communists and turned on Tabacalera, more entrenched and a tougher nut to crack. Briscoe and his staff on one side faced the communists on the other and both bared their fangs in ferocious confrontation. It would be a fight to the death.

Meanwhile, back at Briscoe's residence-cum-consulate, with its huge lion-and-unicorn seal, the officers of the local constabulary and civil authorities had come treading lightly and asked: "What can we do for you? Death certificate. Certainly. Cause of death?"

"Single bullet to the head. Sign it please. Many thanks for coming, *adios, pues.*"

The *alcalde* (mayor), was Señor Smith. Except for that fellow in the family named "Smith" the mayor was 100 percent Honduran. In the coming years I saw that we did not bother the police and they did not bother us. It was *"Ojala"* ("as God wills"), the Spanish cognate of the Arabic expression *"In sha' Allah."* Stern faced but polite, they bowed themselves out.

Day three. Leading the cortège trudging along the dusty dirt road behind the flatbed donkey cart carrying Her Britannic Majesty's honorary vice consul to his grave were two heavily veiled women, the stolid widow, *La Viuda* Briscoe, and a tearful, inconsolable Lucy, a "Daddy's girl." Lucy's uncles, her mother's brothers, marched with steady, dignified tread behind the women.

The first secretary from the British embassy in Tegucigalpa, Mr. Thorne, accompanied the acting honorary British vice consul and new Tabacalera, S.A., general manager Mr. Pell. The entire *cuerpo consulado* (consular corps); Charlie, wearing a jacket and necktie, I, in my new suit, and Josephine in the black dress she had packed on top according to the Foreign Service Institute foresight, came next. Tabacalera expatriate employees and wives followed along with the polyglot expatriate community, local professionals and businessmen.

As we plodded along in the dust, I meditated on the theories of motives for Jack's death other than the accident or suicide theories that were deemed implausible. Was there with us one or two husbands too often cuckolded by Jack wearing sly, self-satisfied smirks? If so, were their pretty wives dabbing red eyes and wiping runny noses now, stumbling along at their sides, wearing worried frowns. Jack had protected his women, ensured they were not mistreated while in his favor, but Jack was gone. In this remote jungle dead end with no way out Jack's discarded women, and their small children, were helpless pawns held hostage in the hands of hurt and vengeful husbands.

In later posts in Africa and the Near East my naiveté was mitigated when I realized that Jack had not been the only raunchy sportsman and predatory male human in San Pedro Sula. Nor were all his women helpless victims. Jack offered excitement to young sexually active but homesick and bored women (the post report had that right.) The end results were predictable and years later Josephine and I were amazed to learn how many and which wives, and husbands, who had seemed so devoted had been exchanged. I realize that the wayward ways of expatriates and ambitious locals in San Pedro Sula and similar insular, self-centered communities, as documented in memoirs, histories, and novels are literal. Josephine and I were moderately intellectually sophisticated in mid-twentieth-century sexual mores; but apparently we were emotionally naive in ways of couples, as they said, "willing to share." Loving, apparently domesticated couples with children were cavorting and "sharing" wildly.

Books such as *Back Garden of Allah* and *Oriental Spotlight* by Major C.S. Jarvis describing life in the British colony in Egypt after World War I are prime examples. These books created quite a stir in Cairo when first published. It is too bad no one has written kiss and tell books about San Pedro Sula but no one knows where it is. Laurence Durrell's *Alexandria Quartet* helped literature catch up with real life.

I wondered if there were not close by a proud Honduran of a noble Andalusian heritage, scion of a family dating from the days of the *Conquistador* who had redeemed his family's honor and name so blatantly shamed by Jack. *La Viuda* Briscoe (the Widow Briscoe), Prudencia Lucinda, was the daughter of one of the revered families of La Ceiba, families with *limpieza de sangre* (clean blood). That meant no black or Indian blood. San Pedro Sula was a hardworking, rough and ready, redneck, blue collar town. Corruption and crime were a way of life. La Ceiba esteemed tradition and culture, prided itself on its colonial legacy, and was justly defensive of the beauty and sanctity of its women.

Fifty years before my arrival in San Pedro Sula, circa 1900, the consulate had been situated in La Ceiba, then the more important of the two towns. One of my predecessors, William Sydney Porter, under his pen name O. Henry, graphically described the city, its nefarious ways, and its people in his amusing book *Cabbages and Kings*. La Ceiba had no harbor whereas San Pedro Sula controlled access to the deep water port of Puerto Cortes; the source of income for Honduras. In due course the consulate was moved to San Pedro Sula. With the expansion of air transport after World War II Puerto Cortes lost its stranglehold and economic power followed political power to the capitol at Tegucigalpa. In La Ceiba I saw that the beautiful daughters and granddaughters of the women O. Henry had known, the flowering *ceiba* trees with long horizontal branches, and the town itself held hard and fast to its long traditions.

Early in his tenure in San Pedro Sula Jack had sought an advantageous connection with the local aristocracy. With calculating honesty he had focused on the forceful Prudencia Lucinda. Paying due regard to custom their marriage, mutually advantageous, was swiftly consummated. Her two brothers, men of the world, had their doubts about Jack and reserved their judgment.

Days ago in the emerging and blood spattered confrontation with the communists, fearful Prudencia had summoned her brothers. As tension mounted, tempers flared inside the residence and Jack was fighting on two fronts. In Jack's death the brothers may have seen that he had gotten his just deserts. They were there for their sister, their name, and not to mourn. La Ceiba's family histories were measured in centuries and unsuitable in-laws were summarily dispatched in time-honored ways. As for the communist agitators, once again the workers rallied to the company. The union organizers were violently rebuffed and with few exceptions the workers returned to their jobs. Under the new General Manager Pell the company remained implacable in its opposition to the communists' demands and scant days later fought the union thugs to a stalemate, which amounted to victory. Without saying which scenario I favor, more palatable to our incestuous expatriate community would be an anonymous professional *agent provocateur,* wearing two hats, as we like to say. One is that of the shouting, placard waving caricature of a union organizer and the other is that of the unobtrusive, practiced, and cunning assassin. He earned his pay by removing an implacable opponent and, theoretically, giving the survivors pause to consider the danger to themselves. With whatever gallows humor assassins enjoy, he would be amused by the thought that the murder weapon was Jack's own J. Purdy rifle worth thousands of pounds—a perfect symbol of luxury, greed, and passion. Looking about before we entered the precincts of the cemetery I realized Jack's funeral was not an official holiday, or even a holiday. From the communists' bullhorn-augmented demonstrations distant shouts echoed down the dusty canyons of San Pedro Sula's mud hut–lined alleys. Nor was it a holiday for Charlie and me. Returning to the consulate, ties and jackets were put aside and Charlie introduced me to a desk piled high with immigrant visa applications and a waiting room full of live visa applicants, both my primary responsibilities. The fancy was over—I was about to become an American vice consul in fact!

My second hat was that of commercial officer and before the first week was out Charlie sent me into town wearing it. "Go and call," he said, "on the merchants you met at the airport."

Most of these were *Turco* (Turks): Palestinian refugees from the 1910–11 pogroms in the Ottoman Empire who had arrived here via British Honduras. By their numbers and work ethic they had made Arabic San Pedro Sula's third language after Spanish and English. The Mayan *patois,* was mostly Spanish. Arabic was the first language among the Arabs and the Jews, the Canahuates, the

Larashes, and Hassan the baker. Despite their Palestinian origins, these two groups did not mingle. Neither cared for a fourth group of ex-Nazis, former prisoners of war, and stateless persons, flotsam and jetsam from World War II—most were East Europeans. After promoting American products, which were without much competition, I strolled around town. The downtown streets were unpaved as were all streets. The cobblestone paving of de Alvarado's day had been ripped up in anticipation of asphalt. One attempt at paving failed when the asphalt of the poorest quality turned liquid in the sun. There were sidewalks, not all were wooden; some were of tile. The road traffic was half oxen and donkey carts and half automotive, mostly American. There was one *Turco*-owned Cadillac. Volkswagen "beetles" and "microbuses" had made a start and were increasing in popularity. They said that beginning in the 1950s the American cars lost out because they were too wide. Three people sitting on the seats didn't rub together.

In our lingual anthropology course at FSI we learned that two Latin males conversing stood seventeen inches, from nose to nose. A male and female stood nineteen inches—you know why—nose to nose. Conversely, brushing together or sitting touching was acceptable, even preferred. In Honduras the traditional salutation for all was a full, four-arm *abrazo* (embrace), a big hug, kissing air, left and right. While crossing the Central Plaza with its tall fountain atop stone steps I wheeled around at a commotion behind me. Past the swarming shoeshine and *Chiclet* boys, I saw that a handsome, young, tall *mestizo* woman had lain down on the fountain steps and, gasping and heaving, her naked lower body exposed to the world, was giving birth. The head was visible. What was I to do? She seemed to be on her own but surely should have had friends or family with her in such a condition. Conspicuous as a lone *gringo* among determinedly indifferent passers-by I moved away. Curiosity soon brought me back. The woman, unattended, reclined, lethargic and silent on the stone steps in a drying, darkening puddle of blood. Her baby was nowhere to be seen.

If this first week was a foretaste of "boring, frustrating, and monotonous," as the post report had predicted, what would the next 129 be like? If the unresolved mystery of Jack Briscoe's death and the birthing by the lone *mestizo* woman in the Central Plaza were portents of life and death to come in San Pedro Sula, what did they portend for me?

As always, life and death flowed seamlessly in a two-sided stream. Four hundred years of murder, suicide, treachery, adultery, and incest had flourished unchanged here among people enthralled by the curse of de Alvarado. Would the curse confound my search for the golden road to Samarkand? What was the answer and the meaning to: "Just where is San Pedro Sula—Mr. Tinny?" Should I worry or put it out of my mind?

Charlie, a no nonsense man always tense and of serious mien, was even less amused when I described the merriment and ridicule at the FSI elicited by the post report, although prepared by his predecessor. I would get to update the post report before my tour ended. How would I change it to reflect my perception of the truth whatever that came to be? Astute Charlie's twelve years' experience at four posts—Prague, Hamburg, La Paz and Stockholm—had ill prepared him for pitfalls lurking in the accursed literal and figurative jungles of San Pedro Sula. I, barely launched into the arcane world of the Foreign Service, knew that battle had been joined and that I could be my own worst enemy. Charlie should have been my best friend and I his.

The influence of de Alvarado's cruel curse of brutal unconcern to life and death hovered over the town like the inescapable swarms of flies. Compassionate Charlie struggling in the vortex of a whirlpool where people and events were rendered irrelevant by a destiny beyond their ken, looked to me in vain for help. Charlie's last two predecessors at San Pedro Sula, Pace and Peake, were gone from the service. A hint of doom echoed in his voice as he reflected on the keynote phrase in the post report defining duty in San Pedro Sula as "boring, frustrating, and monotonous," and said: "Living and dying are neither more boring nor monotonous in San Pedro Sula than anywhere else in our time and place in the world. A sword of Damocles hangs by a hair over each of us. However, until, if ever, you learn what forces you are dealing with here your days here will be more maddening rather than simply 'frustrating.'"

In my ignorance I could only agree; it seemed "so simple."

2

The Visa Mill

The crack of the rifles, *un fusilado* from the Honduran firing squad sounded across the Bay of Trujillo. The thud of their bullets into the pockmarked cemetery wall sounded the inglorious end of the briefly popular and romanticized life of the American filibuster William Walker. His foolish dream of a Southern Confederacy in Central America foundered on his own ineptness. Hounded on all sides he sought haven with the captain of a British warship who promptly delivered him to the Hondurans. Walker was shot on September 12, 1860, at Trujillo. He is buried in the old cemetery, near the pockmarked wall.

Trujillo at that time could trace its modern history back 358 years, plus a month, to August 1502. On his fourth voyage Columbus, who had been cruising the islands of Bonacco and Guanari, sailed south to the mainland and landed on a long, narrow spit of land he named Punta Caxinas. This is the only place on the New World mainland where Christopher Columbus, admiral of the Ocean Sea, actually set foot.

The well-chosen name is the Arawak Indian name of the coco plum tree with edible fruit.[3] The fleet anchored in the bay south of the cape. A few years later, on the south shore of the bay, the Spaniards founded Trujillo which they optimistically termed a "metropolis of colonial Honduras."

Passing around Punta Caxinas Columbus began a long, hard beat eastward but did not get very far. He anchored again on Wednesday August 17, 1502—still on Punta Caxinas— and took formal possession of the mainland. On the occasion, Friar Alexander celebrated the first Mass. It was noted at the time that hundreds of Indians came to watch the "taking possession."

Columbus described the land as "verdant and beautiful with many pines, oaks, seven kinds of palms, myrobalams ... an abundance of pumas, deer and gazelles." The natives were Paya or Jicaque—flesh-eating Indians. They bored large holes in their ears, so Columbus named this part of the Miskito Coast, overlapping La Costa de las Orejas, or "the coast of the ears."

Columbus also inadvertently named a yet unborn nation. Beating eastward for 28 days of head winds and foul weather, Columbus wrote: "It was one continual rain, thunder, and lightning. The ships lay exposed to the weather, with sails torn, anchors, rigging, cables, boats, and many of the stores lost." Turning south at Cabo Gracias a Dios he said, in deference to the deep hazardous waters he had passed through *"Gracias a Dios que hemos salido de estas honduras"* [Thank God, we have left these depths]. He called the area Honduras, thus was a yet-unborn nation named.

In my day, 454 years after Columbus landed to take possession and ninety six after Walker was shot, Trujillo was important to the consulate in San Pedro Sula. It was the way station for our many visa applicants from the three Bay Islands now called Roatán, the main island, Utila, and Guanaja. The first European Bay Islanders were shipwrecked or marooned Elizabethan era seamen. They and their descendants survived on piracy, smuggling, fishing, and other seafaring occupations.

I had become acquainted with these islands, banks, and rocks, which speckled the waters north and east of Honduras and Nicaragua during my navy days in Panama. They were dangerous to shipping as was acknowledged by names such as Quita Sueño Bank (take away sleep bank). The British had unceremoniously dumped the Bay Islands, including a distant fourth, Islas Santanilla (Swan Island), onto Honduras, which had tried to refuse them. I had visited the islands once ten years ago, in 1946, to deliver supplies to an American survey party. Honduras didn't want the islands but had them anyway.

Now, ten plus years after a fleeting visit I became acquainted with Bay Islanders, a fascinating lot. The men still followed the sea and were law abiding at least to the extent of obtaining a seaman's or crewman's visa for merchant seamen. Others manned the many small banana boats calling at U.S. ports. The women stayed on the islands until their menfolk settled, many in my hometown Tampa, FL. The generally attractive Bay Islanders were readily identifiable by language; they spoke distinctive Elizabethan English and would have been wonderful Shakespearean actors. Most had ruddy or light complexions and blond hair, not *castaña*. African blood surfaced occasionally in different aspects.

Seaman's visas were straightforward and restrictive so they were not easily abused. Charlie, ever wary of visa fraud, carefully broadened my duties as vice consul and let me issue seaman's visas along with my immigrant visas. That was logical since many of my immigrants were Bay Islanders. Happily, they had no connection to Don Pedro de Alvarado and his curse.

Nonimmigrant visas were the most treacherous, most easily abused, of visas, which is why Charlie issued them. These visas for business, pleasure, and a myriad of specialized limited purposes required minimum documentation and were validated by a simple stamp in the passport. These visas were a test of our ability to ascertain the applicant's true intentions. Would the applicant leave voluntarily when the visas expired or was their intent to get into the United States only to avoid immigrant visa requirements? The immigration service usually accepted our nonimmigrant visas. The burden was on us; we had to be right.

Conversely, under the McCarran-Walter Act an immigrant visa with its bulky twice-folded application form and attachments was a bundle of paper, comparable in size to a weekly tabloid. It held the life story of the applicant: past, present, and plans for the future. One missing piece would prevent issuance. Affidavits had to show a clean police record, no Communist party ties and no "intention" to overthrow the U.S. Government by violent means. Applicants needed authenticated birth certificates, photographs, marital history records, children's records, and a clean bill of health showing birthmarks and scars with a full sized X-ray showing a chest free of tuberculosis. We prepared a full set of fingerprints. Applicants had to be literate. Proofs of economic viability in the United States promised job offers but other sources of income required close scrutiny. A boon for most of our immigrant visa applicants was that native born citizens of the Western Hemisphere were not subject to a quota.

In 1956 World War II was very much with us. Honduras had not signed a peace treaty with Germany for good reason; there was much sequestrated German property the Hondurans did not plan on returning. Likewise, our quota book, a large ledger-sized hard-cover volume was full. We seemed to have at least one applicant, refugees of one sort or another, from every nation subject to a quota. That was not counting the Asia-Pacific Triangle, the nations of China, Japan, and Indo-China. We also had some from no nation, stateless, unclaimed persons and waifs of World War II. Friends or enemies once, now alike they traveled on a United Nations document, a *laissez passer* [allow (them) to pass].

Desperate refugee and prisoner of war escapees had come to San Pedro Sula seeking safe asylum, an undiscovered hiding place. The hopeful sought surreptitious, easy entry into the United States through a careless or untended back door. They had not reckoned on Charlie, the antithesis of careless, and me, his pupil. Our book included some once high and mighty Nazis, as you will see.

Quotas were severely limited and strictly enforced so when a quota applicant would try an illegal end run by applying for a non-immigrant visa, the exposure could be brutal and dramatic. In rapid succession we had two cases, both East Europeans. One went out and shot himself, the other was more helpful—he simply disappeared into the jungle. Another East European had spent ten years working to obtain Honduran citizenship (most countries have no provision for "naturalizing" foreigners.) As a "Honduran" he thought he was quota-free. He was not. It was good bye and hello jungle.

Most immigrant visa cases, which had problems would hang up on one requirement. For example, each applicant above a specified age had to be able to read one known language. In a country with a 70 percent illiteracy rate this should have been a problem. Immigrant visa applicants' first contact at the consulate would be with my immigrant visa clerk Astrid Funes. Astrid was as smart and efficient as she was pretty. At their first interview Astrid would give the applicants instructions and other forms and unobtrusively ask questions easily answered by reading the forms in front of them. If any doubt existed Astrid would catch it. Frankly, I do not know how many illiterates may have been turned away without my knowledge. If the applicant persisted she would pass them on to me to test. They usually wanted Spanish or English. I had a box of test cards in every major language and more were obtainable.

Despite the 70 percent illiteracy rate in Honduras, of the hundreds of immigrant visa applicants who came down to the wire on this requirement, only one man and one woman, both ordinary middle-class Hondurans, flatly failed. The man, smooth shaven, had short-cropped hair — *castaña,* of course — now turning gray. He wore a neat, clean, open-necked shirt; clean, pressed cotton trousers; and gave his occupation as "carpenter/laborer." He looked like he would be a competent carpenter and had square, strong hands with stubby fingers. They reminded me of hands like my father's who had worked with machinery and wood all his life. Astrid and I agreed the man's affidavits and other papers were in order but she said he couldn't read. She wanted me to make the decision. He probably was a competent carpenter and had what seemed to be a valid job offer. She was right. When I mouthed the words in English and in Spanish he just looked at me blankly. He was hopeless. Learn to read I said and sent him away.

The woman, also approaching middle age, was modestly dressed, neat, and clean. She was not pretty and her face had the smooth, olive complexion with the deep lines of her Mayan ancestors. She would make a good maid or housekeeper in Miami or New Orleans. Again, Astrid warned me to get my cards ready. The poor woman had no concept of *uno, dos, tres,* spelled out in letters. Seated across my desk from me she tried something else. The more she stared at the cards, without twitching or moving a muscle, the deeper and more exposed her cleavage and breasts became. I don't know how she did it or how far she would have gone. She had my attention and it wasn't boring. Astrid watching from the door found it all very funny.

In both of these cases I wanted to issue visas. However, I knew that when they got to the port of entry they would have to read something. Their illiteracy would be discovered and then what?

During my first twelve or thirteen weeks I was fully immersed in immigrants and their visas. Charlie gave me generous leeway on my cases and to my questions said: "read the regulations." Just when I saw daylight over my pile of immigrant visa applications, and some nonimmigrant cases, we were told that an "inspection" had been scheduled. The Foreign Service Institute had mentioned inspections briefly as something you didn't want to talk about. These were make or break, life or death events for everyone from the newest vice consul, like me, to the most senior ambassador. Not even the richest, well connected political appointee was immune from the blow of a bad inspection report and could find himself on the next boat home. A post was given enough time to catch up on the things the inspectors wanted to see. Inspectors came in teams of four or five, each with a different expertise such as political, economic, consular, or administrative. Often the head of the team was a senior ambassador, freshly retired, with nothing to lose. This team went first to Tegucigalpa to inspect the embassy.

After a week or so, two of the inspectors—the leader, Henry Stebbins, who was not retired, and a veteran consular officer, Thomas Linthicum—came to San Pedro Sula. Stebbins had been attached to Embassy London in the fall of 1940 and, with most of the embassy staff, fought fires during the Battle of Britain and throughout the war. He married a Londoner. He was so precise, I once saw him neatly peel and eat a banana with a knife and fork. He later became our first ambassador to Nepal.

The embassy had been no help when they said to us; "Prepare for the worst, you are in trouble." I was scared, tense—here is another test in what seems to be a life of tests. Charlie, as principal officer, had his own problems. He and I had our differences but I had confidence in his experience. Only too late did I realize that neither of us could handle the curse of de Alvarado. I was pitifully little help to Charlie or myself. The inconsequential and unimportant became consequential and ultimately fatal.

On the surface everything looked fine. Our visa, passport, and citizenship affairs were being handled properly. Our political reports were timely, insightful, and broadly sourced in our smoldering Cold War hot spot. Our relations with the Hondurans and the American expatriate community were good. I was the only American citizen member of the local Rotary Club. Our monetary accounts balanced. With our heavy immigrant visa load we were making more money from visas than the embassy.

Stebbins and Linthicum were blissfully unaware of de Alvarado's curse of cruelty but they knew something was amiss. The curse spawned dreadful innuendo and the dire predictions reflected in the post report I had read. The authors of that report, Charlie's immediate predecessors, consul and vice consul, had failed their "tests" and were gone from the service. Hostility, apprehension, and stress in the consulate were almost palpable. Life was a perpetual series of visceral twitches.

In one concession to San Pedro Sula itself, after one evening at my house they recommended I be authorized the immediate acquisition of one window air conditioner. The consulate office building and residence both had multiple window air conditioners. Josephine and I became the envy of our American neighbors; not a good thing. Too late did I learn they were our most important constituents.

In the end my forlorn hopes for positive results from the inspection were unrequited. Charlie was further embittered and the inspectors were so frustrated, they could not get away fast enough. Their report, unread and unlamented, molders in some mammoth bureaucratic graveyard along with the bones of the now defunct consulate at San Pedro Sula. For its part the embassy reluctantly admitted the consulate as a whole had earned a superior rating thanks to Charlie. It is too bad the lessons of Stebbins and Linthicum—two fine, professional Foreign Service officers—fell on rocky soil in me.

The strike threats of September at the United Fruit and Standard Fruit companies were under control with much improved labor relations. The Tabacalera Ltd. S.A. tobacco manufacturing operations were running smoothly. The Cold War simmered fitfully with random sabotage by *agent provocateurs.* These agitators, foreign and domestic, were now the province of a new vice consul and labor attaché, William J. Smith, who arrived in 1957. He was, as you might suspect, from the "other agency," the Central Intelligence Agency. Attaché is a diplomatic title and function, which consulates do not have, so he belonged to embassy Tegucigalpa. He and his wife Anne were likable and gregarious, and tried to be nice to poor folks like Charlie and me.

Smith had been a gung-ho, enthusiastic Marine Corps *Corsair* fighter pilot in the Pacific during World War II and was now an equally energetic CIA officer. He had his hands full keeping watch on the dangerous *agents provocateurs,* recruiting and running his own agents. One of my much-prized immigrant visas was an appropriate payoff for one of his operatives, or as he said, his "good friend." Bill even coughed up the $25 visa fee, which I insisted on. The visa was prepared and I signed it as usual.[4] It was all grist for our mini "visa mill."

Before Smith arrived we had a Communist defector, my first, from a Russian ship docked at Puerto Cortes. We billeted him briefly in Charlie's spare bedroom. In a few days, a couple of security officers showed up to question him and verify his authenticity. They said he was a *bona fide* defector and that we had done well. They spirited him out of the residence and town one dark night. No visa for him and we never heard of him again.

Nonimmigrant visa cases, whether quota or non quota, were usually more interesting than our usual run of Honduran immigrant visa applicants. The first time several Honduran Army officers showed up in the same week to apply for B-1, B-2—tourist/business visas—in order to "take my daughter to school," I took them at their face value. Charlie set me straight when he explained they were plotting a coup d'état and wanted an emergency escape hatch.

My first coup came at the time of my first national elections in the fall a couple of months after we arrived. This was a bloody affair between the Liberales and the Nationalistas—the two traditional major political parties. Throughout Honduras's political history these parties had frequently alternated governing, usually as a result of a *coup*. When we arrived in 1956 Honduras in 130 years of independence had experienced 108 presidents. In one year they had 8 presidents. In this 1956 coup four or five election officials were bushwhacked and shot dead while bringing ballot boxes into San Pedro Sula. The missing boxes had been tied to the rumps of their horses. The horses ambled on their own into town to their home stables. The murders of these prominent civic minded men, fellow Rotarians, were deduced from key words in their obituaries: "died suddenly last week."

National elections were simple with blue ballots for one party and red for the other. Counting votes was even simpler when voters with the wrong colored ballots, the "outs," arrived at the polling place and were forced to eat their ballots by soldiers of the "ins." Of course, "in" and "out" changed frequently and the survivors had ballots of both colors as well as cockades to put on their hats if any fighting had to be done. Until after World War II when air cargo transport became commonplace San Pedro Sula, with control of import duties at the custom house in Puerto Cortes, ruled Honduras.

Coups two and three were perfunctory pseudo-elections. My fourth, last, and my favorite was led by a *junta,* council, of three young army officers. Hector Caracciola, the *jefe de Junta* (chief of the Council), Roque J. Rodriquez and Roberto Galvez. They paved the way for constituent assembly elections in 1957. The assembly appointed Ramon Villeda-Morales (*Pajarito,* Little Bird) as president and then transformed itself into a unicameral national legislature with six-year terms. Charlie and I probably saw more of *Pajarito* in San Pedro Sula, which he favored, than did our political officers in Tegucigalpa. Villeda-Morales was deposed in 1963, with ten days left in his term. I am told the airport in San Pedro Sula (SAP) is now named after Pajarito. Had he completed his term he would have been the first president of Honduras to do so.

Lucky for me, the three *junta* members, especially the *Jefe,* Hector Caracciola, were well liked, popular, and handsome. I added that last comment, true or not, because several Sanpedranos said I strongly resembled Caracciola and, in fact, once in a gathering was taken for him. If he had been disliked by even just one dissident, I might have gotten shot, by mistake, of course. Being shot was a real Foreign Service occupational hazard not emphasized by FSI.[5]

Astrid Funes, mentioned earlier, the young daughter of a prominent, well-to-do Sanpedrano family had come to work at the consulate to replace the absent Lucy Briscoe who, with her mother, had gone into seclusion after the death of her father Jack Briscoe. The elder Funes was a farmer/businessman and a popular *raconteur.* His usual answer to the greeting *"Cómo está usted?"* (How are you?) was, *"Entre jerez y la frontera."* This is a word play on the name of the Spanish town Jerez de la Frontera and was considered clever or even funny. I never did understand it.

Shortly before she came to the consulate Astrid had accompanied her father on a business trip to Panama where he had conferred with the president. My first glimpse of Astrid, who was unknown to me, had been at a lavish house warming party at the new mountainside home overlooking San Pedro Sula of Charles Daniels, a night or two before she started work. Daniels exported Honduran lumber including Honduran mahogany and other exotic woods in exchange for lots of money. His wife Sidney had been a movie starlet in the 1930s, appearing in light comedies and was a favorite of comedy star Joe E. Brown. She had kept her figure, was still attractive, and always beautifully dressed.

At the Daniels' party Astrid, with bobbed black hair and dark eyes, was outstanding in a long, strapless gold lamé evening dress which was close to topless in a garden full of equally spectacularly dressed women, especially the *sanpedranas*. As the evening wore on, Josephine who is very good at these things, sidled up to me and asked how I liked the girl in the gold dress. That was obviously a loaded question so I hesitated.

"Well," she said, "I hope you like her because she is your new visa clerk."

Astrid was indeed worth her weight in gold. Three of our four clerks—Lucy, Astrid, and Lena—were from prominent and well-to-do Honduran families and did not need to work. They did it for the pleasure of having something meaningful to do and for the excitement. A clerk in the Consulado de los Estados Unidos had prestige and power among her peers.

We were fortunate in all of our clerks. Aida Trau, dignified and unassuming, was attractive and had been at the consulate the longest. She worked with Charlie on the more sensitive nonimmigrant visas, American citizenship, and passport cases. Her husband Hector Trau and his older brother Carlos were German-Hondurans and had a successful air conditioning business. Hector had been in the American Army during World War II and had served in Europe. He said that he had met General Eisenhower once and Hector boasted: "we fought together." His army service earned him American citizenship but he had not claimed it. I heard that later they emigrated to New Orleans.

Lena Sunceri came in early 1957 and had been Miss Honduras

in an international beauty contest. Her father, a Liberal Party member—currently the "outs" —was part of the powerful oligarchy of "really rich men," above political party squabbles. When Lena's sister was married by the Archbishop, and blessed by the Pope, the Honduran president Villeda-Morales, *Pajarito*, attended. Likewise, a "summit meeting," between President Villeda-Morales and Guatemalan President Ydigoras-Fuentes was held at the Sunceri residence in San Pedro Sula. Lena later went to the Honduran Mission to the UN in New York.

After the period of seclusion Lucy returned to her job at the consulate and of the four girls attracted the most attention even though still in black. One example; when our regional security officer, newly transferred to Mexico City from Paris, visited us on his first tour of inspection, he met all of our clerks. After meeting Lucy he backed me into my office and closed the door. Standing there, wide-eyed and panting with excitement he exclaimed:

"I've traveled over all Europe, all the world in fact, and I had to come to the worst godforsaken hole I've ever been in to find the most beautiful woman I've ever seen."

In addition to the consulate clerical staff Charlie had one personal servant—a large black Jamaican-Honduran, Rebecca—who was cook and housekeeper. She had a house in the compound. The blacks were far better cooks in general than the Hondurans of Mayan stock although the Hondurans did well with their native dishes. Josephine and I had an Indian girl, Caya, as cook and maid, and she did very well. Of course, we had a lot of rice and beans, especially for "chuppa," her pronunciation of supper. Polocarpus, called Polo, was the consulate driver, customs expediter, and general errand runner. He did well when he was there but he didn't always show up. Zacarias, a Honduran, was the gardener and very adept with his machete. He could trim the grass of the consulate's sizable lawn as smoothly as if it had been cut with a lawn mower. He raised the flag every morning on our tall and prominent pole and at least half the time got it right side up. He took it down at night. Charlie and I both got to the office before he raised the flag. We could not very easily see the pole from inside but someone—not necessarily an American—always telephoned to tell us when Zacarias had gotten it wrong.

Helping and guiding serious and determined potential immigrants to obtain an immigrant visa was my initial principal responsibility in San Pedro Sula but a vice consul has many other duties. The issuance of visas permitting entry into the United States involved foreigners but by definition our first duty was to Americans. This ranged from simple passport renewals to documenting and, oftentimes, handling everything from births to deaths. In San Pedro Sula births to American women were rare because our young matrons went to New Orleans, Miami, or home to mother to have their child. On the other hand Americans did die, willy-nilly. If without some responsible person close by their effects had to be inventoried, shipped somewhere, their remains cared for and all documented. Shipping remains involved embalming and airtight lead coffins.

My first deceased American was a bush pilot working for a fly-by-night (no joke intended) oil exploration company. As far as I know they did not find oil. He was flying a Douglas DC-3 single handed, which could be done but is not recommended. He piled up in our consular district and Charlie said I needed the experience. With Bill Smith's help we packed the man's effects, cleaned out reading and other material of a potentially embarrassing nature, dirty laundry, dirty hair brushes, and counted his money. He had thousands of dollars of traveler's checks carefully hidden in odd places. The reason he crashed was not clear but pilot error seemed unlikely. His flight log book showed an almost unheard of 30,000 hours of flying time. He was an old pilot and he did not seem like a bold pilot but in the end it didn't matter.

My second deceased American in San Pedro Sula was a helicopter pilot for the United Fruit Company. He was spraying a banana plantation (*finca*), with a full load of a highly toxic chemical when he flew into high tension power lines. His craft exploded, burned, and crashed to the ground. In his case the company made most of the funeral arrangements. I got involved when the doctors could not agree on a cause of death. They finally agreed that the pilot received a high voltage electric shock in an exploding and burning aircraft, carrying deadly chemicals, which crashed to the ground, and he died.

Gathering the documentation necessary for an immigrant visa

was a chore for both us and the applicant. Astrid and I averaged at least a dozen a week, each of which may have represented weeks, months, and even years of preparation. Some applicants brought in documents one by one. Others, with our instructions in hand waited until they thought they had everything. Often they were wrong; something was wrong. This was not catastrophic if they were local but bad if they had come a long distance.

One memorable day, Astrid and I put together in final form—signed, sealed, and delivered—fourteen immigrant visas beginning with the newspaper-sized application form, continuing with all the certificates and affidavits gathered over months, finishing with the full sized chest x-ray, full set of fingerprints, and stamp in the passport. This is a minuscule number compared with the output of the "visa mills" like Kobe and Tiajuana, but their staffs outnumbered Astrid and me twenty or more to one. The fates of the hundreds of my visa applicants are unknown to me except for a young girl, one of a family immigrating together. I met her twenty-five years later in Miami as the second wife of the widower husband of my wife's late sister. In discussing her origins in Honduras, San Pedro Sula came up. She brought out her passport and we found my stamp and signature authenticating her visa.

All the while I worried about the "flood" of immigrants I was admitting but my few hundreds over two and a half years in San Pedro Sula could not compare with the hordes of Mexican "wetbacks" wading the Rio Grande each day. Someone suggested I not worry and think of them as "cannon fodder." Another suggested stationing army recruiters along the border.

I tried to make it easier for visa applicants by field trips to distant towns. If they are coming anyway, make it legal. Every five or six weeks, Josephine, the boys, and I piled into the jeep for a field trip up to a village that was home to some of my visa applicants. Sometimes Chuck and Joan Brookwell with their two boys; the Fishers, no children; or Sig and Eunice Lingelboch, one daughter, would come along so we had two vehicles. We had to ford many streams and could always tell when a stream had once been bridged and how many times. If the stumps of the pilings and remnants of the approaches were smooth, finished stone, bridge number one dated from sixteenth century colonial days. If the adjacent stumps were planed and sawn timbers, bridge number two had been built in the early days of independence while trained artisans and carpenters remained. If the pilings were just rough tree trunks covered with bark, poorly assembled, bridge number three was "modern." Each bridge was blown up by a succeeding generation in a revolution. Now, of course, there was no bridge. If the stream looked too deep Josephine would hike up her skirts and wade in front of us to test the depth. Her shapely long legs were the right length so if her panties stayed dry and she didn't step into any potholes, we could ford it. We had alligators, moccasins, and, of course, the boa constrictors. The other women thought she was brave; the men liked the view.

Rats had been a big problem in the cane fields and banana *fincas*. Although native to Honduras some *politico* thought it clever or profitable to import boas from India. It was expensive but they multiply rapidly. A law was passed protecting boas. That was fine because an "imported" boa cost more than a native Honduran *peon*. Boas have small sharp teeth for hanging onto prey—hopefully a rat—their jaws stretch to accommodate large prey and they prefer dry land but are excellent swimmers. We had heard many boa constrictor stories from friends in San Pedro Sula; usually one found in a house as the rats disappeared. Even the oft quoted and much maligned post report had no mention of boa constrictors much less that they were good swimmers, but not one ever approached or latched onto Josephine.

Charlie let me carry our heavy iron and brass impression consular seal, rubber stamps, other paraphernalia, even red tape and sealing wax which we used to attach certain documents together, and blank forms for visas and to register American citizens, reluctant for one reason or another—perhaps dodging the law—to come into the consulate. We visited Yoro, Gracias, Santa Barbara, and Santa Rosa de Copan near Copan de Ruinas. The later was called the "Athens of the Mayan Empire." The Rockefellers had partially excavated Copan years earlier. We thought getting to Copan in four wheel drive jeeps an achievement until we saw that two fat German women and a teenage boy had followed us in a Volkswagen Beatle.

In the nineteenth century, John Lloyd Stephens had drawn beautifully detailed pictures of the carvings. Since 1957, extensive excavating and study has been done in and around Copan de Ruinas.

The morning after our usually late afternoon arrival, I set up shop in a place arranged by the *alcalde* (mayor). A wooden table and two or three chairs, an American flag, and a consular flag comprised my office. Visa applicants and other supplicants quickly gathered and I did as much as I could for as many as I could. The exercise was dramatic in a small way. I felt like a circuit riding preacher or a Roman proconsul visiting the farthest marches of the empire. With the flag flying and my seal in a place of honor on the table I was *el señor consul*. It was a fleeting moment of glory but satisfying. This was not Flecker's Samarkand but perhaps closer than I realized.

The villages were poor but pleasant and picturesque especially at the higher elevations. Once, at over 9,000 feet we had snow flurries. Elaborate church facades and sturdy arcaded government *palacios* (office buildings), with cool, shaded courtyards facing cobble stone streets and the central plaza were the visible legacies of the Spanish conquistadors. We were always well received by the local officials and offered their best by the villagers. This usually meant cots with leather straps for springs and straw mattresses in a bare *pension* room with a dirt floor and a chamber pot. Bathing was done in an outside wooden stall open at the top. A young boy perched on the beams at the top and poured buckets of water into a bigger bucket with holes punched in the bottom so the water ran out shower-like. The same procedure served men and women. Showers were usually brief because water from the mountain streams was icy cold. The women went in pairs but never felt themselves in any danger.

One night after we had dined at a local café and returned to our *pension,* I showed the other members of our party that I had my .45 automatic stuck in my belt under my loose shirt. Whereupon the other men in our party, Chuck Brookwell and one other, lifted their shirts to show they were similarly armed. We felt better but would have been foolish to try anything.

One day we drove across the border into Guatemala on the "Armas" road used by Castillo Armas with Honduran and U.S. aid to overthrow the communist Arbenz regime. We found no Guatemalan consul in Copan, but one wearing pistols galloping up on a horse found us. At his office he prepared for us a hand written visa. Charlie said a hand written visa is acceptable but rare and is to be cherished. He stuck mine in the files and there it sits.

For us these field trips away from San Pedro Sula were mini vacations especially when it was *fiesta* time, which seemed to coincide with our arrival. Centerpiece of the *fiesta* was the *marimba* band consisting of one or more *marimbas.* These are wooden xylophone-like musical instruments that may accommodate one or more players simultaneously.

In Copan we saw a huge *marimba* being played by nine men with two sticks in each hand at the same time without getting their sticks crossed and keeping in time. They started playing in the evening and in the morning they—or replacements—were still going strong. A village in the south near Gracias—Las Minas—specialized in making miniature *marimbas.* Late one night several months after I ordered and paid for one it was delivered. Honduras claimed to have invented the *marimba.* Astrid also claimed the "cha-cha-cha," a Latin American dance, was invented in Honduras. Gracias is noted for its cuisine, which specializes in monkey meat. It is an acquired taste and does not taste like chicken; it tastes like monkey.

Monkeys are also known to inhabit an area where consular officers operated a few miles northeast of Tegucigalpa from 1873 to 1917, presumably under the auspices of the embassy. Part of the La Tigra National Park, the area was in the consular district of the embassy and I had no business there.

That O. Henry was consul in La Ceiba in 1902 is well known. He was 36 or 37 when he went there, about the same age I was on my arrival in San Pedro Sula. I flatter myself that we, both of an age, might have had the same responses to some of the same problems. His book *Cabbages and Kings* is a pseudo record of his one tour of duty as a consul. O. Henry described the northern littoral of Honduras as "presenting to the sea a formidable border of tropical jungle topped by the overweening *Cordilleras*...still begirt by mystery and romance. In past times buccaneers and revolutionists roused the echoes of its cliffs." In his time and mine, we both had "buccaneers and revolutionists"

Village food was always thoroughly cooked and well seasoned.

Often it had surprises. In La Entrada, a small town atop a small hill, European style and gateway to the tobacco-growing region, our chicken stew had the head and both feet of the chicken.

The wonderfully aromatic tobacco from the mountains of western Honduras is the main reason for the British-American Tobacco (BAT) Tabacalera investment. Handsome, tall, lean, and rangy women in black derby hats pick the leaves while smoking huge hand rolled cigars. Paul Riley, the "leaf" man, inspector, for Tabacalera gave us a tour of the fields.

Freshly killed chicken or freshly caught fish from the ten-mile-long Lago de Yojoa taste vastly different from the frozen stuff. Of course, we had to take some precautions. Beer was much safer than the clearest water for drinking. We did find that a liberal amount of scotch in river water seemed to render it harmless. Pasteurized milk, for our two boys, was unheard of but boiled milk was plentiful and better. The *tamales* are crushed meat, corn, red peppers wrapped in corn husks and steamed. A village boy walking along the road with a lunch pail sold his to us. They were the best we have ever eaten.

The scores of immigrant visas we issued at $25 each and other fees earned the consulate several thousands of dollars a month. So, along about May or June when the budget and fiscal officer (B&F) from the embassy came to give us the perennial "sad story" that we would get no more expense money until the beginning of the next fiscal year in July, Charlie and I dreamed up a tongue-in-cheek response. We addressed a standard Operations Memorandum—a printed message form interleaved with carbon paper for multiple copies, used for routine administrative matters—to the department with a copy to the embassy. This was normal procedure. This time, however, we concocted a proposal for using our fees and other income to make the consulate financially independent. Being cowards we did not send the original to the department, but we did send the embassy its copy as though we had sent the original. When the dust settled, no one appreciated our little joke. Lesson number one, do not tease budget and fiscal officers at budget time or the embassy at any time. Bureaucracies are deadly serious, humorless business.

Visa fraud was also serious business, as we were constantly re-minded by directives from the department warning of the threat and instructions for combating it. Charlie also admonished me to be alert to the threat. When my female African-Honduran immigrant-visa applicants began bringing in identical, professionally prepared affidavits vouching for jobs in Miami or New Orleans, fraud reared its ugly head. All were prepared by the same New Orleans lawyer. People who assisted immigrants to obtain visas—maybe legally, maybe not—were called "coyotes." The epithet originated on the Mexican frontier and refers to the wolf-like carnivore, in Mexican Spanish, from Nahuatl, *coyotl*. Charlie agreed it looked suspicious, and over a few weeks I collected a dozen or more samples. When my case seemed convincing, I sent my samples to the department, referencing recent departmental warnings about fraud, and waited. Lesson number two on the thinking of bureaucracies in general was a letter from the commissioner of the Immigration and Naturaliza-tion Service in New Orleans addressed to "Mr. (Phonetic spelling) Tinny." He said he played tennis with Mr. Wolson every week, he was a fine fellow and that I "had better mind my own business." So much for combatting visa fraud.

My favorite immigrant visa applicant was a Bay Islander named Mrs. Williams. Williams is one of the original four seventeenth century Bay Islander names. We, Mrs. Williams and I, had had a lengthy correspondence, the specifics of which I have forgotten except that she was fortyish and had been married four times. Bay Islanders make documenting anything, including immigrant visa applications, difficult for themselves by resisting writing or speaking Spanish. They much prefer their archaic Elizabethan English. Eventually she wrote to tell me she had everything required and that she was coming, via Trujillo, to present herself to the consulate to receive her visa. The appointed day arrived and Astrid announced Mrs. Williams. Eagerly I rushed to the waiting room to greet her and I was not disappointed. She was handsome, tall, and erect with a pale complexion but the distinctive light freckles of an ethnic mixture. Almost regal, she wore a full length, long sleeved dress, boasting a lace bodice— if not Elizabethan, certainly

Victorian—under a wide brimmed elegant straw hat trailing veils and ribbons. I ushered her into my office, which she filled with her presence and an unrecognized but sensuous scent. I inspected her documents including the full sized chest x-ray, which brought on a blush and flutter of her fan. Everything, indeed, was in order except for one subject on which the prudish McCarran- Walter Act was adamant. Mrs. Williams's four husbands, each come and gone, were accounted for as were her four children, one for each husband it would seem. Looking at the children's birth certificates there was the rub and so I said: "Mrs. Williams, you have had four children but not one of them bears the name of any one of your four husbands. How do you account for that?" In her lilting accent with a wink, a mischievous twinkle in her eyes, and an utterly disarming smile she said: "A body's got to have some fun." She was a most charming and remarkable woman.

Astrid, way ahead of me, with no time for McCarran-Walter prudery, had already prepared Mrs. Williams's visa, and I signed it forthwith. We saw Mrs. Williams off to Trujillo and beyond, where, perhaps, husband number five was waiting.

Charlie was right; the post report wrong. The dangers were not that life and death were frustrating, nor from "too much love of living" boring and monotonous. Better ideas were that each life as we knew it, even in deadly San Pedro Sula, produced its own narrative romantic themes. Consular work was exciting, each visa represented hope, joy, expectation; and Mrs. Williams was a prime example.

That cruelest of men, Conquistador Don Pedro de Alvarado, branded his town with the curse of unconcern for human life; no one here was immune. The best and the worst were yet to come.

3

Tres Pistoleros

Whatever else they may say in Honduras, for the first half of the twentieth century it was a land of ruinous anarchy sweltering in an orgy of wearisome destructive revolutions. For these reasons Honduras was either a sanctuary, a place of redemption, or a land of opportunity for the flotsam and jetsam of the bloodiest wars of the first half of the twentieth century; for petty criminals and for soldiers of fortune. As American vice consul in San Pedro Sula from 1956 to 1959 I met some from each of these groups. I found the most colorful and romantic of these categories to be the soldiers of fortune; although not the bloodiest, those were the war survivors. Honduras became the battleground—one might almost say the playground—of three notorious and quintessential soldiers of fortune. O. Henry would have styled them as buccaneers in whichever century they lived. Their days of power and glory had passed but I was happy to know and work with two of them.

Lee Christmas, a Southerner and a former railroad engineer, became the epitome of the soldier of fortune. He was not cast in the mold of the cruel Spanish *conquistadors*, such as Don Pedro de Alvarado, but fought for personal gain and glory and was not by nature cruel or vicious. If it can be said of a warrior, a fighting man, that his wish is to live then he should also be willing to let live. When I arrived in San Pedro Sula Christmas was very dead but not forgotten. A daughter and grandchildren lived on as did the legacy of his exploits—real and imagined.

Lee Marston was a Southerner also, and left the States for the first time during the latter days of Reconstruction when so many believers in the "Lost Cause" sought solace in distant lands. He did go home once or twice. Marston called Tampa his hometown, but he didn't live there and left forever. Marston was my favorite because I knew him best although not intimately. At the end, when I might have made a difference, I let him down. There was nothing to do then but bury him deep and my regrets with him.

Last and youngest of my triumvirate was "Machine Gun" Guy Moloney, a fiery South African bully boy who learned to operate and, most importantly, maintain machine guns during the Boer War and World War I. Taciturn, he spoke in monosyllables. He was the most pragmatic, practical of the three and there was little of the romantic in Moloney. He and Christmas often teamed up together and while Christmas got the glory, Moloney with his machine guns made sure the fighters on the other side kept their heads down. It was me who—in the last days when Marston and Moloney could walk the streets of San Pedro Sula in relative safety—brought these two old, bold gunfighters eyeball to eyeball once and for all. After a few tense moments it was, as the Romans said, "Hail and farewell."

In 1920 my three *pistoleros* were at the height of their power and glory; by 1940 there were two and in 1959 I left Honduras with only one still standing. Now, another half century on, I am sure there are none. What O. Henry does is to set the scene and many of his characters, who remained in Honduras, or "Anchuria" as he called it, would have been familiar to my *pistoleros*. I am glad I knew at least two of them and had read O. Henry beforehand. He showed me where, and I saw how they ran.

"Mr. Marston is here! Mr. Marston is here!"

It was still my early days in San Pedro Sula and the excitement in this cry from Astrid Funes told me more than her words that this was an important event. As she turned away from the door of my office I jumped up and followed her through our large outer office to the waiting area. Breathless she stopped facing a very old man standing on the other side of the counter. Bent and stooped by his 96 years he was still taller and broader than me. His lined and leathery face must have once been deeply tanned but now his complexion was faded but clear. He sized me up through bright blue eyes that bespoke strength and character. His hands resting on the counter were large and powerful. The long barreled Colt .45 caliber *Peacemaker* would have nestled firmly and comfortably in those long and bony fingers. It would, indeed, have brought peace—the peace of the grave.

Once upon a time he had been a dangerous man and possibly still was. Astrid's beautiful face glowed with pride and joy when with a wide, happy smile she announced to me:

"This is Mr. Marston and he has come for his check."

She held out to him the familiar brown U.S. Treasury pension check envelope but she made this one seem special. American consulates around the world receive tall stacks of envelopes like these each month and distribute them to the beneficiaries. Charlie let the clerks hand out most of the checks but some he, and I, liked to handle;, usually those to older U.S. citizens. In addition to hundreds of social security checks there are military pensions, railroad pensions, and others. Like my own immigrant visa applicants the recipients of this American largess were people who had immigrated to the United States legally, lived there all of their working lives, or at least long enough to earn their pensions. Many had become U.S. citizens with all the rights and privileges pertaining thereto but now had yielded to the call of the land of their birth; to home. Others were happy with a green card. I once thought these thousands of U.S. dollar check recipients in dozens of countries around the world had a vested interest in the continued well being of the United States and were on our side. I imagined they had brought home some of the culture and philosophy of the American institutions under which they had thrived and still received American "greenbacks." It is not so. Our way of life does not transplant effectively, certainly not easily, if at all.

The first English colonists to America brought with them millennia of Greek and classical philosophies nurtured and developed in Western civilization. In the British Isles the Anglo-Saxon traditions of "commonwealth," individual freedom, and inalienable rights have very deep roots; the Magna Carta is one. As Rome was not built in a day neither was the United States. Millions of citizens have honed our republican form of government and free enterprise economy. You and I are still working on them. Thirty or forty years of productive living in the United States can be erased in a flash. Returning home immigrants fall into their old ways and the gloss of the American way of doing things is rubbed away. Some citizens register at the consulate, most do not but vanish into the jungle, as in Honduras, or desert or whatever hinterland from which they had emerged. Some we register with an extra passport renewal form and piece of carbon paper slipped onto the typewriter carriage. We see them when the checks accumulate and they need the money; when they seek "Uncle Sam's" protection in a "revolution;" or to renew a ragged, moldy passport dragged out of a damp hiding place.

Lee Marston was the exception. He said he was born in Tampa, Florida about the year 1860; the year filibuster William Walker faced the firing squad in Trujillo. Like Walker, Marston was an adventurer; a mercenary for hire and a born soldier of fortune. Unlike Walker he had no aspirations to be *El Presidente* of an impoverished *opéra bouffe* country or in pursuing America's manifest destiny in a Central American confederacy. Chief of police in San Pedro Sula was good enough.

Marston had left home as a young man and never returned to the States for any extended period of time but he was not unknown in his hometown. He returned long enough in 1898 to enlist in the U.S. Army for the Spanish-American War because it had promised at first to be a real war with a name. He did not actually participate as a soldier but he did get to Cuba on his own. His experiences in Central America and Cuba as a fighter and gunrunner brought him to the attention of Florida's Governor Napoleon Bonaparte Broward who he served as private secretary to from 1905 to 1909.

Before becoming governor, Broward had achieved local notoriety as an armchair filibuster by financing arms to the Cuban insurgents whose activities were a major cause of the Spanish-American War. Out of office, Broward's political successors in Florida disavowed his Cuban warmongering. There was no place in Florida then for Marston so he headed back down south.

Marston's U.S. Army service earned him the monthly checks that were now his major means of support. Adventurers in general and soldiers of fortune don't usually have big savings accounts and plan for long term retirement or old age. Marston achieved the old age many of his friends and most of his enemies didn't. However, he had not had any reason to count on a long life or to plan for one.

Marston had loved a good gunfight and as a gun fighter he was good. How many men had he killed, how many notches were on his pistol's handle? He wouldn't say because probably he didn't know. Before the Spanish-American War he had battled his way to Peru and back. Whether the outcome was win, lose, or draw he had survived to fight another day. In the early decades of the twentieth century Honduras was in political chaos. Savagery, murder, and mayhem among the peasants were sometimes called revolutions and fed upon each other. Political cliques survived by staying at war with one or the other. In the brief cessations of fighting Marston and Lee Christmas were given chances to bring law and order to chaos with their guns; an unrealistic oxymoron. At one time or another both were alternately chief of police in both San Pedro Sula, which with Puerto Cortes had the economic power, and the capital Tegucigalpa, growing in political power. In terms of timing, after Christmas left for one reason or another, Marston stepped into his place. Mercenaries try to avoid shooting each other and may even watch each others' backs.

Marston had a reputation as an honest, trustworthy, and fair man. With rugged good looks and a massive frame, he had charm and bold charisma. His blue eyes were deceptively bright but like a Doberman's never blinked. He carried his six feet four inches of muscle gracefully and was not readily challenged. As a *norteameri-cano*, he was cloaked with all the prestige and authority that title carried in those days. Marston was a man of faith and his faith was in his guns and his innate abilities with them. He did not kill for killings sake; it was just the way he, and others like him, made their living.

To judge from Astrid's awestruck reception of Marston he was not only a man's man, but women found him attractive and appealing. Even now he had charisma. Marston liked women, and one way or another, a pretty woman Marston set his cap for he got. Astrid had grown up listening to exciting tales of gunfights and revolutions featuring Marston, Christmas, and Moloney. These stories and others were related by her father, noted for his knowledge of local history. At the consulate she met Marston in the flesh, handed him his pension check, and was not disappointed. Señor Funes did not know Marston, at least not well, and now she could bring home a new episode with the *"pistolero norteamericano"* every month. Her Marston stories got better until they climaxed in the coming months.

In the first quarter of the twentieth century Marston was overshadowed by the flamboyant Lee Christmas. They knew and respected each other as mercenaries and even when on opposite sides they were not enemies. Christmas had been a railroad engineer in the southern United States, but around 1900 he had been involved in a railroad accident, that caused several deaths. Facing civil and possibly criminal charges he had fled the country and found safe haven in Honduras. He visited the States once in the 1920s and took his first and only ride in an automobile. Politically inclined, Christmas involved himself in local affairs sometimes on the side of the duly elected regime. It was a question of who paid better, if at all.

Although Honduras was the most backward of the Central American states, thanks to the United Fruit Company of Boston, Standard Fruit of New Orleans, and other banana exporters, it had several firsts. For example, before 1909, between Puerto Cortes, San Pedro Sula, and the railhead in Potrerillos, Honduras had the first, and at that time only railroad in Central America. Potrerillos was the end of the line. Half a century and two world wars later, on my first visit, it was the roughest town I had ever seen. It was not only the end of the rail line but also the road for those wanting to get lost. If no one in Washington knew where San Pedro Sula was, no one in San Pedro Sula knew where Potrerillos was—or cared. Second, in 1909 San Pedro Sula also had the one and only industrial-sized ice-making plant in Central America.

A few years later Christmas and his men used huge blocks of ice from the plant to build a barricade on the railroad trestle over the Chamelecon River. With bullets stopped cold by the ice (no joke) they held off the rebels long enough to save themselves and the duly elected regime. Then the ice melted.

Christmas often worked with the husky, no nonsense "Machine Gun" Guy Moloney, machine gunner and mechanic *par excellence*, trained in the British Army. As is so often the case, the poorer, more backward the country, the better armed its people are and the more plentiful the ammunition for those arms. Honduras was no exception. While its neighbors used a motley assortment of castoff rifles, thanks to Moloney and his friends, backward Hondurans banged away at each other with the technologically advanced Vickers and Lewis machine guns. Moloney, much younger than Christmas, the oldest, and Marston, was impetuous.

During one of the 1930s revolutions centered in San Pedro Sula, Moloney and a few men were pinned down with a crowd of women and children in the Tabacalera cigarette factory. This was a city-block-sized fortress-like building with three-foot-thick adobe walls and massive wooden gates. The joke was that the cigarette factory (the cheap ones were named *Buffalos*) was adjacent to the livery stables. Fuming at the humility of the siege—and, probably, the noise of the children—Moloney had finally had enough. He wanted no more palaver. Cradling a .30 or .50 caliber—I don't know which—belt fed machine gun in his arms and belts of ammo over his shoulders, he charged out the main gate alone, with his men covering his back. Blasting away at anything or anybody that moved and a lot that looked like it might, undaunted, Moloney stalked down and back in the middle of Avenida Central.

That scene is replicated in the movie *Professional Soldier* with Victor McLaughlin and Freddie Bartholomew. I don't know if there is a connection between the movie and Moloney. I do know that Moloney's bravado, like McLaughlin's in the movie, ended the siege and brightened his reputation.

This story came directly to me from my Spanish instructor, a schoolteacher who had been one of the children. She said the children knew that Moloney, whom they considered to be the same as a *norteamericano*, could do anything and get them safely out. For them he was a hero.

Lee Christmas died about 1933 in bed, according to his daughter. She was married to our consular agent in Tela, a United Fruit Company town where as a company employee he was located. Tela was connected to La Lima, United Fruit headquarters, by a railroad built for hauling bananas. Passengers moved in trucks fitted with railroad car wheels. Standard Fruit, based in La Ceiba, had a similar rail system, but gauges of the two systems were different, requiring a change of cars.

We had a consular agent in La Ceiba as well. These are American citizens and permanent residents who perform limited consular functions. They are also important for local news, history, and contacts.

Now my *tres pistoleros* had become two. Without Christmas to call the tune, much of the fun, excitement, and, to be honest, security in following Honduran revolutions was gone. Moloney did not know Marston until I came along. In any case, they never took on any revolutions together. Instead, Moloney soon left for Huey Long's Louisiana and police work, for which he was eminently suited. Like Christmas, Long was described as flamboyant, but unlike Christmas, also as ruthless. Long's opposition was stifled and intimidated; many were persuaded to join Long or were permanently silenced. Machine Gun Guy Moloney was as adept with Mr. Thompson's masterpiece with the round, fifty cartridge magazine, as with other machine guns. After Long's assassination in 1935 Moloney continued in law enforcement and retired after World War II as New Orleans' chief of police. Another exception to my theory about the longevity of gunfighters; when I met Moloney he was eighty three. Returning to San Pedro Sula, scene of forgotten triumphs, he quietly owned and operated a flour mill.

One afternoon Moloney slipped in by the back door of the Consulate, with which he was familiar, to see Charlie and to have his passport renewed. He wanted to visit his mother who at 103 was ailing up in New Orleans. While Aida stamped the passport and Moloney sat in Charlie's office, Astrid told me Lee Marston had come in for his check. As I prepared to go out front with Astrid to see Marston, I had a thought and told Astrid to hold the check and stay put. In Charlie's office I told him and Moloney who was in the waiting room. I was sure Marston and Moloney knew each other. I didn't know whether they were friends or if they would shoot it out here and now. Believe it or not, after a lifetime of shooting their way around Honduras, these two gunslingers had not met face to face.

"Well, then," I asked Moloney, "would you like to meet him now?"

Moloney's eyes took on a faraway look, as if he saw something at a distance but I figured it was more likely back in the past. When he came back from wherever he had been he growled out, "Yes."

"Please wait here." I said as I turned and closed the door. When at the counter I asked Marston if he knew Moloney, he guessed what was coming and stiffened. I asked if he would like to meet him waiting now in Charlie's office. Again came the same long, far-away gaze, the same hesitation.

"Yes. Out here," he said as he laid both hands on the counter and, straightening, stood tall; his blousy shirt hanging loose outside his trousers could conceal most anything.

Back in Charlie's office I told him and Moloney what Marston had said and done. Moloney said that he means we meet on neutral ground, unarmed. With that Moloney leaned down and pulled a .45 automatic out of one ankle holster, a .38 snub-nosed police special out of the other and laid them on Charlie's desk. I figured he had a third someplace but was not about to ask. Tense, I took a deep breath, held it, and walking in front led the way out to where Marston stood.

Usual consular work creates stress and tension, but this was different. Now I felt as I had when the Koreans had zeroed in on the *Dextrous* and were trying to sink my ship and kill us all.

When these men, two legendary *pistoleros* who had survived because they shot first and asked questions later stood eyeball to eyeball, none of the room full of noisy visa applicants made a sound or twitched. Sanpedranos who live or die on instinct know when to be still and this was such a time.

Marston, ninety-seven, and Moloney, eighty-three, were equally self-assured and confident. Neither blinked nor smiled nor shifted his gaze, and when Moloney laid his hands on the counter they didn't touch Marston's. Moloney was dapper in a double-breasted blue wool suit, white shirt, tie, and polished leather shoes. Marston wore only a locally made cotton shirt, baggy pants, and sandals. One was self-sufficient, the other a welfare case. That was not an issue between them. Their fights were not with each other—at least not now—they had agreed to that. I invited them into my office to visit for as long as they liked, but they declined. What they might have said was left unsaid, maybe they had nothing to say. They had agreed to let the dead bury the dead. They left as they had come; strangers to each other.

Astrid had sat at her desk entranced, wide-eyed, her chest heaving. Now she would have a new story to tell her father. Marston waited—cool as a cucumber—at the counter while Moloney returned to Charlie's office. Moloney left as he had come. When Astrid took Marston's check to him, her eyes never left his face. I don't know what we might have seen; we were pawns of the curse of de Alvarado.

In the 1930s between stints dodging bullets as a twentieth-century buccaneer in revolutions and *opéra-bouffe* governments with stints dodging bullets as a lawman, Marston had to make a living. For a while he and two partners joined in a brief flurry of Honduran "gold fever," and went prospecting near Yoro in the rain forests and high mountains on the southern slopes of the *Cordillera Nombre de Dios*. One day his partners took their stash of gold into San Pedro Sula, a three or four day trip, to cash it in and buy supplies. Marston stayed to guard their diggings by the mountain stream they were also panning.

When *banditos* looking for easy gold jumped Marston, he shot one dead right off the bat, winged another, and then, himself wounded, scared off the rest. As he lay there by the stream waiting, unable to walk and in agony, he found consolation in the grandeur of the beautiful vistas before him. Blue skies contrasted with green mountain ranges spaced by misty valleys covered with towering pines, twelve feet or more in diameter at the base. The views reached out in all directions, deepened into distant rich purple, and stretched the limits of believable beauty.

We are not often given the time and place of our choosing in which to die. Marston decided: "If my time has come there can be no more beautiful spot on earth to die."

If, in accepting death, Marston found a deeper meaning in the Name of God Mountains, I cannot say. Nor can I challenge the manifestation of the wondrous handiwork of God he saw there.

His partners had not deserted Marston and returned in time to cart him off to a doctor. While recuperating he decided that revolutions were safer than gold prospecting and went looking for work.

***

For me Marston's monthly visits were a welcome diversion. Astrid made sure I knew he had come and after she handed him his pension check he and I visited for a chat that was always far too short. The day in January the woman I knew as his daughter came instead of Marston because, she said, he couldn't make the walk, caught me unawares. I grabbed the envelope from Astrid, piled the "daughter" into the consulate jeep to direct us, and with Polo driving headed for Marston's place. It was one of a row of rusty corrugated iron shacks on a muddy track, the main drag of San Pedro Sula's miserable *barrio,* on the barren slope of a garbage-strewn windswept hill. He was sitting on a crude wooden bench watching his "granddaughters." These were two fair, dirty blond — both dirty and blond — girls of five or six at play nearby in a group of children. He seemed glad to see me and grateful for the check. He declined my offer of help — he was an American citizen, and I should have tried harder. He apologized for any trouble he had caused.

After work one day in February, I took my wife with me when I went to deliver Marston's pension check. With her long legs tantalizingly revealed by a short skirt, her bobbed dark hair disarranged by the wind, and her pretty face flushed, Josephine looked especially attractive. When Marston looking up from his bench, saw her get out of the car, he struggled to his feet. His ninety-seven-year-old, six- foot-four-inch frame straightened up as the years and decades magically fell away. His gracious younger self showed as he took her by the arm and politely escorted her to his bench. Should I be jealous of a ninety-seven-year-old *pistolero*? Yes. Astrid, herself not immune to Marston's charm, had confided to me that in his day Marston had been notorious, as a man-about-town ladies' man. Now, perhaps for the last time, with a beautiful woman at his side, a touch of his charm and charisma showed through the ravages of age. In my mind's eye I saw him tall and dignified. I saw him a half century ago at a money-raising *soirée* for Cuban revolutionaries at the governor's mansion in Tallahassee; then with a pretty matron in San Pedro Sula, or in between with one of the renowned beauties of La Ceiba. The tableau on the bench gave me a glimpse into the private life of a bold, exciting man. My wife and I treasure that moment with Marston in the twilight of his life.

I saw Lee Marston alive one more time. In March I took my whole family and we went to deliver his pension check. Josephine held our three-month-old *gringito* (young Gringo), our own *sanpedranito* Gregory Cone. Marston's two "granddaughters" stood passively while they and our oldest, Clayton, seven, and David, five, sized each other up. Perceiving no threats they began to mingle and joined in the universal language of childhood. Feebler than before, Marston was especially attentive to Josephine and apologetic for having no refreshments—nothing to offer us. Leaving the conversation to Lee and Josephine, no telling what they talked about. I was chagrined at the realization I had not brought something for them. It was bad manners and thoughtlessness. What hurt even more was what Marston thought of me. The American vice consul comes calling and doesn't bring even a token for the host or hostess. What a blessing toys for the girls, groceries, and a full ice chest might have been. What a difference it might have made to Lee, what a difference to me!

Before Marston's next check was due word came that he was in the hospital. I should have rushed there at once but Astrid told me not to worry. Dr. Martinez, she assured me, would take care of Marston. Not going was my mistake, I can't blame Astrid. The next morning the hospital called to say that "the old *norteamericano*, Marston" had died in the night; choked on his own vomit, alone and unattended. My fault, but in my frustration (that word again), I could have choked Dr. Martinez.

Bitter, anguished, and although of small recompense, I arranged the best funeral I could. A bright, brand new, unused Veterans Administration American flag draped his coffin, loaded onto a flatbed donkey cart. Following his "daughter" and two "granddaughters" came a cortège of *norteamericanos*. The *cuerpo consulado* (consular corps) was represented by Charlie, wearing a necktie; me in my new suit; Josephine, pretty as a picture in her ever-ready black dress; and a tearful Astrid. Behind us came as many of the prettiest American expatriate matrons I could dragoon into coming. None of the women knew Marston even by name, but I thought he would have liked having them walk behind his coffin for auld lang syne.

They came because I asked them to and they knew it was important to me. No Hondurans came, not Astrid's father, nor "Machine Gun" Guy Moloney. From Potter's Field the "daughter," flag tucked under her arm, and the two girls disappeared. I wish they had let me help them but they didn't.

Trudging along behind Marston's coffin I remembered the day a year and a half earlier when we had followed Jack Briscoe, honorary British vice consul to his grave. How different had been the lives and deaths of these two men, yet, in the end they were equally dead. Marston had lived most of his life on borrowed time; Briscoe was shot down with his best years ahead of him. Marston, the soldier of fortune, the crack *pistolero,* an O. Henry–type buccaneer, died naked in bed. Death came to Briscoe, the dapper *bon vivant,* on his feet, ready to fight, in the blast of a high-powered rifle. Briscoe was a success, rewarded with money and honors. Marston had been good at what he did, but what had he done? Who could remember in which revolution and whose side he was on? Forgotten, old, he was surrounded by lesser, weaker men. I too, who might have held off death a short while longer, had let him down. Was it the "boring, frustrating, and monotonous" way of life and death that corrupted and put the cruel hex of de Alvarado on men and women in San Pedro Sula? Was the assessment of capable and highly regarded Consul John Cameron Peake and Vice Consul Joseph Pace, who completely revised the post report dated February 1956, right after all? It is sad to report that neither Peake, Pace, nor Paine, my predecessors and contemporaries, survived their tours in San Pedro Sula. Was that post a graveyard or a dumping ground for consular officers? *Gracias a Dios,* they closed it soon after I left.

Did the director general of the Foreign Service when he assigned me here know what he was doing? Is that the import of his ominous question, "Just where is San Pedro Sula—Mr. Tinny?" Had I stood and said "Ambassador Hare, sorry, I don't know—either." what would he have done? Had he answered his own question and said "Go find out," how might my life have been different?

My all too brief acquaintance with Marston and sketchy knowledge of his life—a gunfight here a battle there—and bandits and renegades everywhere told me San Pedro Sula was accursed. Perhaps my *tres pistoleros* and Jack Briscoe were worthy successors to

Don Pedro. None were sterling characters and in the end all is forgotten, nothing is forgiven. Why didn't Marston and Moloney have anything to say to each other? Murder and mayhem are indigenous to San Pedro Sula. Without a *pistolero* like the ones I knew to add class it became sordid. I left one standing; now, fifty years later, he must be gone too.

Like the story of the man trying to escape death by fleeing to Samarkand, my *pistoleros* couldn't escape and neither can anyone else. We know death has many guises; does it masquerade as the farmer's wife with her butcher knife in hand who pursues us to cut off our tails?

No, Don Pedro de Alvarado, life in your town—caught between it and death as the farmer's wife—is not boring, not monotonous. We are, I hate to say it, frustrated. One out of three is all you get. It is poor comfort, and I do not expect absolution for not being more help to Marston at the end. As I grieve, my prayer is that in his last hours Marston saw not the grimy walls of a stinking hospital ward, but instead saw in his clear mind's eye the blue skies and bright green of the Name of God *cordillera*. With wounds healed, muscles taut, head held high, and step springy, he becomes the man he was. It was in such a place, he told me, he faced death and thought it a fitting place in which to die. Again he challenges death.

His gun is ready, cocked, and primed; but this time with the instinct that brought him ninety-seven years, he knows it is useless. Whether he sees God, I don't know. I have been to the Name of God Mountains and do know he sees lush valleys shaded by majestic pines laced with icy streams paved with gold nuggets and shadowed by misty rainbows. Lee Marston stands tall, gazes at distant mountains of purple grandeur, one after another, that go on forever and ever, and steps forward.

4

Götterdämmerung

Nazi grand strategy for global conquest envisioned domination of the heartland of the Euro-Asian landmass, hegemony over the Atlantic nations, and sooner rather than later over all countries on the outer rim of the civilized world. One Nazi strategic ploy that touched San Pedro Sula was the insertion of Deutsche Luft Hansa, Germany's national airline as it was then called, into the air travel passenger market of Latin America. In the mid-1930s their technically advanced Dornier flying boats challenged existing technology.

These streamlined, high-winged seaplanes used two inline, water-cooled, diesel engines, mounted tandem, atop the single wing in a "pusher-puller" configuration. Futuristic in this era of biplanes with wings held together with wood struts and wires they were, with their long upturned noses, in profile reminiscent of Dutch wooden shoes. They were nicknamed "flying shoes" or "flying Dutch shoes." The Nazis encouraged use of the word "Dutch" and jokes and cartoons to divert suspicion of malicious intent or ulterior motive. Meanwhile, these "flying shoes" were setting records; for example, flying 5,200 miles nonstop across the Atlantic from start point Devon to Caravellas, Brazil. They were widely publicized all across Latin America, overtly "surveying for routes." In fact, by flying into places inaccessible to land planes, the "flying shoes" were gathering new meteorological and geographical data for Nazi Germany. Luft Hansa aircraft also ferried people and maintained clandestine contact for Germany's network of covert operatives.

Overt operatives, those in quasi-official positions, "trade missions" for example, were blatant future Nazi Leaders, designed to build a local "Party" from the grassroots. Guatemala, El Salvador, Nicaragua, Costa Rica, and Honduras, although prime targets, did not rate the exotic Dorniers and were serviced by the boxy, corrugated, tin Junker 52 planes. Enthusiastic Nazis, proudly German, accompanied by handsome, sturdy, fecund blond wives, fair skinned and enticing—true Valkyries—slipped smoothly into the local society. They were friendly, handy, and proficient in everything; adept at ingratiating themselves into the prevailing culture while maintaining an enviable Teutonic identity.

They successfully recruited converts, especially in the military, to the demagogic, forceful philosophy of National Socialism. They evangelized a nationalistic goal of a "strong central government," the *Füehrerprinzip* (leadership principle), in economic, cultural, and political activity. Throughout the 1930s they worked hard at selling their creed. Then, the war overtook them and with the collapse of Nazi Germany and chaos in Europe, these agents' original reasons for being in Central America ended. Some returned to Germany others made for themselves new homes and new lives; some had private and darker agendas. Private contacts openly whispered in my ear that eleven years after the end of World War II, the "would be Nazi Party leader" for Central America, once headquartered in Guatemala, was known, liked, and living well, right here in hot, dusty, and accursed San Pedro Sula.

Hans Mueller appeared to be a "good German," as opposed to the stereotypical Nazi thug. He was industrious, intelligent, obviously of good stock, with a high gloss of European culture and sophistication. When I met him in 1956, he was in his late sixties with a mature charm and grace. His shiny bald head framed by a neat fringe of white hair, his ruddy cheeks, round face, ready smile, and clever repartee, topping a tall spare frame, made him attractive and pleasant company. Wearing my commercial officer's hat, his importing agency was one I routinely visited in town. He represented German manufacturers re-emerging with Marshal Plan aid, but the bulk of his business was American.

Not only did Hans push American products; he ostentatiously delighted in everything American. At first I had no clue to Hans's

Nazi past until Charlie gave me the consulate's bulky dossier on him. In that file, plus the whispered innuendo and stories in town, his two roles—the efficient Nazi Party leader of the 1930s, and the popular local businessman of the 1950s—became one. Although we never discussed it in so many words he knew I knew who he had been. I wasn't sure which one he really was—the whole story. Hans was athletic and in good health and had been, in the 1920s and 1930s, a serious soccer player.

One achievement he claimed loudly and boasted of most readily was to have introduced soccer into Central America. Murder and mayhem, he assured me, had not been his job. He had not worn the uniform of the *Wehrmacht,* the army, at least not in World War II, and certainly not of the *Schutzstaffel (SS).* Rather, he had sowed the philosophy of Nazi Germany's superiority and ability to create a better world in the fertile fields of Central American militarism. Hitler, he preached, would unite the West and together the Aryan race would destroy the Communist barbarians from the East. He had proselytized the leaders in the indigenous societies who thought of Europe, particularly Spain, as their motherland. Not a pilot, Mueller knew Spain from the days of the Spanish Civil War.

Through connections with General Hugo von Sperrle and his deputy Colonel von Richthofen, cousin of the World War I Red Baron, leaders of what became notorious as Germany's Condor Legion, his job as a Nazi propagandist was made easier. German culture and mystique had an intrinsic appeal to militaristic politicians in the Central American countries where the largest organized power base was the army. There the generals dreamed and plotted government overthrows in three languages—army coup d'états, putsches, and *juntas* led by them, proclaiming the promise of future elections as "reform" and "democracy."

As an expert on Central America, Hans was recalled to Berlin after the war began in September 1939. Following Pearl Harbor the Central American republics—some coyly reluctant, perhaps due in part to Hans' machinations—followed the United States into the war. There they learned the joys and profits of sequestration of alien property and never let go. In 1956 Honduras was still at war with Germany.

* * *

Frieda, one of the statuesque, blonde *Valkyries* in her prime, was now a handsome, sturdy *hausfrau* who kept an immaculate house and supported all that her husband Hans said and did. Haughty, or the kinder "typically German," are words which best described her. Once, not so casually, she mentioned that her brother was a general in the *Wehrmacht*. Apparently, Hans had married up. Bruce, their sixteen year old son, a well-mannered, good looking boy who idolized his father lived with them when not in boarding school.

The Muellers had had an older son, Werner, who had just reached his teens in the spring of 1945 as the Russians were pounding Berlin into rubble. While the Third Reich visibly collapsed, he and other teenage boys were drafted into military service, either into the Hitler Youth, *Hitlerjugend,* or with old men into the *Volksturm,* usually as anti-aircraft gunners. In the debacle at the end of the war Werner was lost in the maelstrom of refugees and rumors. The Muellers heard from other boys who had deserted or been captured by the Russians and released that Werner was still held and with wishful thinking would be released. Worse than capture were rumors that as the war was ending many German "deserters" were summarily and wantonly executed on sight by the SS. In any case, the Muellers never saw Werner again.

Hans' position as a staunch Nazi party functionary and government official, once so important, was now his greatest handicap. It was no surprise the Soviets were blatantly hostile. Hans tried everything; pursued every lead. Reports that Werner had been "seen" in a prisoner of war camp somewhere set them off on another frantic, heartbreaking wild goose chase. Again, not surprisingly, the Allies brusquely turned deaf ear to Hans' and Frieda's entreaties. As a known Nazi Party official and government functionary, he could not plead innocence or ignorance of the facts.

Americans were the least "unhelpful" and Hans got the idea that if he entered the United States he would find sympathetic ears. Unfortunately, his prewar and wartime activities detailed in his dossier meant denazification didn't extend to "would be Party Leader" Hans Mueller. The McCarran-Walter Act is specific about the admission of Nazis. Frieda and Bruce could have gotten visas but they wouldn't leave Hans because Werner still might be alive in Russian hands. Hope, however vain, is not to be denied. Mueller needed a safe haven and the insignificant backwater of San Pedro Sula, known from prewar days, seemed perfect. From here he had access to Germany; it had a polyglot expatriate European community with a strong German contingent, some also known from prewar days. Better yet, San Pedro Sula was a lightly guarded gateway to the United States because it had an obscure, "Just where is San Pedro Sula?" small, poorly staffed American consulate. Hans was further cheered by the appearance of a naive and inexperienced vice consul—me. The bad news is that after a decade of costly searching, eleven years after the fighting stopped and with dwindling hope, Hans had expended his resources so his business failed. He went to work as a store clerk, in a final irony, for burly, swarthy Boris Goldstein; a devout, Orthodox Jew, a survivor and staunch Israeli supporter. Hans didn't know he was beaten, yet. Boris had come to San Pedro Sula in the early 1900s, with other Jews and Arabs, such as the Rosenthalls, Canuhuates, and Laraches fleeing the Ottoman pogroms in the Near East. These people were now the *Turco* business community, unique in Central America and a major part of commerce here. Boris was a generous supporter of, and frequent visitor to Israel. I liked Boris and cannot say for certain, but it must have given him satisfaction to have as his hireling a former high-ranking Nazi. The only comment on Hans I ever heard from him on that subject was that he was a good worker.

If Boris was tough, Yankel Rosenthall was tougher. Escaping from Palestine with many others, he landed first in British Honduras. He started by selling alligator skins from alligators he caught himself. His method was simple; armed with a large knife he had whetted to razor sharpness and wearing a white straw hat he would swim out into the lagoon at dusk. When the alligator, attracted by the white hat, approached Yankel sank down in the water leaving the hat floating on the surface. As the alligator passed overhead Yankel eviscerated it. He was not one to be taken lightly—not by alligators, not by anyone. Now he sold American automotive products; the money was better and he stayed dry.

I reacted favorably to Hans's friendliness and overtures, and constantly had to remind myself that it was not me personally he liked, but the American vice consul. Charlie, seeing our rapport, along with a clear warning, consigned the Muellers and their dilemma to me. My wife Josephine and I enjoyed their company. On evenings when the busy social pace of "cocktails" and dinners left a gap, the Muellers and the Tinnys played a few rubbers of bridge. Frieda played a "blitzkrieg" style bridge, counting the trumps aloud and playing her cards like a barrage from an 88mm cannon. They always got the bid. Hans was always dummy and they rolled over us like a couple Tiger IV *panzers*. After an evening of that I marveled we had won the war.

Our best times together with the Muellers were spent at a remote swimming pool hidden high in the verdant hills above town. Built before the war by another German "businessman," it had been preempted by Hans—perhaps legally, perhaps in another Nazi-style *anschluss*. Ever the good German, but also a good Nazi, Hans found that old habits are hard to break. A simple, fairly large, concrete rectangular box, mossy and crumbly now, the pool was fed by a swift mountain stream of icy water. The two Muellers, the Tinnys—Josephine, Clayton, David, and me—and a few select others spent many delightful afternoons there. Periodically, Hans would decree it was time to clean the pool. This became a game, and after opening sluice gates on the downhill side we shoveled out the silt and brushed the walls with stiff, push brooms. Hans was *Oberst* (Colonel). At pool-cleaning time he and his female lieutenant kept us working; it was good, clean fun (no pun intended).

The pool sat amidst coffee bushes, shaded from direct sun rays with banana trees. It was a veritable Garden of Eden with a variety of citrus and avocado trees, grape vines planted years earlier, but no apples. There were snakes like the poisonous *fer-de-lance* (spear-head), with a fatal bite. The silent trembling of a banana leaf marked the passage of a boa constrictor. Garden of Eden must have a snake.

Afternoons fueled by cold fried chicken—freshly killed and plucked—corn on the cob, fruit directly from the tree, and excellent Nacional beer from master brewer Sigmund Lingelbach's brewery, cooled in the mountain stream, were memorable. Sig, from a family of proud master brewers, with his wife Eunice and one daughter

Clay's age were from Racine, Wisconsin and also good company and good friends.

The shaded pool had an idyllic cathedral-like setting formed by towering pines admitting slanting rays of sunlight accompanied by the gurgling of the stream and murmured conversation. An occasional excerpt from Richard Wagner's *Der Ring Des Nibelungen* on Josephine's portable record player added class to the scene. We talked about everything except the war and what we should have talked about.

Deer and other animals roaming the area added to the enchantment. The women, in bathing suits which set off fair skins and shapely figures, even statuesque Frieda, heightened the glamour of the scene. Josephine was for most of the summer of 1957 heavy— she said huge—with our third son, soon to be a pseudo "Sanpedrano." The Muellers were excellent hosts and these quiet, contemplative, and seductive afternoons, reclining beside that mountain pool, were a world away from the chronic heat and dust, hideous chaos, and cruelty in San Pedro Sula below. Black panthers, growling and coughing in the distance but slinking closer at dusk signaled when it was time for us to go. We took coffee beans home to be ground, roasted, and brewed. Once Hans explained to me how they had made the coffee in Guatemala. There, rather than roasting beans in an oven as we did, and grinding them in the Osterizer, the beans were boiled down to a gummy black *esencia* (essence), which was mixed with water or milk, and sugar to taste.

Professionally, and Hans was a true professional, he described as follows how Guatemala farmers grow their coffee, the right way: Start with fertile, in our case jungle, soil at an altitude between 1500 to 5500 feet, a bit higher than his pool. Better coffee grows at higher altitudes but in smaller quantities. First, plant the coffee beans in a nursery bed and when they sprout, move them to a secondary bed. Shield the sprouts from the sun with a canopy of brush and cornstalks. When the plants reach two feet set them out under shade trees. If there are already suitable trees good, if not, plant banana trees which mature in a year. A coffee grower will try to plant 111 acres the first year and so on. During the third and fourth years the oldest coffee trees flower with white, star shaped blossoms and there will be some berries. The trees reach full bearing capacity in five or six years. Each 111 acres may produce over 100,000 pounds of berries and require gangs of Indians as pickers. These—the berries, not the Indians—are dumped into tanks of water. However, if the tank is not too full of coffee it may serve as a bathtub for the Indians. In separate processes the berries are stripped of two hard shells and a softer inner shell. This is done by a hulling machine, by fermenting, drying them in the sun and stripping them of the inner shell. Someplace in the process the berries become beans. Broken beans are rejected. Polished beans are blended with beans from Brazil, Colombia, and El Salvador—roasted and ground. Finally, in the kitchen the grounds are boiled in the percolator. Honduras was not big on coffee. The best coffee, Hans said, comes out of a Maxwell House coffee can.

Ilse Koch, Hans' female lieutenant, was one of the "others" who came to the Mueller's pool. Despite the similarity of names, she was not the notorious "Witch of Buchenwald," wife of the SS Commandant of that camp. Ilsa Koch, a sometime librarian, was a sadist and nymphomaniac who made lampshades, gloves, and book covers from the tattooed skins of Buchenwald inmates, each skinned alive. In sex orgies she inserted glass rods into the prisoners' penises and then, using both hands, bent and pounded the penises breaking the rods into pieces.

Unfortunately, our Ilse looked the part. She had a full figure of medium height, muscular really, and could have been attractive except for a mouth half full of bad teeth—the other half was empty. Her English was good but she was loud. Now safe and at home in the warm climate the Northern races seek, she wore the flimsiest of clothes with no underwear. Her bathing suit was akin to Gunga Din's uniform, "…a piece of twisted rag before, and less than 'alf of that behind."

Her husband, Herr Koch, the name he used, sold German tools and trinkets with samples he dragged around in trunk sized luggage. He sweated profusely in a double-breasted wool suit and I wondered if he still worked for Hans and if he knew WWII was over or if it was for him. What he did when he wasn't selling trinkets was a mystery. In answer to my question he said, *"Ich spreche kaum Englisch.* He didn't speak much English, and I, likewise, don't speak much German.

* * *

Ilse may also have once worked for Hans but now she worked for Max, director of the Honduran-American Bi-National Center. Max, an Orthodox Jew lived next door to us. Ilse, who never acknowledged that there was nothing she couldn't do, claimed to be an accomplished masseuse. That must have been true because more than once I heard sounds of vigorous massaging mixed with Max's grunts over the narrow space and low brick wall that separated our house and bedroom from his.

Ilse's status with the Muellers was unclear to me. *Frau* Mueller, it seemed, tolerated her because she was German and she worked for an American. For *Frau* Mueller and Hans the war would never be over and they were ready to exploit any opportunity to learn the fate of Werner or to get into the United States. Ilse was unrepentantly German, if not Nazi, with unyielding loyalty to Hans and all he stood for.

Hans, broke, dependent on Jews, had every reason it seemed to me after two years of frequent socializing, to be bitter. Loss of his son could only become a heavier burden with time. Driven by a forlorn hope of learning the fate of his son, he was dealt an ace, if not a trump. Proud Frieda's brother, General Hans Johann Cramer, last commander of Erwin Rommel's Afrika Korps, was coming to San Pedro Sula.

Colonel Hans Johann Cramer's Eighth Panzer Regiment was in Rommel's Seventh Panzer Division which "blitzed" the French Army and the Allies in May 1940. Cramer followed Rommel to Africa and his Eighth became one of the Afrika Korps' crack regiments and Rommel's favorite. March 5, 1943, General Cramer became the last commander of the Afrika Korps. On his surrender in May he said in messages to Rommel and to Hitler: "Ammunition expended...The Afrika Korps has fought until it can fight no more, as ordered. The Afrika Korps must rise again!"

In January 1944 Rommel took command of Army Group B in the West. In February Rommel became a party to the plot to remove Hitler. Cramer was never implicated in the plot although staunchly loyal to Rommel. He was, believe it or not, repatriated to Germany at the height of the War by the British who had taken him prisoner in Tunisia in 1943 because, they said, of his bad asthma.

After the war Cramer was quoted in *The Times* of London as saying Rommel had considered the war in North Africa a "gentleman's war" and had taken pride in the clean record of his troops, and ours. Rommel, Cramer said, had strong views on correct conduct and observance of the soldiers' code as did the majority of German regular officers, particularly those such as Rommel and Cramer, who predated the Nazis. Rommel did not allow any SS troops in Africa. Cramer condemned both what he called the murder of Rommel and General Maisel who carried it out. Now General Hans Johann Cramer was coming to San Pedro Sula—why? Was he now coming in his own time to commit murder "as ordered?"

Is life a zero sum game; for every birth there is a death? A real Wehrmacht general was coming and echoes of World War II, Africa, and Hitler would reverberate in San Pedro Sula, and relieve the "boredom." Would the Sanpedranos hear these echoes and would they care if they did? The answer to both questions in a word is "No."

Why is that? In two and a half years of living amongst them nothing had mitigated my first impression of Sanpedranos. True sons and daughters of Don Pedro were ambushed by other true sons and daughters and left to die on a muddy trail while their horses trotted on home. Coup d'états were festive occasions, at least for the new office holders. To be fair only a few voters with the wrong color ballots were made to eat their ballots—or else. Sanpedranos are a callous lot and took World War II in stride.

In some places it would have been the "dog days" of summer, those miserable days of late August and early September when Sirius, the "dog star," rises and sets with the sun. Since almost every day in San Pedro Sula is miserable there isn't much to distinguish dog days from other days. One difference was that this was our third and last summer here. Frieda was in charge of General Cramer's visit and kept putting me off when I asked to meet her brother. The day, or as they say in German, *Der Tag,* arrived and he slipped into town with no fanfare. Perhaps he met with the local army commandant—the real power in San Pedro Sula; perhaps one who had been cultivated by Hans. I don't know. He was soon due to leave, according to the time table I had ferreted out of the Muellers, and I had not yet met him. Frieda relented:

"I will bring him to your house tonight if you promise not to ask about the War."

I agreed with the proviso that if he brought the subject up I would respond. She did, he did, and I did. Actually, Cramer's visit was short and only Frieda came with him. We three sat together but that was enough. His forbidding presence filled the room. His remarks were mostly of the sort Frieda would allow. In appearance he was every inch a German *Junker,* a typical Prussian soldier. Tall, like Frieda, he had an air of command, no doubt, a family trait. He addressed me in German, Frieda translated, and every sentence sounded like an order: *"Ja, Generalfeldmarschall Rommel..."* Yes, Field Marshal Rommel (was a great soldier). He made no mention of his surrender of the Afrika Korps, Rommel's death, or the plot to kill Hitler. Abruptly, he stood, and with a click of the heels and a stiff Prussian bow he was gone.

That same day I had seen Hans briefly. He was preoccupied; busy arranging papers in his office and sullen to the point of brusqueness. He was not the Hans I had known for two years, proud, not boastful, but defiant. Finally, he was a beaten man, a dead man and he knew it. A trump was played but it was not his. Can you look a man in the face, know he is about to die, and be cheerful?

At first light the next morning a Honduran soldier knocked on our door and asked me to come to the Mueller's house. There, Frieda and Bruce were sitting, silent and stolid, in the front room. police and others were standing outside.

Hans was curled up on the floor in the hall bathroom; one pistol shot to his head had ended his life. Whether the mess of blood and brains on the wall and floor corrected the mess of his life is not for me to say. A nickel-plated officers Walther P-38 pistol was still clutched in his hand. The sound of the shot had awakened the household but Hans' body had blocked the door. Young Bruce had been obliged to climb through the window and move the body of his beloved father before anyone could enter. Frieda, Bruce and I—

the general was not to be seen—sat silent and composed, saying only what had to be said.

How much time had Hans been given to say good bye to his faithful wife and devoted son? Had he been given any time at all? Had Frieda known beforehand? I don't think so, she had held steadfast to Hans but she was also a Valkyrie to the core. Had he been given the choice—poison or the pistol? Rommel had taken poison. What was Hans' crime? Was it his glorious Nazi past now ended in failure which branded him a pariah? Had he betrayed his past, committed treason? Had Hans been implicated in the plot to kill Hitler? Hans had been in Berlin at the time and because of his years in Central America could have brought that point of view to the table. Did General Cramer bring news of Hans' first born, Werner? That he was dead? No, Hans already knew in his heart; Werner was dead.

Here again I questioned myself. Should I have mentioned the possibility to General Cramer that Hans might someday receive reprieve from the United States and a visa. Other Nazis had found relief, but I was guessing. Robert Newbegin who next year, in 1958, would be named ambassador to Honduras had written earlier, soon after the war, that it was silly for the United States to insist others deport Germans while we imported Nazi scientists and intelligence agents. Was it the curse of Don Pedro de Alvarado that prevented me from uttering that thought in the back of my mind to General Cramer? The curse had kept me from racing to Lee Marston's side a year ago as he lay dying or from reaching up to give Charlie a friendly hand. Hans would have done well in the United States. He would have been more of an asset than most of my immigrants.

Another day, only half of the *cuerpo consulado*—the Honorary British Vice Consul Pell declined. My wife in her black dress and me in my two year old new suit accompanied Hans' undraped coffin on the donkey cart and walked behind Frieda and Bruce, along the familiar dusty road to the cemetery.

Charlie, transferred to the Department of State, should have been a memory in San Pedro Sula but would soon return on his own. He knew life and death in San Pedro Sula were frustrating but not boring and he was returning for his wife to be, the lovely Leonor Gavidia. With due credit to Charlie, that sentiment is in my revision of the post report. A new consul, Harold Wood, originally from Boston, who now called the charming little town of Eagle Pass, Texas home, had taken his place. Harold and I got along fine.

Harold Wood had served in a U.S. Army artillery company in World War I in France. His company captain had been Harold L. Ickes, later secretary of the interior for Franklin D. Roosevelt and Harry Truman. In 1922 Wood made a high grade on the written exam for the Foreign Service but was offered only a staff position. At our first meeting he showed me the original report of his grade on the exam I had to take three times to pass. They never told him why he was not made an officer. I didn't attempt an answer when he asked me. He was never content to let it rest.

One handicap Harold had was an unbureaucratic sense of humor. His first question on meeting someone was; did they know where Eagle Pass was. In forty years only a man in Buenos Aires knew. The man said in a recent movie one cowboy had said to another "You go to the ranch for help and I'll head them off at Eagle Pass!" His second question was why was he not given an officer's commission?

He served thirty-three years in Mexico beginning at Guaymas and going on to Salina Cruz, Mexico City, Veracruz, Puerto Mexico, Piedras Negras, Guadalajara, and Tampico. The three decades in Mexico were at the height of the interminable "revolutionary" period and the continuous smuggling of whiskey from Mexico to the United States during Prohibition. He stayed there during World War II. In 1956 he was posted to Buenos Aires and in 1958 he was assigned as principal officer at San Pedro Sula.

San Pedro Sula would be his last post and the title principal officer his reward for forty years of consular service. Harold was the other side of the coin which made it my first post.

Born in 1897, Harold died in 1981. Together in San Pedro Sula he and I represented a beginning and an ending of Foreign Service careers. My quest for an answer to the director general's question was beginning. His quest was for the reason for his failure to earn officer rank, despite his high grade. Harold's forty years in the wilderness led not to Samarkand, but to San Pedro Sula. He might have been a great ambassador. Was that the answer I did not want to hear?

With all due credit to Harold he did seem to be satisfied. He was the principal officer of a little known, but busy, well-established consulate competently staffed and furnished with comfortable furniture. After three decades of consular work he was on familiar ground. His appraisal of San Pedro Sula was the opposite of mine; he thought it was a fine place. It would have been helpful to me to have had more time with Harold and benefit from his long experience. His quest to learn why he had been refused officer rank was his unanswerable question comparable to my conundrum.

Harold had been briefed on Hans Mueller and had a right to his personal opinions. On this occasion, he pleaded "diplomatic illness." This afternoon in his very rigid daily routine he was riding his Sears Xercycle. He could think about Mueller, or perhaps not, as he drank the three tall gin and tonics set before him every evening by Maria, his Mexican wife from Chiapas while she shaved his head. Ramrod straight with a bull neck and bald head, no white fringe, he looked more like a "Nazi" storm trooper than did Hans. He had told me he would not, on principle, attend a funeral for a Nazi. Harold never had a chance to swim in the Muellers' pool or lay on the grass beside it. Frieda did not know Harold, or miss him today, but he signed her visa. Apparently, she couldn't bear to look at me.

There were two other funerals I did not attend, the same day; both of them Germans and part of the flotsam and jetsam of World War II. They were officially "stateless" traveling on a United Nations *laissez passes* (permits), and faceless to me. They were listed in our visa quota book, and I drew a line through their names. I didn't know their connection to Hans, but Cramer did. Was that what Hans was, flotsam? I hated to think so. Had General Cramer been sent to insure the execution of Hans and the two others? They always send a general. Cramer hated General Maisel who gave the poison to Rommel. Did he hate himself for what he had to do to his sister's husband and nephew's father? Germans are tough.

Let the dead bury the dead they say; and if he was accountable, General Cramer had done his work well. How deep, I wondered, was the connection between Hans, Rommel, Cramer and the plot to kill Hitler? Five thousand Army and government officials were executed for the plot. The Gestapo claimed seven thousand. How many conspirators were victims of their own ineptness, or worse yet, innocent?

Were these three more of the same? What is the connection that brought the plot to kill Hitler down to San Pedro Sula, the most unlikely spot in the world—or was it? The curse of de Alvarado knows no bounds and brought a certain ghoulish attraction to San Pedro Sula. Paid assassins, *pistoleros,* renegades of all sorts came. A veteran State Department security officer said he found the most beautiful woman he had ever seen there. The connection between de Alvarado and the Gestapo is not surprising. How fitting that the Gestapo track down one more conspirator to "Just where is San Pedro Sula—Mr. Tinny?" The Gestapo had an answer.

Did ever a failed plot destroy more victims? They ranged from Rommel, a national hero, who was among the highest, down to the lowest. Was that Hans and was he the last? Who were the other two anonymous Germans? What about Ilse and her trinket salesman husband? I never saw them again, did they burrow deeper into the jungle? There may be still other plotters, guilty or not, but if so they are not in San Pedro Sula. General Hans Johann Cramer was a very good general and had won battles for Rommel in France and in Africa. He had his orders and would have taken care of them as ordered, as he did Hans.

Could I have done more for Hans—temporized, found excuses and given him an extra bit of time? Harold had absolutely no excuses for Hans's past, nor for Frieda or Bruce, and rightly so. Did even a tiny role in the plot to kill Hitler earn Hans consideration? Charlie's insight into the matter was lost; we never discussed it. Life in San Pedro Sula was indeed frustrating. The post report was right on that. Except for the birth of our third son—and he is a blessing— would anything else good come out of my tour in "Just where is, what's its name?" From whom, where, when, or if ever, will I find the answer?

5

Adios, pues, San Pedro Sula

My colleagues in the A-100 class at FSI were ostentatiously delighted that it was I who was assigned to the unknown jungle consulate at San Pedro Sula, not one of them. Those halcyon days of our first dip into Foreign Service life were brightened by their thoughtless banter inspired by the dismal Post Report, which branded the post a veritable career death trap. They consigned me to a smelly path of consular drudgery never to surface. So insignificant was this forgotten post that Ambassador Raymond Hare surprised us all, and condemned the post to oblivion when he asked the simplistic, pertinent, and yet to be answered question: "Just where is San Pedro Sula—Mr. Tinny?"

Surprise, surprise! In that august body of naive, budding diplomats only yours truly knew the answer. Alas, to know, to touch, is to be caught in the curse of the town's cruel founder and brutal patron, the polite Conquistador, with the chestnut, *castaña*-colored hair, Don Pedro de Alvarado.

Actually, some of the fondest most vivid memories Josephine and I have of the Foreign Service are of San Pedro Sula. As I said to the relief of the flustered young lady, the personnel officer who mistakenly revealed the name of my first post to me, "Let us keep San Pedro Sula our secret."

Despite the gloomy post report that branded San Pedro Sula as "boring, frustrating and monotonous," Ambassador Hare knew that every post is what you make it. He also knew that challenges and opportunities for all of us would come in many guises. Finally, if he did not know the latitude and longitude of San Pedro Sula, he did know it was not Samarkand. Unlike the Walrus he didn't talk of those things. FSI gave us a hint, through a glass darkly, of the stresses of Foreign Service life. We had to make our way along the golden, but narrow and uneven road to Samarkand.

The public and bloody birthing by the naked *mestizo* woman in front of me and the world on the fountain steps in the Plaza on my day six was, I now know, not extraordinary for the time and place. With that birth, and if the result of birth is death, then the murder of Jack Briscoe on day one gave me a hint as to "just where is San Pedro Sula?" The murders of Briscoe (Day One) and Leroy (circa Day 4015) were like bookends bracketing my search. How often had I witlessly, like a comedic antihero, escaped my own murder and the definitive answer to Ambassador Hare's conundrum? The great *pistolero* Lee Marston might not have died so abjectly when he did had I not blinked. To my eternal sorrow I was slow on the draw. Lee was fast, never blinked, and dodged death for ninety-seven years. At the intense, Wagnerian finale of the sad saga of Nazi Party leader Hans Mueller, what was my role? Was handsome, aloof Frieda, the *Valkyrie* who guarded his soul, innocent? Why didn't she want me to sign her visa? Her brother, a Wehrmacht general, last commander of the Afrika Korps, on Hitler's posthumous orders brought death and the ghost of Rommel to San Pedro Sula. We lived and died in the wake of Don Pedro's curse of cruel unconcern for human life.

The omnivorous, promiscuous ear of the Walrus has heard many things, but not all things. Granted, I must confess, Sanpedranos and we pseudo Sanpedranos have become a cynical, callous lot. We accept flying shoes and airships, sealing wax, cabbage palms, and if not kings, *los presidentes*, with equanimity. O. Henry told the story of consular life in his *opera-bouffe* novel *Cabbages and Kings*. His town of Coralio was comparable to my mid-twentieth-century San Pedro Sula. He brought in Thalia for comedy, whereas Melpomene for tragedy was my guardian angel. On the last day, as on the first, frantic frustration, bitter boredom, and mournful, monotonous death darkened my years in this unknown, unlamented, and God-forsaken hole.

In the long days and short years of our tour in San Pedro Sula, so often it came down to my wife in her basic black dress—she looks good in black—me in my new suit, and Charlie wearing his necktie, all following one coffin or another. When the native Honduran and Sanpedrano grandparents of our esteemed senior consular clerk, Aida, were literally hacked to pieces with machetes and their house ransacked by *banditos,* the police commented: "They were old."

Four election officials, fellow Rotarians and community leaders, were shot dead on a muddy highway during my first coup d'état. Their obituaries offered condolences to the widows. Voters had a choice: eat the ballots of the wrong color or be shot. Sanpedrano voters chewed and swallowed hard.

The death and burial of Lee Marston, chief of police and mayor, whose guns sometimes brought a modicum of law and order to San Pedro Sula, might as well have taken place on the moon as far as Sanpedranos were concerned. Lee Marston and Lee Christmas, once local heroes, had lived and almost died here for two lifetimes, were lovers of the ladies, and friends of their blindsided cuckolded husbands. The *pistoleros* may have called themselves "Sanpedranos," but they were not; they were, and would remain, *norteamericanos,* with the power and prestige that name bestowed. Marston left a woman who called herself his daughter and two little girls who were her daughters and possibly his granddaughters. Lee Christmas left a daughter. Machine Gun Guy Moloney left no one to regret his leaving or hail his return—except me and I am glad to do it.

Louis Ware, my 1930s boyhood neighbor—I talk about him later—and a forgotten fugitive from the law, revealed himself to me but left no forwarding address. Our meeting after a quarter century tells us we each live in a small world. I wondered about his bare legged sister Clare who looked good in shorts and with an impish smile in those long ago neighborly days.

What mark did I leave in San Pedro Sula? Rather, what deep crippling wounds did the detour to the town of de Alvarado carve into my hide? I can show you the scars.

Would any of my family and colleagues leave anyone to note we had come and gone? I doubt anyone in San Pedro Sula had heard of or read O. Henry's account as vice consul in "Coralio," and few

Americans have. Charlie, for one, did better on that score than the rest of us; he went back.

Twice married, twice divorced, Charlie courted and married Leonor Gavidia, daughter of a Sanpedrano physician. She was an American citizen by virtue of being born on one of her parents' visits to the United States. Charlie and Leonor had two beautiful daughters, innocent victims of de Alvarado's curse. Despite her passport, Leonor was a sanpedrana and her roots to blood and place were strong.

As for me, what would be my legacy? Suppose I had refused a visa to an applicant who felt he should have one or had pried too deeply into the history of a scared fugitive? Louis, whose history I knew, might have feared being reported by me. Men have died for less. Fugitives flee to Honduras to get lost not found by an over-zealous but naive vice consul.

Our street with permanent ruts, usually hub deep in mud, had little through automobile traffic. It was a pedestrian path for Sanpe-dranos who lived in shacks and tiny farms up the first slopes be-hind the town. The short distance from the Consulate to my house was dark and desolate. I often wondered on the few times I carried my trusty .45 if I would have the guts to shoot first. For anyone who wanted to find me, where we lived was known. Would my obitu-ary contain those ominous words "he died suddenly, one night on his usual walk home"? The voracious pi-dogs would destroy any clues.

More useful than the .45 was a solid stick, like a cudgel. It was good for keeping the yelping, ravenous, cowardly but aggressive feral pi-dogs at bay. There were hundreds of them, and they were a real threat. Howling started after dark on one side of town, trav-eled in a wave across town, faded into the distance on the other side, and then began again somewhere else. Spotting a lone walker, they circled ever closer, until several on opposite sides charged in simultaneously for the kill. One tense encounter with pi-dogs from which I got away unharmed taught me a lesson.

Complementing the pi-dogs were the *zopilotes*, vultures, who often roosted on the peak of our roof where they scratched around noisily with their vicious claws and beaks. When the *zopilotes* were there, and we always knew when they were, more than likely packs of pi-dogs lurked nearby. Prey for the dogs was food for the vultures.

Conversely, Sanpedranos could also be courteous, friendly, and hospitable to guests. When we arranged to have our third son born in the *clinica* on the slope above town, they were pleased. American wives had traditionally flown to New Orleans, or home to mother, to have their babies. The *clinica's* doctors and owners were the Bendaña brothers. Guillermo was the oldest; Sergio, in general practice, my wife's pediatrician; and Rene, the youngest, the pathologist. All were American educated and impressed me as capable, conscientious doctors. Guillermo had lost interest in treating human patients, but kept his hand in while he concentrated on veterinary medicine. He also managed the family cheese factory, entirely separate from the *clinica*. Bendaña's popular cheeses sold in fifty and one hundred pound wheels throughout Honduras and neighboring countries. Sergio took an interest in us after Josephine declared her intention to have her baby in his *clinica*, and one night may have saved her life.

She was devastated by an infestation of cattle ticks encountered in a careless moment on an archeological site, an ancient Mayan village discovered by the United Fruit Company. After the official survey, the company archeologist oft times invited us to visit the site. Pottery shards and obsidian knife blades were sometimes were to be found, and Josephine once found a human bone.

This time she wandered off the cleared site—a big mistake. By that night her beautiful body lay sprawled naked across our bed, arms and legs akimbo, unconscious, burning up with fever and covered in red tick bites. My panic phone call brought Dr. Bendaña, and we coated her in a salve he brought in a double handful of little glass jars stamped "sample." By morning her fever had broken. She was sleeping comfortably, oblivious to her ordeal, on the way to full recovery.

In preparation for the baby's birth—we did not yet know the sex—we visited the *clinica*; a long low building of heavy adobe construction, with a roof of handmade tiles, located high enough in the hills to be above the volcanic dust and almost volcanic heat.

The woodwork, the doors, windows, and furniture, were beautiful Honduran mahogany, lignum vitae, and other exotic woods.

Josephine received a gracious reception and was shown "her" room-to-be, adorned with a life-sized portrait of the Virgin with one arm outstretched, the other clenched over her heart. The room was clean and cool, with a dramatic, panoramic view over the jungle toward the sea, unmarred by the town sweltering below.

Josephine's contractions began in the very late evening of December 13, 1957, after the annual Christmas program of the international school at the Casino Sanpedrano. After a cup of coffee we were off to the *clinica*. The three Bendañas rotated night duty so one was always there. That night I turned her over to the vet and cheese maker, Guillermo. When I asked if I should wait, he said in his brusque, raspy voice: "Come back at 6:00, it will be born then." At precisely 6:00, December 14, 1957, I stepped through the door to hear the birth cries of our third son, Gregory. They called him *Gregorio lindo* (beautiful Gregory). Sanpedrano friends were anxious to see the *gringito* born in San Pedro Sula. He was a ten- pound baby, born in a perfect delivery. Veterinarians do these things right.

In the preceding months, Gregory's impending advent had been the subject of much planning. He was the first child born to a consular officer in San Pedro Sula in recorded history. Not even O. Henry, a bachelor, had speculated on such an event. Some Americans warned us that, if a boy, he would be subject to service in the Honduran Army. Charlie and I knew better; the consulate was American soil, and he was born 100 percent American. The one baby necessity not available in town, one on which Josephine insisted, was American baby food. She wanted the gooey stuff in little glass jars with the picture of baby Humphrey Bogart on the label. Six cartons of assorted flavors were promptly ordered from Henry Fransen's *supermercado*. Surely, cheaper ocean freight—we had seven months—would be good enough. Wrong, ocean freight was nineteenth century, skip ahead to the twentieth century; use airfreight, always!

Seven months later, early in December, the chief of customs at Puerto Cortes, Army Colonel Morales, telephoned to say my baby food would arrive at noon on December 24. Hopefully, the baby, due before then, could survive a few days without Bogart's help. Col. Morales was one of the army officers who had gotten escape-hatch visas "to take my daughter to school," just prior to the recent *coup.* Perhaps, he felt he owed me a favor, or was preparing for the next *coup.* Furthermore, he said: "If you are on the pier, I will have the six cartons loaded directly into your jeep. If the boxes get separated, none can be released until all are brought together. I will handle the formalities. As for you, *'Adios, pues!'* goodbye, and off you go."

This is how business can be expedited here, with the proper incentive. He expected his next visa to be issued just as expeditiously. "I'll be there," I said.

The distance from San Pedro Sula to the port in Puerto Cortes is little more than thirty miles, but the road is unpaved and crossed time and again by unbridged creeks. When Josephine was along she hoisted up her skirt and waded in on her long legs to test the depth. With a ten-day-old baby she was not coming on this trip.

Charlie insisted I drive the consulate Jeep, despite a leaky radiator, because it had four- wheel drive. Going was downhill and easy; coming back would be a test of Jeep and me. Food, drinking water, my household pistol, the .45 Colt, seemed appropriate; a machete, rope, a spare tire, and a new straw hat seemed adequate equipment. No bucket was handy so the hat would do double duty.

"Promise to be home tonight," my wife said, as early on a dreary, drizzly Christmas Eve morning I hit the road. Major traffic concerns were slow-moving ox and donkey carts piled high with hay or vegetables, and fast-moving lumber trailer-trucks, laden with huge pine logs and exotic hardwoods roaring down from the mountains of Yoro and La Esperanza. The trucks' brakes barely slowed them down as locked wheels skidded on a road lubricated with slippery mud or talcum powder like dust, and the trucks fishtailed wildly. When a big rig came roaring up behind me, I snuggled over to the shoulder, however narrow, and stayed there.

To hit a cart could be a matter of life or death for the driver of the car, depending upon the severity of the accident. Damage to the cart could cost only the repairs to the "luxury" cart. Damage to the animal could be very expensive to this "one of a kind" beast. Injury to the cart's driver, or worse, to a pedestrian, could mean real trouble. Instantly a mob gathered to pelt the driver with stones, or in the case of a really bad accident, butchered with machetes. After an accident, keep going to the next police checkpoint, or better yet, just keep going. The killing of a *norteamericano* is dismissed with a shrug of the shoulders.

I reached Puerto Cortes well before noon. In his hot, stuffy office in the Aduana (Customs) compound, Colonel Morales greeted me. Two snub-nosed .38 caliber Smith & Wessons on his desk served as paperweights—and to settle complaints. He said the ship was due *prontissimo*, very soon. An hour later he said, go to the hotel for lunch and a cold *cerveza*. "Go enjoy Puerto Cortes."

Seated at the hotel bar with bottles of *cerveza* in front of them, were two of the lumbermen whose trucks I had dodged and who knew what *prontissimo* meant. One, Plowden, owned a sawmill near the rail head of Potrerillos, the end of the road type town which made San Pedro Sula look like a Sunday school. He cut timber from the mountains to the south and east. The other man, tall and boney, worked for him and handled big and fast rigs. We got into conversation and I asked where they were from. Both said "Tampa," my hometown. Interested, I asked the tall one "What section?"

"Seminole Heights." That is where I had lived. "What street?" I asked.

"Paris Street," he said. That was my street! "What number?"

"706," he said, two doors from 702, my house!

Then he said, "I'm Ware, Louis Ware," and it all came back to me.

He had been the neighborhood troublemaker, not mean, just always into mischief. Older than I. In 1933 when we both lived on Paris Street, he was then in his late teens. With a few dollars in his pocket, an A-Model Ford coupe, *sans* muffler, he was a local character. Gregarious and likable, sometimes Louis would give me a ride in his car. We got along, despite the age difference, or maybe because of it. Clare, his tomboy kid sister, older and bigger than me, was my nemesis. What tortures she inflicted afterward are lost in the dimness of faded memory. I think Louis, not always around and who thought it all very funny, came to my rescue.

The summer of 1933 saw the final, hectic days of Prohibition. "Revenuers" were making a last ditch effort to stem the rampant bootlegging. One night Louis was delivering a load of whiskey to the "Blazing Stump," a neighborhood bar close by at the corner of our dirt street and the hard road. As he drove up he was waylaid by deputies. Trying to elude capture, turning in the deep sandy ruts his car overturned and his friend riding shotgun in the front seat was killed. Louis was uninjured and charged with manslaughter and bootlegging. Scared, he jumped bail and ran. His parents, taking Clare with them, thank goodness, left town never to be heard of again. Now, twenty four years later, Louis sat on a bar stool next to me. He knew me and that I was government. I was, he said, "the law." The way he said it was a question; "What was I going to do about the manslaughter and bootlegging charges?"

Charges against Louis had not been pressed but by then he was gone, on his way, it turns out, to Honduras. He saw good prospects in lumber and stayed. He didn't give me details of his life, the less said the better, but the question remained.

Louis' accident had been almost a quarter century ago. Without knowing the law I was sure the statute of limitations had taken effect. He didn't need to worry about a twenty-four year charge of manslaughter, or bootlegging. I told him: "If you want to go to Tampa, come in sometime and get your passport renewed." He probably knew that too but seemed happy to hear me say it.

A messenger from the colonel told us that our ship was in so we all headed to the docks. While the lumbermen took care of their logs, the ship lowered a pallet with my cartons of baby food down beside my Jeep. The colonel was as good as his word. In the late afternoon with an "*Adios, pues,*" I started home.

Laboring up the inclines in low gear the Jeep's radiator drained quickly and, with much hissing, steam poured out from under the hood. Each time that happened I would stop at the next stream and, using my new straw hat, refill the radiator. As it was getting dark about midway, but with the inclines ahead getting steeper, the radiator started hissing at a spot with no stream and not much of a shoulder to pull off on. With the engine off, the jungle became noisy with unidentifiable but ominous sounds. Black panthers were not uncommon in these jungles. We had seen them with their long, thick tails on field trips. They and other carnivores would be coming to the streams to drink. Wild boars in fast-moving herds were vicious, unpredictable, and exceedingly dangerous. Gangs of unruly two-legged predators, loitering about ready for any opportunity to cause trouble or for loot, could be worse. My .45 would make them go crazy. If one chance passerby spotted me, a lone traveler, and my presence became known, I would be a tempting, easy target. When I needed help most Louis and Plowden roared up the road. In the glare of their headlights, I flagged them down.

"How about a tow," I shouted.

They quickly grasped the situation and hooked a logging chain onto the Jeep. For a second time, Louis was there when I needed help. It was slow going but before midnight they dropped me off close to my house. After brief "so longs," they headed up into the mountains. I never saw either again. The big trees and big money are there; it's hard work but a good place to hide. Besides, Louis, a born mischief-maker, may have had other misdemeanors and charges he forgot to mention to worry about. It was after midnight when I got there but I was, as promised, home for Christmas.

Gregory did not like the baby food and never did eat much of it. I didn't like it either. He thrived on the boiled milk Honduran families with babies always kept in a pot on the fire.

This was our second Christmas here and would be our last. On the Sunday after that next Thanksgiving, I would read a third Thanksgiving message from President Eisenhower at the church, this time my own *"adios, pues"* to San Pedro Sula.

All of that was still eleven months in the future but living in San Pedro was now routine. We were not given stateside vacations each year, as were most of the expatriates in the private sector. In fact, while researching to update the post report, I discovered that the lowest-paid American employees of Tabacalera and United Fruit were paid about twice as much as I was.

We did take a short vacation after a consultation visit to Tegucigalpa but could not really relax. We were headed for Costa Rica, which I had visited in navy days, because that was as far as the Pan-American Highway reached. We got as far as Managua, Nicaragua, where car trouble forced us to turn back. The Nicaragua we saw was flat, hot, and dusty, and not everyone carried a machete as in Honduras. There were no Turcos, Arab escapees, now businessmen, from the Ottoman pogroms.

We had other compensations; United Fruit let us use an oceanfront vacation house on a glistening white sand beach at Tela, on a space-available basis. They also let us use (when available) their lodge at Lake Yojoa, a freshwater, ice cold mountain lake, ten miles long, half as wide, and full of accommodating fish. Of course, and this was our secret, we had the Mueller's mountain pool.

In April 1958, I got my first chance to be on the receiving end of a "friendship visit" by a U.S. Naval vessel when the USS *Bigelow* (DDL 942) came to La Ceiba. The *Bigelow* was the first of a new, larger, and more powerful class of destroyers called "Destroyer Leader," (DDL). Embassy Tegucigalpa delegated responsibility for the visit to consulate San Pedro Sula. Charlie and I were pleased and flew to La Ceiba to make the arrangements and to meet the *Bigelow*.

Why the navy chose La Ceiba was never explained to us. It could have been because the Standard Fruit Company, founded by the Vacarro Brothers of New Orleans, shipped their bananas from La Ceiba and the company had influence with the navy. It could have been because the communists were less obstreperous in La Ceiba than in San Pedro Sula and Puerto Cortes. Two years ago the communists had almost closed down United Fruit with strikes and sabotage in the ports of Puerto Cortes and Tela. At this same time, both companies were in a long-term fight against "Panama disease," a ruinous banana fungus. The two: Panama disease and the communists almost wiped out the industry in Central America. That would have meant the literal end of the "Banana Republics." Both threats were defeated. It could have been that the navy wanted to stay away from San Pedro Sula because the consulate was there. There had been only a consular agent in La Ceiba for fifty years.

The navy knew the consulate was no longer in La Ceiba, because it had used San Pedro Sula as its center of relief operations for hurricane damaged British Honduras in 1954. After the hurricane navy officers helicoptered in and landed on the lawn at Sig Lingelbach's Cerveceria Nacional brewery. Driving through San Pedro Sula, which was undamaged by the storm but appeared its usual trashy bedraggled self, they had exclaimed "My God! What devastation!"

By contrast, La Ceiba was an attractive town isolated from the rest of Honduras by ocean, forest, mountains, and the personal preference of La Ceibans. To the north lay the clear deep Caribbean, the beautiful *hondos,* the depths known to and feared by Columbus when the wind was wrong. They were fertile fishing waters sheltered by the Bay Islands. Approaches from east and west were hindered by thick forests in which Columbus reported "many pines, oaks, and seven kinds of palms." There were *ceibas,* hence the name, flowering trees with stout trunks and long limbs which reach out horizontally. Southward, the eight-thousand-foot-high range *Cordillera Nombre de Dios* (Name of God Mountains)separated Atlantida, the *departmento,* province, and its capital, La Ceiba, from the contagion of the rest of Honduras.

Clouds from the north heavy with moisture were forced to drop their rain on the fertile coastal plain. La Ceiba had a corner on exotic lumber from the mountains which they uniquely, and quaintly, exported on Swiss flag vessels. These ships called Basle home port but in fact used Dutch ports. Entranced by the *cordillera,* I prayed that its beautiful, distant vistas had comforted the last earthly thoughts of my favorite *pistolero,* Lee Marston.

Finally, the insularity of La Ceiba has been cherished and fostered over the centuries by the preference of its inhabitants. They prided themselves on what they had, and they wanted to keep it.

The pride and joy of La Ceiba is threefold, of which the first is its relatively "pure" Andalusian Spanish blood, *limpieza de sangre,* with minimal African and Indian input. Second is the observance of colonial era Spanish customs, traditions, and manners preserved through usage. They do this much as the Bay Islanders try to preserve their Elizabethan era English identity. Third is a confluence of the first two, which has produced beautiful, gracious women of whom it is justly proud and jealously defensive.

First, Charlie and I had to establish ourselves with the local authorities. We called on the *Alcalde Municipal* (the mayor); Colonel Marcelino Ponce; the *Gobernador-Politico,* the governor of the *Departmento,* Atlantida, Colonel Napoleon Cubas Turcios; and finally, the real wielder of power, even in insular La Ceiba, the *Commandante de Armas,* local commander of the Army, Major Raul Diaz Garcia. All were gracious with the dignity of old power; they knew who they were. Charlie knew from experience that it was not us they honored but the United States. The ship was met by some of the officials standing on the pier. Afterward, we took the *Bigelow*'s Captain, Commander Audley H. McCain, to call on them.

Charlie hosted a party on shore the first night for local officialdom who came arrayed in uniforms or sashes of office, and many leading citizens. Other officials included Major Ruben Hernandez Lopez, deputy army commander; Captain Jose Joaquin Garcia, chief of police; P.M. Miguel Suazo, a political leader; and Doctor Salvador Godoy, police commissioner. The renowned beauty of the faces and figures of the women was in full display in fashionable, lavish *décolleté* gowns. The pomp and ceremony I had enjoyed so much in my navy days, and greatly missed in San Pedro Sula, was refreshing. The *Bigelow's* officers and crew were resplendent in dress whites and a credit to the captain, their ship, the navy, and the United States. The three cases of whiskey Charlie had brought were consumed *con mucho gusto*, with great pleasure. It was an event to be long remembered by one and all and I am sure it was. I do.

The *Bigelow* responded with a luncheon for fifty one guests on board the next day with as much protocol and formality as it could muster. There were side boys for the guests, with the Boatswain piping them aboard. The officers wore swords. The ship even produced a band. There were guided tours for the La Ceibans. There was a "Limbo pole," a long rod held horizontally and danced under leaning backwards, balanced by legs and arms, by the daring, then gradually lowered. The limbo pole was introduced from a port call in Jamaica. To sit on the bridge in the captain's chair or to stand in the Combat Information Center (CIC) with its electronic screens glowing were thrilling new experiences for young and old.

Standard Fruit gave the crew a train tour of a banana plantation and hosted a swimming party. The company also arranged other sports, sightseeing, and shopping in town and at the company store.

In my report I said that the visit was an unqualified success for both the U.S. Navy and La Ceiba. When the ship shifted its berth I got to ride along and reported that the ship "is a dream, fully air conditioned… a marvel of electronics and automation." Then, my "dream" was over and it was back to San Pedro Sula and reality. In October 1963, five and a half years later, I again hosted the *Bigelow*; this time she was on a routine visit to Aden and was then the flagship of Destroyer Squadron Sixteen. We hosted many port calls in Aden but not one was as memorable as my first in La Ceiba.

***

April was a good month in another way. I got promoted. The numbering had been changed so I went from class seven to class six. The promotion list showed that everyone in our A-100 class had been promoted and that only one man, J. Harden Rose, had left the service for bigger things. Some said he had bettered himself, however impossible that seemed to us, because his first post was a prize. He would have started at the top; in the Secretariat, the office of the secretary. Harden was a Princeton man, made in the F. Scott Fitzgerald mold, engaged to Georgia Rockefeller. My promotion meant an annual pay raise of $600. Today that doesn't sound like much, and frankly, it wasn't much then.

Foreign Service life is hard, strenuous and always stressful. The State Department is a demanding taskmaster putting our lives, and careers, as we had been warned, on the line. We are always subject to the exigencies of the service. Our first tours were not over, and already we were learning that truth. Twelve years later when my time ran out, most of the nineteen had disappeared. Only one of our class, Thomas Smith, our only Harvard man and only World War II Marine, made ambassador; but despite that success his was a sad, hard luck story. In a freak accident he fell down an elevator shaft and was permanently crippled. He hung on and served in Tunis, Paris, University of Wisconsin for postgraduate study, the National War College, London, and, finally, Lagos, as ambassador. During his tour there he contracted the African virus that killed him. Tom was smart, knowledgeable, cultured, and handsome, picture-perfect ambassadorial material. Better yet, everyone liked him and took vicarious pride in his success. He was everything a Foreign Service officer could wish to be.

More excitement came in June when our ambassador, Whiting Willauer—who, like Ambassador Hare, apparently didn't know where San Pedro Sula was because he never came—resigned. Willauer had been a political appointee and was a talented man. He had been number two to General Claire Chennault of the World War II Flying Tigers in China and afterward in the Flying Tiger

Airline. The stateside press described him as our "skin- diving ambassador" because he did a lot of diving off the north coast using his own tank and aqua lung. He also recovered the body of a boy drowned in the river near Tegucigalpa. His diving trips were a source of envy to me as a diver.

At the end of the Korean War I had trained with the Underwater Demolition Team Five, UDT, in Coronado, California. However, Ambassador Willauer was not interested in me or my diving skills. I did get one up on him when I had a couple of days diving on the reefs off Punta Ycacos, British Honduras. United Fruit invited me to go up on their yacht the *Chamelecon.* Ambassador Willauer lost part of his stomach when he drank from a water can filled with gasoline. Finally, in a period when many ambassadors spent months away from their posts, Ambassador Willauer held the record by an American ambassador for the most time out of country, 108 days. In a sad ending to a generally unsatisfactory tour of duty, his beautiful twenty-two year old daughter contracted polio—endemic in Honduras—and was evacuated on a stretcher. Tending to her in Tegucigalpa must have taken a heavy toll on his time and energy.

Our new ambassador, Robert Newbegin, was a veteran Foreign Service officer familiar with Latin America. He had opposed U.S. insistence that Latin American countries deport Germans while we secretly smuggled Nazi scientists and intelligence agents into the United States. Too bad he never met Hans Mueller and confronted his problem. Newbegin could have backed up his words with help from Hans.

Soon after his arrival Ambassador Newbegin drove up to San Pedro Sula; Charlie and I delighted in showing him the sights. To the places previously mentioned we added the brewery and the prison, the latter a four centuries old Spanish fort deep in the swamps. The prisoners' families had to bring food for them. He came once and apparently saw enough of Honduras to satisfy his curiosity. Besides a new Embassy and residence were being built in "Teguc" and that diverted his attention.

Lawrence S. Eagleburger, a new officer, class eight, who had recently arrived in Tegucigalpa, accompanied Ambassador Newbegin. Larry was a handsome young bachelor, very popular in the embassy, already recognized as a nascent star, destined for a great career. By the time I was in class five, eight or nine years later, he was class two. Larry became a protégé of Henry Kissinger. His goal, which he achieved, was to be ambassador to Yugoslavia. That was his first stop on his way to becoming a respected secretary of state. He is the only career Foreign Service officer to be so promoted. He knew where San Pedro Sula was and was smart enough, except for one visit, to stay away.

More memorable than our funerals were our weddings. When the sister of our non-immigrant visa clerk, Lena Sunceri, was married the President of Honduras Francesco Villeda-Morales attended. They had two wedding cakes, flown down from New Orleans, and 100 bottles of champagne for starters.

Poor Charlie, with transfer orders to the department in hand, he lingered too long in San Pedro Sula, without power and not much prestige. His replacement, Consul Harold Wood, whom I described in the last chapter, with his orders as principal officer in hand piled in on top of him. Wood had a wife and valued his prerogatives and privacy. Harold could be demanding. Charlie wanted to stay and tie up some "loose ends," so he moved out of the consulate residence into the Hotel Bolivar and out of his office into the file room. It didn't matter; the curse of de Alvarado had doomed Charlie long ago. Even I sensed something amiss. Charlie didn't ask for my help and my plate was full. Could I have done more for Charlie, *pistolero* Lee Marston, and the "good" Nazi, Hans? In every case, what could I have done to avert what in the end was not averted? As they say in San Pedro Sula, *"Que sera, sera,"* what will be, will be.

In the beginning, Charlie seemed to have much going for him. An army veteran of WWII; he was from a good family; and a direct descendent of a signer of the Declaration of Independence. Charlie was fluent in Spanish and German, with degrees from Yale in Music and Classical Languages. He had bad luck in his first two marriages—although, his second wife, whom he met while posted to Prague, was from Czechoslovakian nobility. He said she was a "princess." Charlie left in 1958; came back and married Leonor Gavidia, one of his smarter moves. We certainly wished them well and they stayed together until he died in 2002. In Washington Charlie was retired from the Foreign Service and settled nearby. They should have stayed clear of San Pedro Sula but could not because Leonor's family was there. Charlie did social work for the state of Virginia and lived a long, useful life with an unfortunate and sad ending. One of his beautiful daughters, Claudia, was killed in a horrible automobile accident and the other, Susanne, has a debilitating illness. Once embraced by the shade of de Alvarado, his blood soaked curse follows you and those you love to the grave. So, what of me, you might ask.

"The time has come, the Walrus said," and I thought it had. Our reward for these years in San Pedro Sula was orders to Cairo. What good news. In the State Department's classification, Cairo is a class A embassy. My orders read "Second Secretary of Embassy and Vice Consul." My job would be assistant general services officer. As second secretary I would be on the diplomatic list, ahead of third secretaries, and as vice consul I would get a consular exequatur. Thus, I may perform consular functions, something officers with only diplomatic commissions cannot do. Perhaps to make up for the ignominy of San Pedro Sula the department gave me a break. If anyone asks, "Just where is San Pedro Sula," what can I say? After this detour I was on the golden road to Samarkand. Flank speed ahead!

After reading President Eisenhower's Thanksgiving message a third time—as Fidel Castro was blazing his way out of the *Sierra Madre* Mountains in southeastern Cuba—and an embarrassing number of farewell parties, we bid San Pedro Sula *"Adios, pues,"* goodbye, then. Indulging my high threshold of pain, I had persuaded my wife to drive back to the States. Somewhere south of Tegucigalpa we turned northward and found the Pan-American Highway unpaved, barely improved, and in some places unmapped. We were on the road about three weeks; first through El Salvador, which was no problem. Every time we crossed a border, David, our second son, would ask "Are we in the United States yet?"

Clayton, our eldest, was seriously affected by with asthma-like symptoms as we traveled through the clouds of dust in San Pedro Sula. We sent him to Tampa to stay with my parents. Gregory was in a car seat/bed on the front seat between Josephine and I. As always we had a couple of pistols in the bed. The procedure was that if stopped by bandits one or both of us would reach into the bed, pullout a pistol and start shooting.

Road travel in Guatemala was famous for the cities of Chichicastenango, Huehuetenango, and especially, Quetzaltenango; popular in pre–World War II days with the *Auslandsdeutschen,* the Germans abroad, but infamous now for *El Tapon* (the cork). This sheer, deep ravine was a major obstacle to the completion of the Pan-American Highway. We made it across on a hastily thrown up bridge of two rows of planks not much wider than our tires and a gang of road workers who practically carried the car. Josephine, carrying Gregory, and chasing David scrambled along the bottom of the ravine. Then between Cuernavaca and Mexico City, in the shadow of the volcano, *Popocatépetl,* we slid down a mountainside, spinning around four times. Fortunately, the power of Hernan Cortes, mentor of de Alvarado, trumped de Alvarado's curse of San Pedro Sula.

That, and the time a carload of exuberant, laughing Mexicans ran us off the road—a very narrow mountain road—were close calls. Fortunately, we were never stopped by bandits. These Central American countries are beautiful and rich in all manner of physical assets. If their befuddled inhabitants could overcome the handicaps of culture, religion, and disinterest they could be among the richest countries in the world.

All the while my eyes were on the pyramids and the great sand sea beyond. In the clean, dry, desert air of the Sahara there would be no jungle rot and cattle ticks. Cortèges to forlorn cemeteries—playground for boys who once stoned Josephine and Joan Brookwell doing watercolors—will give way to picnics among the tombs of the Necropolis and cocktails in Sahara City, the diplomatic enclave in the shadow of the Sphinx.

We'll toast Mother Nile, which has brought life and death to Egypt for thousands of years, with champagne. Josephine won't need to test the depths of icy mountain streams with her long legs.

When we crossed the border at Nuevo Laredo the Texas Ranger charged us tax on our half empty bottle of *Crème de Menthe.* Now, we could say to David, "Yes, this is the United States." We had bid goodbye to Don Pedro de Alvarado and his benighted city, San Pedro Sula. The thought that his curse was lifted from us now and couldn't harm me or mine now was cause for rejoicing.

Our first stop in Texas was a visit to Ruth Beard in Waco. Retired from the Foreign Service because of a health problem she was optimistic with great hopes for me. She said, "Keep in touch."

Surprise! I had not vanished into the sweaty, smelly jungle as my colleagues had envisioned. This is not the end of the story. That we had enjoyed San Pedro Sula not only because it was our first post is a secret. How foolish of me to think the curse of San Pedro Sula could be so easily dismissed. What bitter lessons there were to be learned the hard way. If I had not yet learned where San Pedro Sula was and the meaning of his question, I could ask former DG Hare himself, because he was our new ambassador to Egypt.

6

Cairo

As we barreled in from the airport on a chilly midnight at the tail end of 1958, Josephine, Clayton, David, one-year-old Gregory, and I stared long and hard through the dusty wind blasting through the open windows of our taxi, anxious not to miss any of our first views of the city. Cairo was a mesmerizing kaleidoscope of the truly ancient, the old, and the new. The latter were harbingers of things yet to come. The dingy alleys, warrens of unpaved narrow streets and crumbling buildings, layered remnants of former cities, were more imagined than seen through the gloom and darkness. The old gave way as we entered the new parts of the city, still dramatic and proudly conscious of Egypt's heritage of a dozen millennia. We passed by antiquities older than recorded time, leavened by elegant, stately apartment buildings with a patina of decades and one tall, modern building; a finger pointing to the future. The city radiated a mixture of ancient glories, pride, and burgeoning self awareness of a life span of dramatic length yet still dynamic.

Across the Nile the Pyramids stood watch over their dead Pharaohs at the edge of the Western Desert as they had for thousands of years. Little more than twelve centuries ago, in the seventh century, an unannounced and irresistible wave of Arab tribesmen had swept out of the Arabian Peninsula and across North Africa. As conquerors the Arabs consolidated an empire on half a continent, as apostles of the one God they made it their own. Two hundred years later, on the banks of the Nile—atop the ruins of Fustat, a Roman garrison town—the schismatic Moslem Fatimid dynasty of Egypt founded an Arab city, Al Qahira, Cairo. Named for the planet Mars, then in the ascendant, it was destined to become the beating heart of the Arab World. Moslems called Cairo *Misr*, which means Egypt, as it is written half a dozen times in the Koran. When Mary, Joseph, and the baby Jesus fled Bethlehem they went to "Egypt" but their hiding place is in what is now Cairo. In intervening years Cairo, and Egypt, have been totally Arab in thought, word, and deed. Yet, the fact and fantasy of bygone Pharaohs, their people, and their way of living and dying, forever preserved in their monuments, linger in the air and the dark, swirling waters of Mother Nile.

Bringing life and death from the heart of black Africa, the Nile has flowed through Egypt from times beyond telling. Thick with fertile alluvial mud and dangerous pollution the Nile we saw from our taxi window glistened like silver as it roiled in the silent moonlight. Here in Egypt is the answer to my hopes for a career, the beginning of my golden road to Samarkand—perhaps Samarkand itself.

Our taxi, its lights flashing and horn squawking, whipped around lumbering camels, so loaded with hay they looked like mobile haystacks; only their feet showed. Plodding donkey carts were piled high with cabbages stacked neatly in truncated pyramids. Groups of furtive men, clothed in the long *gallabiya* (robe), common in Egypt, scurried along the roads. I marveled to think that political turmoil born and nurtured here is so explosive it sets the world on edge time and again. The dimly lit streets and staid, solemn circles seemed immune and remote from the frantic jostling we had seen in Washington only hours ago. Egyptian President Jamal Abdul Nasser, a new Saladin, four years into his reign as the charismatic leader of the Arab World, had brought Arabs everywhere to their feet with his call to arms. Were it not for three sleepy boys and a tired wife I would have gone straight to the embassy, ready to do battle.

The obscure consulate in God-forsaken San Pedro Sula we had left in October had been an unappreciated but instructive initiation to perils on the Golden Road. Orders to Cairo were a godsend and the next day I would present myself at the American embassy to take my place as a second secretary and vice consul, with all the duties and responsibilities pertaining thereto. When on the lowest rung of the career ladder the only way is up. I was happier to be here rather than anyplace else in the world.

First things first; report to the embassy. Then my wife and I had to follow the routine for a new, reporting officer. We would call and leave cards on the senior officers, among other things so diligently pounded into us at the Foreign Service Institute, unused until now but vivid in my mind. Last but not least, I had to find a convenient place to live and get us comfortably and safely settled.

One of the embassy's local employees from the travel office, George—our welcoming "committee" at the airport—had swiftly sped us through the formalities of Customs and Immigration. Our destination now was a small *pension* frequented by Americans and Europeans. At my wife's entreaties, George had managed to find a can of evaporated milk to make some formula for our one year old. At the *pension* we were welcomed and made comfortable. They thought we were Germans because I wore a fedora.

My orders read that I was the first incumbent in a new position: assistant general services officer. At the Embassy the next morning I met my immediate supervisor, the general services officer (GSO), and the head of that department of the embassy, congenial Charlie Bakey. Charlie and I became friends and remained so until he died in May 2005.

Soon after Pearl Harbor, Charlie enlisted in the army. Two years later he landed on Utah Beach on D-Day, then communications officer on General Eisenhower's staff. After V-E Day he turned up in the Berlin Document Center of the military government of Germany. Fourteen years later in the State Department his thinking was still very much "army."

His greatest coup in the army was the discovery of Eva Braun's diary intact. Although, he did also walk away with Charlotte Gearhart, the top notch private secretary for John J. McCloy, military governor and later President Truman's high commissioner for West Germany. Charlie and Charlotte had two beautiful daughters. Charlie joined the State Department in 1949 as a staff officer but did not get commissioned a Foreign Service officer until after Cairo in the 1970s. His wartime and post war army experience had many similarities to general services functions for embassy Cairo.

General Services and the Budget and Fiscal office are two large departments in the administrative section of the embassy, here headed by genial Walter Chapman, counselor of embassy for administration. The smoke from Chapman's pipe obscured the tension behind an amiable facade. Administration is subjective, dealing with our own people and their problems. Political and economic officers face host and third country nationals and can often stand aloof and be objective.

The GSO is responsible for the physical maintenance and well being of the post. For those purposes we employed eighty five Egyptian gardeners for the Chancery compound, the ambassador's residence and two other official residences; house servants for the three government residences, a dozen drivers in the car pool, gatekeepers, telephone operators, and last but not least janitors. Most all were Egyptians. Then we had commissary and mail room clerks, including one American staff officer for pouches and classified mail, half a dozen travel agents, including George, a full sized printing press with printers, plus plumbers, electricians, painters, and who knows what. Most were skilled artisans, often "Alexandrian Greeks" —a clever breed of indigenous Greeks with French as first language. We also had Italians and Pakistanis. General Services is not a sought-after, glamour job but it was not boring and had advantages. In a private joke, when American visitors unfamiliar with embassies, asked what I did I replied: "Assistant Chief Janitor." They laughed but it was truer than they knew.

The aerial photo of the Embassy compound is centered on the Chancery—the large, square building in the center. The ambassador's office suite is on your left as you enter; the deputy chief of mission (DCM), political and economic counselors and most of their staffs are within easy reach or just above on the second floor. The commercial section is on the second floor, front. The "spooks," agents from the Central Intelligence Agency, are hidden, although not very well, on the second floor, rear and in the attic. It was always a minor triumph for me to get information from my working level contacts the "spooks" were unable to get. Political and economic officers were always suspect; on the other hand I was only the "janitor."

General services with Charlie's office, the commissary, travel section, and all our other services, including me and my desk (no office,) were in the basement. The consulate occupies the ground floor of a modern—World War II years that is—three story building, left center, just inside the main front entrance; convenient for consular services visitors. The army, navy and air attachés offices have the top two floors. The adjacent courier building, home of our regional courier office, in addition to mail and pouch facilities held Mr. Chapman's office suite. It had been the stables around the turn of the century when the Chancery was a residence. The budget and fiscal office—the bottom floor of a long, portico fronted building behind the Chancery; a wartime structure—was once Attaché Row and had also held a U.S. Army unit. Upstairs were various overflows from elsewhere: the health unit with our nurse and the security section. The Rollo Building behind the Chancery, actually fronting on the next street over, housed the U.S. Information Service library and the cultural attaché. To its right behind the Chancery is the Palm House, which housed the Voice of America and the agricultural attaché. The Khanki Building to its right had the public affairs officer, printing press, and information agency offices. On the far right, partly cut off, is the building that had been a school when bought that summer. I wanted it called the "Tinny Building" because as acting disbursing officer I signed the sales contract and check for 80,000 Egyptian Pounds. It wasn't.

Other buildings in the photo, similar in design were residences. A twelve-story building in the upper center is the Egyptian General Government building with the Ministry of Foreign Affairs to the right. The British had a large and beautiful building, built to be an Embassy, located five or six hundred feet behind where the photographer, who took this photo from a helicopter, was located.

Some of the interior walls and ceilings in the old buildings had quite splendid tiles and mosaics and we were able to preserve many of them. The agricultural attaché's office had a magnificent ceiling and walls—Ambassador Hare insisted we protect it, the office, as was.

The floors in these old Cairo residences were as solid as the Pyramids but we did have one squeaker; the grand and beautiful wooden staircase in the ambassador's residence. It had been Ambassador and Mrs. Hare's headache and on my familiarization visit she cheerfully charged me with fixing it. To get under the treads to add cross bracing was impossible; to dismantle it, out of the question. I suggested she think of those stairs as an alarm system. New, thick carpeting and pads did not solve the problem but did deaden the sound. Mrs. Hare bravely looked the other way.

Our most visible and sensitive function, and most important to the embassy's American staff, was managing and operating the embassy's cooperative commissary, with its diplomatic, duty free import privileges. This was important to staff employees without duty free privileges. Employees bought a $50 share for each person up to four in a family in the commissary; our working capital. Individual orders were consolidated in one large monthly order. We all paid in U.S. dollars.

We were not a supermarket, but stocked popular American staple canned, frozen, and some-non food items. Items of similar quality were purchased more cheaply in Denmark or England. Local fresh meat and vegetables—not commissary items—were acceptable, especially artichokes, peas, and beans.

Embassy Athens was at this time, in the waning days of the Greek Civil War, State's largest overseas post. With an estimated 2400 personnel, including the military contingent, it naturally had a huge military post exchange, *cum* commissary, where everything from auto tires, maybe even autos, to peanuts was available. State Department people in Cairo were granted shopping privileges, if they could get there. Our air force attaché's plane, a C-47, made periodic flights to Athens and would carry State and other departmental people on a space available basis. Josephine and I were added to the list when we arrived.

Seven or eight months later, having heard nothing of our turn to go to Athens, I had forgotten about the list. One day while helping the wife of Colonel Pope, the army attaché, en route to the airport arrange her luggage in an embassy car (my responsibility) I asked where she was going. She said: "To the commissary in Athens, for the fourth time this month" she took a long drag on her cigarette, "and I am sick of it." Josephine and I were on the wrong list—the black list.

Maybe the problem was the Johnnie Walker Black Label Scotch whisky episode with Col. Pope. Black Label was the best scotch the commissary carried. Other good scotch brands were available. Our supplier, Sacony and Speed, rationed our supply of Black Label according to the volume of other cases of scotch we ordered. Ambassador Hare gave orders to Bakey and me, that the Black Label was to be dispensed only with his approval. It was reserved for "representational" functions; those involving the host and other countries. For Charlie and me—he was army, I was navy—orders were orders. Col. Pope, who knew better, was giving a going-away party for his secretary and nothing but the best would do.

The good colonel was one of the embassy's most colorful. A shop in Cairo's market, Khan al Khalili, was famous for tailoring vests of quite spectacular Egyptian cotton. The colors and patterns of the material seemed inexhaustible. I could afford three. Col. Pope proudly boasted thirty-nine such vests.

Sitting in Charlie's office, in uniform, the colonel ordered me to sell him some Black Label. Charlie was on home leave. I said certainly colonel, after the ambassador authorizes the sale. The ambassador was out of touch. The chargé d'affaires, Norbert Anschuetz, deputy chief of mission and a good number two, was not sticking his neck out for the colonel's secretary. I was the assistant janitor.

"Sorry colonel, you know as well as I, orders are orders." Goodbye shopping in Athens.

Since Americans do not readily take to *gamoose* (water buffalo) milk, which was rich in butter fat, we imported and sold from the United States and northern Europe milk in powdered and evaporated forms. As you might expect, sooner or later, "someone" suggested we get an industrial size mixer, for the commissary and sell ready mixed milk. Dutifully Charlie ordered a machine we initially called "the cow." It arrived in Customs weeks later, duty free but not "clearance" free, which took longer. Finally, all was ready, they said, and I was sent to pick up "the cow" in person. Seven signatures and half a day later Customs let me have "Bossy." Gleefully, I raced back to the Embassy and prepared a trial "milking." Made of shiny stainless steel "Bossy" made perfect milk flawlessly. The tasting committee consisting of Charlie, Mr. Chapman, and others declared the milk delicious. Then the same "someone" who suggested buying it, questioned the care and feeding of the machine, noting it must be sterilized before and after each use.

"What if," he cried, "anyone gets sick from embassy milk?"

Mr. Chapman, panic-stricken at the specter raised, told me "Do not use it; the 'cow' is dead."

I suspect that in the half century since someone else has resurrected "Bossy," put her to work mixing milk and no one has gotten sick from our stainless steel cow.

Mr. Chapman, who had the ultimate responsibility for the commissary, was super cautious. We once burned hundreds of pounds of meat because someone had suggested it might be tainted.

The commissary handled all orders for liquors, whiskeys, and wines and met normal needs. Special needs were another kettle of fish. Commissary goods, especially liquors, always limited by the logistics were often a matter of great concern and dispute among our diplomats. Rank has its privileges and often makes onerous demands. Fortunately, there is often a higher authority; here, the ambassador. Redoubtable Ambassador Raymond A. Hare had been named to head American missions many times in thirty years of service. President Eisenhower sent him to Egypt in a moment of Near East turmoil arising from Nasser's Egyptian Revolution of 1952 and the consequent 1956 Suez Crisis. In that debacle Britain, France, and Israel had tried to occupy the Sinai and regain control of the Suez Canal in a joint attack the Egyptians called "the aggression." The three allies failed. President Eisenhower called their attack to an abrupt halt and Nasser nationalized the canal. The British and French predicted that was the end of the canal. The army colonel Nasser appointed to run the canal did a good job. Ambassador Hare's job, the job of all of us, was to assuage the Egyptians and get things back to the *status quo ante*. The United States was in good standing with the Egyptians, a real plus.

While Ambassador Hare, Norbert Anschuetz, Claude "Tony" G. Ross, political counselor, and others dealt with the highest levels of the Egyptian government life went on at our lowest level, the basement, where Charlie held sway and I had my desk. It was an "upstairs, downstairs" world. The two levels met and interacted but our focuses and routines were quite different. In the long summer months, when Charlie was traveling on home leave and I was acting GSO, the levels interacted and sparks flew. Perhaps my thinking was too simplistic, too unsophisticated; our employees were my constituents.

The first time was one of those "morning-after" affairs. Ambassador and Mrs. Hare had attended a high-level dinner party and one of the wines served was an excellent but unfamiliar *rosé*. This was unusual because conventional wisdom says *rosés* do not travel well. He had been able to ascertain from his Egyptian host that it was Portuguese but nothing more. Ambassador Hare knew this wine would soon be in great demand in the diplomatic community and he wanted to get some first and for his exclusive use. When his secretary informed me what it was he wanted "now," it was clear that my Golden Road to Samarkand was paved with bricks in various sizes, and colors.

"Yes, ma'am," I replied, "name, vintage, year, anything?"

"You have all the information we have," she said, "go find it,"

Downstairs I got onto our suppliers of wines and liquors; a big slice of our business at the commissary. In a matter of hours an exporter based in Malta told me they had "my *rosé*" in fact, and confidentially, that they supplied it to the Egyptians. By this time everyone in the embassy knew of my search (so much for security) and, perhaps, my success. Some of the more aggressive, senior officers asserted to me that they also had a special need for some. My position was clear and my answer was a polite but unequivocal, "Yes, sir, Mr. Attaché I'll take it up with the ambassador." I believe the *rosé* episode came before the Johnnie Walker Black Label rhubarb with the colonel. This generated sparks among State officers and fire among senior officers of other federal agencies and departments.

"Bingo," I told my supplier, "how many cases can you send and how soon?"

We agreed on a number, a date, and the number of cases of complimentary items. These were inexpensive and largely advertising items such as drinking glasses distributed on request.

Upstairs I told the secretary who replied: "Tell the ambassador, yourself."

This access would have been an advantage had I known how to

use it. It has been a sobering pill to swallow that as I stood before Ambassador Hare, he admitted to no recollection of the 1956 summer day in Washington, when he had asked the question, traumatic then, which haunts me yet: "Just where is San Pedro Sula—Mr. Tinny?"

I gave him my answer, innocent of the world and import of his question. The true meaning for me was a long time coming but it came, as you will see, in the end.

This day Ambassador Hare smiled when I told him his wine was en route and that he would get it "as soon as humanly possible," to be held for his use or distribution.

"Thank you," he said. "Now, don't worry about it, Mr. Tinny." He pointed to a beautiful tile plaque prominent on his desk inscribed in Arabic script with one word, *Sabre* (patience).

"This is Egypt and in Egypt you must learn patience; many don't, but I have."

I promised myself that the next time we talked I would ask the question burned into my subconscious. That occasion came very soon when the ambassador undertook to tour all the many elements in the Embassy compound. When he came at last to the basement my tongue failed me. Charlie was on home leave. Whether he remembered the *rosé,* San Pedro Sula, or neither, I don't know. His focus was elsewhere. Skipping the gardeners, drivers, and janitors, I introduced him to our travel and office staff. I introduced him to our Greeks, Alexandrians and otherwise, Italians and Pakistanis. Again he had one question directed at me: "Where are the Egyptians—Mr. Tinny?"

The implication was clear but this time I did not venture an answer that would not be what he wanted to hear. Instead, I promised him to find the answer and do what should be done at once.

About the time of the *rosé* wine episode, early spring, 1959, my commission as a vice consul, with the concomitant *exequatur* from the Egyptians, came into play. Spring is the season; everyone transferring wants to get going and everyone eligible for leave wants to head for wherever they go. Charlie, my boss and mentor, had waited a month or so—long enough to get me started—before taking a long, overdue leave. Next to go were the consuls in the embassy's consular section, or consulate.

The consul, John W. "Jack" Foley Jr., lived in Ma'adi and we carpooled. Like all the colonels I have worked with he was brusque, kept me on my toes, and made sure he came out on top.

A marine lieutenant colonel in World War II he had earned two Bronze Stars in five Pacific assault landings. Before the war he graduated *summa cum laude* and was Phi Beta Kappa in history and political science at Dartmouth; studied international law at the London School of Economics and earned a Masters degree in international relations from Yale. In 1946 he joined State as a Japanese Peace Treaty and NATO Treaty analyst. In a photo of one of the American signers, Secretary of State Edward Stettinius, of the NATO treaty I recognized Jack standing alongside but unidentified. He was posted to Cairo a year before I was and a good consul; left the consulate in tip top shape. After a stint as deputy assistant secretary of state for Africa, Jack retired in 1976 and lived in the Watergate. He died at age 92 August 5, 2008.

Mr. Claude "Tony" G. Ross, counselor of embassy for political affairs, third ranking officer in the embassy and collaterally responsible for the consulate, discovered I was the only officer present who had a consular commission, consular experience, and had already received an *exequatur* from the Egyptian Foreign office. Many of my peers had a low regard for consular work, considering it demeaning. They thought it drudgery. I did not object when it fell to my lot. Consular work gave me my best days in the Foreign Service and brought me closer to Samarkand than I realized.

The Rogers Act of 1924 combined the Diplomatic Service and the Consular Corps into the Foreign Service but preserved certain differences. With my commission as vice consul and my *exequatur* I could sign passports, issue visas, and other things officers with only diplomatic commissions: secretaries, attaches, even the ambassador, could not do. I was ordered to divide my time between general services and the consulate. Why they let both consular officers take leave at the same time is a mystery to me. With my vice consul's hat on American citizenship, immigrant and non-immigrant cases were familiar. Echoes of the North African desert war years of World War II and Rommel were as loud and clear in Egypt as in San Pedro Sula. Wars don't end for everybody just because the shooting has stopped.

As second secretary I was entitled to be on the diplomatic list. However, our protocol officer decreed that the list was already too long without me. Two other officers, third secretaries: Barrington King, II and James R. Sartorius were the last and the most junior entries on the list. For a moment they considered putting me on the list in place of one of them but Barry was in the political section, Sartorius was in the economic section, and both "needed" to be on the diplomatic list. I had a consular commission; they did not, so I went on the consular list. The duty free privileges and other perquisites were roughly the same. They went to more parties. King and Sartorius had diplomatic plates on their cars while I had consular plates, a blessing in disguise—the police knew it was consuls, not diplomats, who issued visas and approved other mundane things.

I felt good about being near the top on the more exclusive—because it was shorter—consular list. Another advantage discovered as I got into things was that I was not suspect as a "diplomat" which in these paranoid countries means "spy." That was the second Arabic word I learned, *jaasoos* (spy). As assistant GSO and vice consul, my opposite numbers in the agencies I dealt with, for example, the electric authority, the telephone company, the ubiquitous P.T & T. of British colonial days, and local merchants, were of my level. We were not the decision makers. In one instance our agricultural attaché, from that department, who dealt with Egyptians on a policy level, hosted a large official party at his residence in Ma'adi. Not one invited Egyptian guest came; he was too "political," or in other words suspect. At my less prestigious parties my Egyptian guests had the word "assistant" in their titles as did I; they came. Not a diplomat, *jaasoos*, to them, but a consul; I could issue visas. I invited "assistants."

These assistants and I often interacted closely. When the International Cooperation Administration (ICA), the original "Point Four" for foreign assistance under President Truman's Marshal Plan, moved into a new building Mr. Chapman was worried the telephones would not be properly connected. If that happened, the ICA people would scream bloody murder and complain that the embassy, the umbrella for other federal departments, was not giving them good service.

The crucial connection was scheduled to be made on a Sunday, an Egyptian work day, and my family came to town with me. Josephine took Clayton, David, and Gregory, who had fallen and cut his chin, to the embassy to get tetanus and penicillin injections from our nurse. I dangled my legs over the edge of the manhole in the street where the lines from the ICA building met the main lines and watched. Afterward, I assured Mr. Chapman they got the wires' colors to match. They must have because before I left we tested every single line and at that moment—Hallelujah —they worked fine. The men on the sidewalk were secret police but my contact in the telephone company, an assistant director, knew me and why I was there. One of the police in a lumpy black overcoat brought me a chair.

By the same token, I had no trouble visiting the World War II battleground at Alam Halfa and the cemeteries at El Alamein. Our military attachés; army, navy, air force, also too political, could not get permission to go there because they were "restricted military zones." I was happy to brief them on this and my other trips around the country including down into Upper Egypt, Assiout, and Luxor.

Carrying the diplomatic pouch to our constituent posts, consulate general Alexandria (Alex), and consulate Port Said was one of those chores junior officers shared. A big pouch came from Washington by diplomatic courier. Then our mail room prepared pouches with mail for the two posts. On my first courier run in early March Josephine came along and we got two pleasant surprises. In Alexandria we saw a beautiful European city, stretching along miles of snow white beach, highlighted by black, basalt rocks, facing a Mediterranean of the bluest blue I have ever seen. Alexandria was laid out with a broad boulevard, the *corniche,* and sidewalks, not "boardwalks," facing the sea with elegant hotels, apartment blocks, shops, and the city on the landward side. Everyone had access to the water and as we saw in the summer most everyone took full advantage of that privilege.

Second, in consul general Heyward Hill we met a model FSO whose diplomatic career had begun early in this century. A gentile, southern gentleman, independently wealthy, and educated in

Europe, Hill was enamored by the Japan of the early 1930s. A Far East expert and an "old Far East hand" before World War II he now faced honorable retirement with the rank of consul general. His residence was a treasure house of Far Eastern art.

Hill was a gracious and hospitable host to Josephine and me. A world-class cook and gourmet, he introduced Josephine and me to the unique Egyptian delicacy of the tiny birds caught by the hundreds in the marshes south of Alexandria. A royal prerogative still observed as a conservationist measure; only a select few are permitted to net the birds.

Embassy Damascus, my next pouch run, was not a constituent post, but Cairo, as regional pouch center, received mail for them and the responsibility for delivering it. As with Alexandria, Damascus surprised and impressed me, so I wrote home:

> Dear Folks, this is a very clean place; even the poorer residential sections and *souks* are amazingly clean. The main *souk* is fabulous, more extensive, and with more to offer than the better-known Mouski and Khan al Kalili— the main *souks* of Cairo. I walked down "the Street called Straight" and saw the window through which St. Paul escaped.   Josephine didn't come because of the militant measures the Egyptian Customs Police were taking to prevent the return of 50 and 100 Egyptian pound notes (LE) taken out during the 1956 Suez "aggression." After a fast approaching deadline these notes cease to be legal tender. Millions of dollars worth of Egyptian pounds are involved.

The 50– and 100–Egyptian pound notes had been leaking back into Egypt since 1956. One of our diplomats, an attaché from another federal department, was caught smuggling these notes into Egypt. The Egyptians did not arrest him since he had diplomatic immunity. Declared *persona non grata*, "unacceptable person," he was deported. The United States did not arrest him because he had paid income tax on his profits and had not broken any U.S. law.

My return flight, from Damascus was held up nine hours, as my letter continued:

All luggage, checked and carry-on, was unloaded and gone through three times. Mine was unloaded but not searched. I had the return pouch chained to my wrist. People deemed suspect were strip searched and women's shoes with platform heels and soles were cut apart. At Cairo Airport they did not open the pouch or my luggage but would not let me, or it, enter. The miscreant attaché had made us all suspect. I had to stay in 'no man's land' until the deadline for demonetizing the notes, 12 hours away, had passed.

I got home hot and bothered but otherwise unharmed. It was a good lesson in protecting the sanctity of "the diplomatic pouch."

The importance of meeting couriers was emphasized when, about this time, the plane carrying courier Johnny Powell crashed trying to land at Vienna and the person scheduled to meet him had not arrived. Johnny, a very pleasant and gregarious man, survived the crash. However, when rescuers tried to move him away from his pouches he refused aid until embassy personnel arrived and took the pouches. The department decreed personnel meeting couriers must arrive at least a half hour before scheduled flight arrivals. For departing flights personnel must remain at the airport until the plane is "out of sight."

My first pouch run to Port Said the northern terminus of the Suez Canal, in mid July was shorter, quicker, and less formal than going to "Alex." Consul Chester E. "Chet" Beaman and his wife Mary had been stationed in Cairo when we arrived and were very helpful to us and to our boys in many ways during those early days. We had carried little more than hand luggage and the boys had no toys. For example, the Beaman children shared their toy dinosaurs with our children. Chet had recently been promoted to consul and was politely anxious to let me know what he wanted the GSO to do. To visit with the Beamans and their children Josephine and Clayton came along.

The Port Said office and residence building was U.S. property and the responsibility of the GSO Cairo—me. The high ceilings and tall French doors of the ground floor offices made them airy and cool. The second floor residential quarters—five bedrooms, sitting room, music room, drawing room, study, baths, and kitchen/

pantry—were the same with a broad colonnaded veranda facing the port and canal turning basin. The consulate—classic mid nineteenth century Egyptian, British colonial architecture—had been built to be the American consulate. It needed painting and some upkeep but had a new wrinkle.

A rifle bullet had passed through the open French doors from the veranda into the dining room and had struck the opposite wall, over the stone fireplace. It happened during the brief fighting in November 1956 and we don't know whose bullet it was or if they were actually aiming at the consulate. A man standing in the way would have lost his head. I wanted to attach a frame around the hole with a brass plaque to identify it but Chet wanted it patched. We patched it; so much for history.

Chet ended a successful career as deputy chief of mission and chargé d'affaires in Malta in the early 1970s. We stayed in touch and he died May 3, 2007, at age ninety-one.

Port Said centered around a bustling waterfront with bright colorful shops facing the canal hiding treeless, narrow, sandy streets with blocks of flats. The steady ship traffic contrasted sharply with dignified, sophisticated Alexandria and its lyric heritage of Alexander, Caesar, and Cleopatra. Even the cacophony of passing ships' whistles, tugboat horns, and the shouts of bumboat men—the excitement of the canal—could not disguise its tumble down shanty town air. In the heyday of post World War II ocean traffic Port Said was where sparkling white cruise ships—rails lined with gaily dressed passengers—crossed paths with shabby but fascinating rusty tramp steamers. The clash of Occidental and Oriental worlds begins here. It always has and always will. Kipling spelled it out for us in his poem *Mandalay*:

If you've 'eard the east a-callin', you
Won't ever 'eed naught else.
Ship me somewhere east of Suez
Where the best is like the worst,
There ain't no Ten Commandments
And a man can raise a thirst.

Going to Port Said from Cairo our route up took us to Ismaliya, thence north between the sweet water canal carrying Nile water to Port Said and the Suez Canal. Here was my chance to get one up on Richard Halliburton. He had swum the Panama Canal and the Hellespont. I had swum in the Panama Canal when stationed there in World War II and would soon swim the Hellespont. He had not swum in the Suez Canal, so I did. It was a good, clean swim, neither the length nor the breadth of the canal, but enough. After all, the Red Sea must have more sharks than any other ocean of the world. It is a thrill is to see the superstructure of a ship sail along in the midst of pristine sand dunes.

The consul general's residence in Alexandria was the opposite of the consulate in Port Said. "Alex" had a rented, beautifully furnished mansion and in August it would be vacant for an interim of several weeks between Hill's departure and his successor Charles Cross's arrival. The department's parsimonious bureaucrats balked at paying rent on a vacant house. The embassy knew well we should pay to keep it or lose a desirable, historic mansion. So, Charlie, Mr. Chapman, Marty Manch (budget and fiscal officer), and I divided the interim period between ourselves, paid our shares of the rent, and used the house in turn, taking local leave. Mr. Chapman gave me ten days; all I could afford to pay for anyway.

At this very moment Laurence Durrell's sensational *Alexandria Quartet*, four novels were published simultaneously. Three of the four books, *Justine*, *Balthazar*, and *Clea*, covered the same events from three subjective points of view. The fourth, *Mountolive*, an objective narrative of the plot, brought in a suave diplomat, Mountolive, around whom the story revolved. The story was set in the days covered by World Wars I and II and the intervening years, the dramatic last days of the British Raj in Egypt. One theory was that Heyward Hill had been the model for Mountolive. For weeks the *Quartet*, and the real identity of its characters, were subjects of guessing games among the diplomatic corps and our Egyptian colleagues. Exotic Alexandria was a perfect venue for the sensuous and intriguing *Quartet*.

The consulate residence in Alexandria was more than convenient, it had been owned by one of King Farouk's bridge playing cronies. My favorite Farouk story is this: One night shortly before

1952, during a card playing session, Farouk presciently laid out the four kings on the dining room table and said:

"Someday soon there will be only five kings in the world that matter, these four and the King of England." It is arguable but he is right. I thought of that story every time we sat down to eat.

The residence was on Sharia Shitta (Winter Street), and not on the seafront. My sons found that a deficiency, which resolved itself in the form of a luxurious beach cabana. A wealthy but apolitical member of the old regime, Ali Assem, one of my contacts not in the diplomatic circuit, let us use his. Ali's grandfather, or great grandfather, had been granted by the khedive all the Alexandria ocean front property he could cover in one day riding on a donkey. He had a fast and cooperative donkey.

These *cabanas* are a European innovation. Built at the back of the beach, they give the owner direct access to the water. The Assems' spacious cabana—with a kitchenette and bathroom—was on the beach front of the king's Momtaza Palace. We had access to the sea and also to the palace grounds. In Egyptian terms—and considering the Coney Island sized crowds on the public beaches—our cabana on palace grounds, fronting a private bay, was real luxury. Actually, the Alexandrian sun was almost too much. Gregory, our fair-skinned youngest, now almost two, suffered from the sun. During our ten days in "Alex" we spent a little bit of time at the beach every day, except one.

I was anxious to see the World War II battlefield at Alam Halfa and El Alamein, so one day we headed west on the beach road without any military clearance. Litter from the critical battles of October and November 1942 could not be found; the desert was barren of war detritus. We did find monumental cemeteries built by the British, Germans, and Italians to honor the soldiers who fought there. I wrote home:

Dear Folks,

Each of the three major combatant nations has built memorials to their men in forms expressing and reflecting their national psyche and ethos. They are very different.

The British cemetery is a wide open area of dozens of acres with rows and rows of white crosses centered on a

Cross imbedded with a Sword (Excalibur, no doubt) monument on a raised marble plinth. Engraved on a raised marble monument was this message:

Within this cloister are inscribed the names
Of soldiers and airmen of the British Commonwealth
And Empire who died fighting on land or in the air,
Where two continents meet and to whom
    fortunes of war
Denied a number their honorable grave
    with their fellows
Who rest in the cemetery. With their comrades in arms
Of the Royal Navy and seamen of the Merchant Navy
They preserved for the West, the link with the East,
And turned the tide of war.
    —Winston Churchill

As in an English garden, rose bushes are placed at strategic corners of rows. ("Never blows the rose so red as where some buried Caesar bled." [Omar Khayyam])

The white crosses have names and dates and one, with a wreath of bedraggled flowers leaning on it with a faded note attached, caught my eye. I forget the name but the soldier buried there was 22 years old. The note read, "To Buddy, With love, Mom'

The Germans built a solid, granite fortress, *Festung*, squatting alone in the desert with battlements and towers, dark and foreboding. A tall solid wood, iron bound gate and portcullis guarded the entrance. The fortress is divided into rooms with names and dates, carved on the walls. A perfect setting for Rommel's *Götterdämmerung*, at El Alamein. A "twilight," not for a god but for the Desert Fox.

The Italian monument is a miniature cathedral with a deeply religious atmosphere not present in either of the other two. The smell of incense and candle wax can be imagined or maybe it is real. The design was 'modern,' tall, and square. Hundreds of doors, big enough for an urn in the walls, as in a columbarium, are inscribed with names and dates of the soldiers.

Only the British cemetery had a visitors' register. I signed, adding the Roman valedictory: *Ave atque Vale,* Hail and Farewell."

From the beginning, life at embassy Cairo was a dream come true. Our room at the *pension* where George had dropped us the night of our arrival was small and cramped for five. After a very short time we moved to an apartment in one of the elegant buildings I had seen coming into Cairo. The apartment, five floors up, in a building with an open European style elevator, overlooked the Midan Tahrir (Liberation Square), the heart of Cairo. The bedrooms were large and the living and dining rooms were huge, with crystal chandeliers and tall French doors opening onto wide balconies. The daytime activities in the Square—parades and political demonstrations—were exciting. Nasser, often accompanied by either Nehru or Tito, led many parades standing in the back of a convertible. They were touting their Third World as a political force. Late at night, after the crowds and din had thinned, the horns of hundreds of taxis, little Mercedes diesel sedans, emitting clouds of smoke sounded like high flying flocks of squawking ducks.

"They are signaling to each other," my wife said, standing on our balcony as we tried to decipher the messages. Were they giving routes, warnings, describing passengers? Often an insistent squawk coming from one direction, usually east, in the old city slums, would be picked up by dozens more to travel in a wave across the city to echo off the Pyramids in the far west. It reminded us that barking, feral "pi" dogs in San Pedro Sula had done the same thing as if choreographed. Today, the harsh squawking horn of a foreign car evokes for me visions of 1959 Cairo at midnight.

For my part that grand apartment on the *Midan* would have been a fine place to live. However, my colleagues, including Charlie, insisted that with three young children we get a house in Ma'adi to be close to the American School, the Sporting Club and American Mission (Protestant) Church. Besides, most of the embassy staff—the army, navy and air force attachés, the navy medical unit, agriculture and other federal department attachés lived there. Ma'adi was a beautiful and pleasant place in which to live.

Beside the Nile, ten miles south of downtown Cairo, Ma'adi

had been built by and for the second level of the British overlords who ruled Egypt from the 1880s until 1952. Other European expatriates and Egyptians found it preferable. Ma'adi, with its wide streets—no sidewalks, we walked in the street—shaded by beautiful flowering trees and separate houses with yards was in atmosphere vaguely like a middle class American suburb. Each house had a well-established rose and flower garden, and fruit trees, such as apricot, pomegranate, and varieties of citrus, which produced delicious fruit. Some grass grew but never quite enough to make a real lawn so they didn't waste time on it. I never understood who arranged for the gardener who cared for our garden and certain other gardens. He had access to Nile water from a canal, which he used to periodically flood different sections of our garden divided by little dikes, serviced by ditches. We never touched Nile water deliberately or accidentally and managed to avoid the dread *bilharzia*—the disease that plagued Egypt. Fertile, fresh mud covered the section just watered and dried quickly. Potable water for house use came from a different source. So far, none of us suffered from "Gypy tummy;" the local idiom for upset stomach and diarrhea. Missing were the itches, bugs, and jungle rot of San Pedro Sula. However, sanitation learned there, and potassium permanganate, served us well.

Zamalek, older and closer in to town, on Gezira Island in the Nile was the most exclusive living area. Garden City, on the east side of the Nile was a diplomatic enclave for embassies and ambassadorial residences. Ambassador Hare lived in Garden City; Deputy Chief of Mission Norbert Anschuetz and Roberta, and Political Counselor Tony Ross and Andrea lived in Zamalek.

Nile water was dangerous particularly because of the *bilharziasis schistosomes*, parasitic worms, also called blood flukes. These parasites entered the human body through the skin and attacked the liver. Bilharzia was endemic in Egypt, probably up to 100 percent, the same degree as polio. The latter usually attacked very young infants and left no noticeable or only slight ill effects. By keeping our three sons out of the mud in the garden, the nanny and gardener more than paid for the keep." The U.S. Navy had a large medical unit (NAMRU) attached to the embassy studying *bilharziasis*. Some years subsequent to our time in Egypt, NAMRU did develop an antidote to *bilharzia*.

That spring of 1959 saw two important developments in the life of our youngest son Gregory. First, after having been carried by a succession of servants all his first fifteen months, he had gotten too big to carry. His Egyptian *ayah* (nanny), Amina, set him down and, on March 21, he put foot to ground and walked. We all were glad — especially Gregory because he could participate in his first Easter egg hunt. We once asked the *ayah* why Gregory wasn't talking baby talk and she answered:

"Oh, but he is. It is all Arabic baby talk."

Another *ayah,* supposedly European, in a fit of pique threw David's kitten out of a window. She was on the ground floor, and the kitten was unhurt; but the spectacle of his kitten flying out the window was traumatic for David. Her immediate replacement, the Egyptian, was also a prima donna and therefore sent by the police. She was the best we had; she was good with Gregory, and he liked her.

Cooks came and went with great frequency and like *ayahs,* were major concerns. We finally got a good Sudanese cook — no doubt sent from the secret police, if not an actual policeman. However, we were warned that all servants, good, bad, and indifferent reported to the police. Our security officer told us our houses were "bugged," especially bedrooms and bathrooms. After six months we had settled with a good cook and nanny, and, of course, a *suffragi* (houseboy).

One high-ranking embassy wife said: "It's fun to think my toilets are being cleaned by a secret policeman."

Regular police were among my contacts and were ubiquitous. Any time, day or night, I could look out and see a uniformed policeman standing at the street corner near our house. At embassy parties police were out front in force. Once, talking to a police officer, I gave an erroneous number of cars. He proudly set me straight, gave me the exact number of cars, license numbers, and identified the guests. Every time I had occasion to be at an embassy party, usually in a GSO capacity, I was on a first name basis with the police. I enjoyed surprising our political people with the numbers and names of their "political" guests.

Easter in 1959 fell on March 29 and Gregory's second milestone came that day when he was christened in the American Mission

Church. The church was called "interdenominational" which, to me, meant "non denominational," since it was neither one thing nor the other. Our rector, born a German, was now an Episcopalian and in the fourteen years since WW II had become an American citizen.

The rector, call him Manfred, was fortyish and a tall, sturdy, strikingly handsome man. Blonde and blue-eyed he was a picture perfect example of the Teutonic, Aryan man the Nazis had tried to portray. He had been a member of the Hitler Youth and had gone on to become a paratrooper in an elite Wehrmacht paratroop unit. When Germany invaded France in 1940 his unit landed ahead of the advancing *Panzers*, which were irresistibly driving the French and British forces back. For Manfred it was another story; everything went wrong. Shot up by gunfire from the ground; as he came down he landed badly and was further injured. Lying helpless, a French farmer discovered him and with the aid of his family took Manfred to his home. During a long convalescence the care and solicitation in the midst of the War of the French family completely changed his outlook on life. As in the cliché Manfred was "born again." I don't know what happened in the interim, but at the end of the war and after the trauma of the denazification programs of the late 1940s ended he was granted a visa to the United States. He attended a seminary and became an Episcopal minister. Now, he had answered the call to the American Mission Church in Ma'adi.

On March 29, 1959, Easter Sunday, Manfred, former Nazi paratrooper, baptized our third son. Gregory has no recollection of the event, or of Manfred, but they both must have done it right because all of his life Gregory has been an honest and sincere Christian. He is a good son and he and his wife, Amy, are good parents to our grandchildren, Gabrielle and Clayton, II. He has never had a problem he could not handle and he has never been a problem to us or to anyone. *Danke schön* (thank you), Manfred.

In early March we got settled in our house in Ma'adi. Smallish by Ma'adi standards and solidly built, it had four floors, a garage, and a typical flat roof suitable for entertaining or sleeping. A massive fireplace dominated the main room but the house had no other source of heat. On some of our cold nights we built a small fire, fire wood was scarce. It was the first time our boys had seen a fire in a fireplace.

The house was owned by the Swiss company that owned and operated Egypt's Tura cement plant, located in Helwan south of Ma'adi. Our contact, in effect, our landlord, was Herr Rhinefranck, the plant maintenance and construction manager. He was a pleasant man but stiff and formal, always dressed in a double-breasted wool suit. He looked like a candidate for a heart attack with his flushed and sweaty face. Sadly, despite warnings he had a fatal one just before we left Cairo.

He gave me a tour of the plant while Mrs. Rhinefranck fed Josephine and the boys Swiss chocolate and other delicacies. He showed me the plant's five rotating kilns which produced a hundred thousand tons of cement per month and described his plans for five more kilns. Several thousand tons of cement a month were exported to the United States. The plant was as efficient as a Swiss watch and very international.

Power capacity was being expanded—Rhinefrank's job—with French built free cylinder gasifiers to run turbine powered generators. The electrical systems were Swiss while most of the heavy equipment was German. The mobile equipment was American. An overhead cable car track a mile long brought in the raw material. A conveyor belt carried the bags of cement to railway freight cars or barges in the river.

When we rented the house a two bedroom, two bath apartment in the basement was occupied by a German engineer working at the Tura plant on a temporary basis. He soon left which gave us more rooms, the coolest ones in a house with no air conditioning. We put the boys and nanny in the basement. The Egyptian custom was to open the outside wooden shutters at night to let in the cool air, then close them during the day to keep the hot air out. The air temperature variant was large.

In the cause of international peace a collateral duty of all embassy families was to entertain, on a rotating Sunday basis, a contingent of soldiers from the United Nations peacekeeping force in Suez. Rhinefranck, his wife, and their four attractive teenage daughters—as did most Swiss—spoke German, French, Italian, and English, which surely would be enough. So, when it came our turn to entertain the UN troops we invited the Rhinefranck girls because they were girls, they were pretty, and surely they could converse with soldiers from any European country. The UN sent a contingent of handsome, tall, and very blond, young Swedish soldiers. They spoke one language only: Swedish. As luck would have it, for all of our planning, the only language the Rhinefranck girls didn't speak was, you guessed it, Swedish.

Using a complicated mixture of hand signals and whatever else came to mind, a good time was had by all. We tried to do numbers in Swedish until, at my turn; I reached "seven." The Swedish "seven" cannot be pronounced properly, at least to Swedish ears, by anyone else—especially me. Amid gales of laughter, I gave up. The soldiers were quite pleased with the company of the girls. Our three sons were excited to be with real live UN soldiers with their perfect military bearing, blue scarves, and blue helmets.

In Ma'adi Clayton attended the American School, starting in March. David, five, entered the French kindergarten, the Lycée François, staffed with nuns but under Egyptian management. The Suez Crisis had prompted the Egyptians to sequester all British and French schools, churches, and other property. David did learn French and looked very French in his short blue smock, which he wore with perfect *savoir faire*. Later on, at a birthday party for a classmate, Josephine was surprised to hear David rattle on in Arabic. Talking was one of David's chief pleasures and if he couldn't do it in one language he would do it in another. For the boys getting to school was fun because they rode on the backs of bicycles pedaled by two sweet teenage girls, from one of the navy medical unit families.

Another reason for living in Ma'adi was the club. The club had a huge swimming pool and Mustapha who taught swimming four days a week. His method was to first throw Clayton and David into the deep end. It didn't work too well at first but Mustapha was unrelenting. Later on they both became excellent swimmers. Meanwhile, Gregory would find a warm puddle on the terrace and just splash water on passersby. Later he took to diving in before he learned to swim; that taught him.

Mustapha also taught golf a couple times a week so Josephine and I took lessons. We did not have time to pursue golf although after several months I did play one full round. Like golf courses in all desert countries it had "browns," oiled sand, instead of greens.

It was my only eighteen holes. Josephine never did get all the way around.

Another advantage of Ma'adi was that of an express train, which originated in Helwan—the populous suburb and home of the cement plant. The track ran through the Ma'adi station, close to our house, to a station convenient to the embassy. The fare was low and the cars, made in Germany, had extremely comfortable, large leather seats. In June when my car pool was unavailable I tried the train and always found a seat. Unbeknownst to me it was also the Moslem month of Ramadan when all good Moslems fast during the day. Egyptians are nothing if not good Moslems and during Ramadan they take a holiday or stay home. The day after Ramadan ended I could barely squeeze onto the train. The inside was packed full; the roof and sides were festooned with riders hanging on for dear life. Infants carried in their mother's arms had rings of flies around their eyes so thick they looked like horn rimmed glasses. It was a scene from Mark Twain's *Innocents Abroad*. I never rode the train again.

By fall I was comfortable in my "upstairs" office in the Consulate building. When I wore my consul's "hat" I was "upstairs" although it was actually ground floor. A telephone call from the British embassy gave me my first missing persons case here. These can be exciting but more often end in tragedy for the people involved and for their families at home.

For some inexplicable reason, the British embassy had been alerted to investigate the disappearance in the desert of two young Americans and two young Frenchmen—college students all, aged between eighteen and twenty-eight—who had ill advisedly planned to drive from Paris to Johannesburg. This was to be their Victorian era "Grand tour" before settling down to a mundane life and careers. One American was studying Chinese literature. My British opposite number passed the ball to me.

When last heard from in a letter dated some weeks earlier, the boys were in the town of Isna, twenty miles south of the tourist center of Luxor, but on the opposite, or west, bank of the river. They were headed for Wadi Halfa, at least 230 miles farther south the first town in the Sudan. They had hired a young Sudanese boy to guide them and were in good spirits. Alarmed now by the subsequent long silence, and fearing that no news was not good news, the families of the two Americans, John Armstrong and Donald Shannon, had asked the State Department for help.

As consul I set the wheels in motion to ask the Egyptians to make a search. The Egyptians alerted the camel patrol. This was exciting news to me because the camel patrol headquarters was in Ma'adi not far from our house. Of course, patrols would not be sent from Ma'adi to the Sudanese border, eight hundred and more miles south, but it gave me a reason to visit the patrol's headquarters. I inspected the huge camels they use and took a short ride; a seminal experience in sand dunes and camels. In Egypt you can be one step away from the desert, literally have one foot on the sown, watered land, and the other on desert sand. How wonderful it would have been to ride out on a desert patrol.

In the end, the desiccated bodies of three of the young men — minus one of the Frenchmen, but with the Sudanese guide — were found north of Wadi Halfa, still in Egypt and east of the Nile, near their cars, two Citroën, 2CVs. They had foolishly, or mistakenly, headed across the open desert where the river bends. Speculation on what they thought they were doing is pointless. Their vehicles, the reliable, air-cooled, two-cylinder French Citroën 2CV, *deux chevaux vapeur* (two steam horses), can be adapted well for this sort of off road travel but these two had not been properly equipped. In fact, they had not been prepared at all! Whether they had run out of water or the *deux chevaux vapeur* out of gas first was unanswerable. They were out of both and a third when they had certainly run out of luck.

Their desert equipment was a *National Geographic* map. The guide had paid for his ineptness; he had lied about his desert lore, with his life. There was no evidence of foul play. The four bodies were parched skin stretched over bones scattered by buzzards and animals, shrouded in remnants of clothing.

Ambassador Hare told a group of us, in a *post mortem*, apropos of the dead and missing men, that when he was posted to Cairo in the 1930s, a popular occasional pastime was "desert yachting."

With cans of gasoline strapped on the running boards of their cars, spare tires nestled in front fender wells, they headed out into the Western Desert on day long—or longer, but not eight hundred miles—"yachting" trips. Model A, but especially Model T, Fords were good for this because they were light and could skim across the sand at high speed, rarely bogging down. When one did stick, the others circled to find a hard spot and park. Then all hands helped dig out the stuck car. In Cairo I never found anyone interested in trying it. Besides, in 1959, slab sided cars did not have running boards and were too heavy.

Consular work also gave me a part in Egyptian-American political finances. Mr. Ross, "Tony," took me with him to deliver large sums of Egyptian pounds to visiting congressmen. I was both witness and bodyguard; unarmed. These were part of monumental surplus funds lent to Egypt which could only be spent in Egyptian pounds, meaning in Egypt. As in our arrival, all flights into Cairo seemed to land at midnight. My first experience was with Senator Bourke Hickenlooper, a typical case. Congressmen expected their money then and there. Midnight exchanges of stacks of money to be counted were tense. One such payment would have covered the rent on the consulate residence in Alexandria all summer.

Tony and I got along well and he said these chores were part of the life we lead. He was right. If I had been smarter and worked closer with Tony, my part of that life might have been much happier.

In 1940, when still a new Foreign Service officer, Tony met and married Antigone Andrea Peterson and they spent their honeymoon at his first post, Mexico City. From there in 1941 they went to Quito, Ecuador where they spent the war. In 1945 they went to Athens, then Nouméa, Beirut, and Cairo, where I met them. Fluent in foreign languages both spoke French, Spanish, Greek, and Italian. I saw in them an enviable Foreign Service team. From Cairo they went to Conakry, Guinea. He got off the sand dune circuit, whereas I was enamored with the desert, so we never served together again. That was my bad luck. Tony tried to take an interest in me. From Conakry he had three posts as ambassador, first the Central African Republic, then Haiti, and Tanzania. After retirement Tony served on selection boards and as a Foreign Service inspector. Josephine and I met occasionally in Washington with Tony and Andrea, until they died; she in September 2004 and he a year later. A loving couple, they spent their honeymoon at a Foreign Service post and it seemed that new posts for them were part of one lifelong honeymoon. They had two sons, one of whom is Ambassador Christopher Ross.

George, our best travel agent was another one of those clever but temperamental "Alexandrian Greeks" and, for reasons which eluded me, suddenly quit. Replaced in the consulate, when John W. Foley, Jr. returned from leave, I took over the actual travel arrangements, customs clearances, and shipping of effects. Also, I was now acting disbursing officer. Embassy hours are six hours a day, five days a week, with one ten hour day to make the required forty hours. Compounding our travel problems was the fact that we had two fiercely competing American airlines: Pan American World Airways (PanAm) and Trans World Airways (TWA). We had to share our business equally and I had to do it. The local employees could not resist an insistent American who wanted one airline when it was the turn of the other—I could.

When the airline club, which included all airlines servicing Egypt, gave a party on a Nile cruise ship we went as guests of TWA. We attended the next function as guests of PanAm. Belly dancers were always featured at these and other parties especially at the Sahara City—the diplomatic enclave of semi-permanent embassy tents near the Pyramids. Once, Nasser decreed that belly dancers had to cover their bellies. The dancers, mostly Italian, got around that order one way or another. So much for the decrees of dictators when popular demand decrees otherwise. Egyptians can be hard-headed.

Thanks to the Information Service (USIS) we did not lack for evening entertainment, usually movies. We saw *Some Like it Hot* with Marilyn Monroe and *Middle of the Night* with Frederic March. Everyone in the embassy was expected to buy tickets because the proceeds went to a current worthy cause, such as the YMCA. Many

Egyptians were leery of attending U.S. political "propaganda" movies since the Egyptians considered Hollywood Jewish—in other words Israeli—dominated. We ended up "propagandizing" ourselves. Although not by courtesy of USIS, I did meet a movie star.

The Hilton Hotel chain had a grand opening of the Nile Hilton at this time. Conrad Hilton came and in his entourage brought Bob Considine, other noted newspaper journalists, a starlet named Linda Crystal (new to me), and Jane Russell! She had achieved fame in Howard Hughes' *The Outlaw.* It was showing in 1946 when I returned to the States. She was still popular in 1959. She came to the Embassy to pick up her escort for the ambassador's *soirée* for Hilton at our tent in Sahara City, the afternoon of the party. He was the lowest ranked American in the embassy. No, not me, he was our regional pouch staff officer for handling pouches and other classified mail. Good looking, gregarious, personable, and alcoholic, he and Russell had been childhood neighbors and school classmates. Even after she became famous they had kept in touch. She picked him up at our mail room office, adjacent to the Consulate, so we all met her. Charlie, ever the operator, had gotten himself (but not me) invited to the *soirée* and had his picture taken dancing with Russell. Charlie was one up on me but I got even on the next go-round.

Michael Ponti, a popular young American pianist touring Europe under U.S. Information Agency auspices, was diverted to Cairo by the head of our U.S. Information Services (as it was called overseas) for one concert. We missed that one but at the last minute decided to attend a second concert, a return request engagement, offered after his first had been sold out. USIS had given general services six complimentary tickets for work we had provided preparing for the concerts and Charlie was not interested. The seats were a cancellation and USIS wanted every seat filled. In addition to Josephine, myself, and our older sons, Clayton and David, I invited the Egyptian couple, the Ali Assems, who had lent us their beach cabana at the Momtaza Palace in Alexandria. His family was out of favor under the Nasser regime. They were a handsome, sophisticated couple, the epitome of the cosmopolitan elite Egyptian with old prestige, old connections, and lots of old, but good, money.

USIS told me our seats would be good but not how good until

we got to the imposing original Cairo Opera House. Khedive Ismail had built it in La Scala–style for the 1869 opening of the Suez Canal and Verdi's *Aïda*, written for that occasion, had subsequently premiered here. We were lucky because in 1967 rioters burnt it to the ground. Had the rioters waited two more years they could have destroyed it on its hundredth anniversary. No one ever said rioters care about history. They also burnt the Rollo Building, adjacent to the Embassy Chancery, which housed the USIS Library with its thousands of books.

For Ponti's concerts in this November 1959 the opera house, with U.S. assistance, was resplendent. Our good seats were the best in the house. We had the royal box, the king's box, on the right side, over the stage! The queen had an identical box across the theatre. Velvet covered the walls and furniture; the drapes and curtains were sable and ermine. The suite had a marble bathroom with gold fixtures. The king's "throne," and *bidet* were marble with gold fixtures. An ante room and a secure staircase gave privacy. Michael Ponti got a standing ovation; in the most visible seat in the house, I stood up first.

We decided to leave by the public stairs and hallway because our car was out front. It took a few minutes to get us organized. When we emerged from our box the occupants of all the other boxes were waiting in their doorways to let us pass first. Ali, who was familiar with opera house protocol, urged that we proceed ahead as expected. With commendable foresight Josephine had dressed the boys in suits and ties. Poised and presentable, they passed inspection by Cairo's literary and musical intelligentsia with flying colors. Charlie danced with Jane Russell; I got the royal box and used the king's golden "throne."

The life of Lillian Hunt Trasher, born September 27, 1887, in Jacksonville, Florida, was overshadowed by the death, months earlier, of a much beloved older sibling also named Lillian. Lillian Hunt never got out from under that shadow. After twenty years of anxiety and soul searching, in October 1910, Lillian—a tall, dark-eyed beauty—sailed for Egypt where she was to remain the rest of her life and be buried. She accompanied the Brelsfords, who were sponsored by a missionary society and had a mission in Assiut, on the Nile, 235 miles south of Cairo. Three months after arriving she opened the Lillian Trasher Orphanage with one orphan. When critics scornfully said that she would fail, Lillian defiantly replied: "An American girl can do anything if she tries hard enough."

After fifty years, this October 1959, and 6,000-plus orphans, widows, and blind children, Lillian Trasher, now the "Nile Mother," and her orphanage, were well-established and well-known institutions in Egypt. Nasser's signed, framed, letter, dated early in his revolution, enjoined Egyptian authorities to aid her and no one to interfere with her work at their peril.

The anti "foreigner" riots of 1919, which almost destroyed Assiut, forced her to leave, and she returned briefly to the States. She took that opportunity to ally herself with an American missionary society. She returned to Assiut and seldom left again.

In January 1960, Lillian's fiftieth year in Assiut, we planned to drive down to Upper Egypt, Luxor, and Aswan. I was prevailed upon to take a load of clothes, canned food, and other items the public affairs people in the embassy and military attachés had collected for the orphanage. My 1954 Oldsmobile, still fitted with heavy duty truck tires from San Pedro Sula, was jam packed inside; the trunk was full and boxes were tied on the roof. Josephine, Clay, and I barely squeezed into the front seat. The embassy was a minor source of support but this was little enough to do for her current 1200 orphans.

The road was paved to Assiut and a long day's drive. My first impression of the town was its super abundance of 1929, '30 and '31 Model A Fords in beautifully restored or maintained condition. Body styles ranged from open coupés to stylish Victorias. These cars had probably been assembled in Ford's impressive assembly plant in Alexandria. All were privately owned. One led us to the orphanage.

In a walled compound Lillian had twelve major buildings; some were named for benefactors, others were variously funded. The hospital treated ailments from isolation cases to minor injuries. The boys' dormitory covered half an acre and adjoined the boys' school. The Clark Memorial Church could seat one thousand. The Clayton and the Lambert buildings held living quarters and schools. She had a nursery for two year olds and another nursery and office building where Lillian lived. The Lillian Trasher Cottage held the newly born. The twenty-five head of cattle, mostly milk cows, had a barn. The new Maurice Doss Bey swimming pool was the gift of a wealthy Egyptian still accorded the honorific Ottoman title of *Bey* (Lord).

Lillian, a gracious hostess, treated us royally. We ate with the orphans and attended church services. For two days she gave us her quarters with the largest bed with curtains and all, I had ever seen. Josephine, Clay, and I, all together, could play games in it.

From Assiut south, the road was marked and ran along the top of a dyke. The verges dropped off into flooded farmland. I stayed in the middle and let oncoming traffic edge around me. Consular license plates were my ace in the hole in my persona as consul when dealing with police who just waved me on. Overloaded, overtaking, or head on jitney buses were 1937 Buick seven passenger sedans with original, straight eight cylinder engines; they added leaf spring suspensions. Camels careened right into us; no harm done. I adroitly dodged the donkeys. After a long day on the road, in the black of night, the brightly lit Cataract Hotel was a welcome sight. An embassy tour group, mostly attachés and assistant military attachés, had come by train. We were not included. Never mind, I had gotten us separate reservations.

Egypt is a land of superlatives and Luxor is high on the list. Since the Old Stone Age, more than 100,000 years, the Nile Valley here has been inhabited. The Valley of the Kings is like yesterday. The Temple of Karnak lived up to expectations and Clay had a field day; running all over the place. We went into King Tut's tomb to see the young man himself. As I wrote "Dear Folks," we did the touristy things.

Bathing at the hotel was exciting. The showers were in one huge room with rows of individual topless stalls divided by high wooden walls. It was just like San Pedro Sula—except with more stalls. Every adult, male and female, came in accompanied by at least one child as chaperone. On the left might be a junior army attaché's wife and on the right the navy attachés wife. Before happy hour we tourists washed off the dust of thousands of years. As one wife loudly exclaimed, it was "good, clean fun."

We started for Aswan but the dykes became impassible. After backing out of one more long *cul de sac*, with Josephine in her usual role of guiding me from outside the car, we headed north.

This stretch of the golden road and my introduction to the sand dune circuit was brought to an end in January 1960 with orders to the Arabic Language School in Beirut. In a foretaste of worse to come I was leaving Cairo under a cloud because Mr. Chapman accusingly said I had requested the school to get transferred out of general services. That was not true. In fact, all I did was put a check mark beside "Arabic language" in the annual routine preference form. Charlie knew that but couldn't, or wouldn't, convince Mr. Chapman. In fact I had enjoyed general services. My transfer seemed all for the best because I mistakenly thought my golden road lay in the glamorous political jobs. During the summer I had been acting GSO, done donkey work in the travel section, had filled in for our female disbursing officer when she was indisposed or otherwise unavailable, had turns as duty officer and was the embassy consul. Not a single day was boring, frustrating, or monotonous.

When I left the general services section, it would be in better shape because two assistant GSOs had been assigned to replace me. A third may be in the offing. Mr. Chapman's "empire" was growing and Charlie benefited from my departure. Notice of my assignment to Arabic language school ended thusly: "You are to be congratulated on your selection since the department, after careful screening, has been able to act favorably on only a small fraction of the many applications for 'hard' language training."

Mr. Chapman finally and begrudgingly conceded it was a good break but was still peevish and unhelpful. Jim Cortada, the energetic, rambunctious commercial attaché, and a "star" in the embassy hierarchy, told me "You're on your way now."

Jim should know; he had attended the school and at class 2, four grades ahead of me, was poised for further advancement. When he arrived in Cairo he, and two other FSOs, were featured in a long *Life* magazine article on Foreign Service officers which made him a marked man. Down the road, in 1964, while he was chargé d'affaires in Ta'izz, Yemen, and I was vice consul in Aden, we succeeded in rescuing a contingent of British soldiers captured by the Yemenis. Jim received honorable retirement as consul general in Barcelona. In retirement he became active in civic affairs. He was twice elected mayor of Orange, Virginia. He died November 1, 1999.

It was time to go. Mr. Chapman let me leave Wednesday, January 20, eleven days before the language school convened on February 1. The trip on Misrair would take an hour and forty-five minutes, so he was either being uncharacteristically generous or anxious to be rid of me.

In another instance his pettiness back-fired. In my departure fitness report, and still frustrated, he could think of nothing helpful to say about me so he wrote he would concur with my last previous report. That report had been written by Harold Wood on my departure from San Pedro Sula. Harold and I had gotten along famously and he had written: "In my forty years in the Foreign Service, Mr. Tinny is the finest consular officer I have ever served with." Thank you twice for that, Harold.

Our car was left on consignment to be sold, household effects were packed, and suitcases had been weighed. Clayton and David each held a Siamese kitten; going away presents from Santa Claus. All were in good health, Josephine was pretty, as always, and at 170 pounds I could get into the "new" suit which had served me so well for funerals in San Pedro Sula.

We were ready and spent our last night comfortably in our house. The cook, nanny, and houseboy—courtesy of the secret police—were staying on for the next tenants, an embassy couple we knew. We traveled tourist class but were given the first class luggage allowance; thirty-six pounds instead of twenty-four, and one carry-on bag; a gift from the airline.

Wednesday morning, after the boys and luggage were in the embassy car, Josephine and I took a last look so as to leave nothing behind. Then we saw it and stared in consternation. Josephine broke the silence and stated she was not about to leave behind a Christmas gift—an "antique," large white porcelain chamber pot, with lid, empty, shining in its enameled glory. What did it mean? Did it symbolize my hollow achievements in my first stop on the golden road and this a cautionary note on the past or was it an augury for the future? Here was another yet unanswered question.

I boarded the plane, empty chamber pot clutched protectively in my arms, hoping to find in Beirut that I was, as Jim Cortada had predicted, "on my way" to Samarkand.

Photo Gallery

John and Josephine Tinny, circa 1956.

American Consulate and Residence, San Pedro Sula, Honduras. June 1957. Consulate Office is at left.

Conquistador Don Pedro de Alvarado, who founded San Pedro Sula in 1526 with his enduring curse of cruel indifference to human suffering, life, and death.

The large American Embassy Chancery Building is in the center of the
Embassy compound encompassing several adjacent buildings.
Cairo, Egypt, 1958.

138

The American Embassy in Beirut, Lebanon, at the west end
of the *corniche,* facing the Mediterranean, 1960. The Foreign Service
Institute Arabic Language School was on the fourth floor of the left wing.

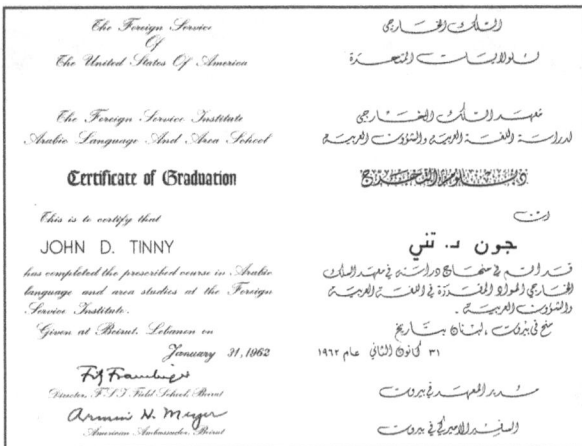

Certificate of Graduation, January 31, 1962. I did pass and graduate, but
that was not good enough.

American Consulate, Aden, 1962. The Consulate office was on the ground floor along with two small staff apartments under the deck on the right. A larger apartment for the principal officer is on the second (top) floor. The building in the background is not part of the Consulate. The lawn and garden had trees, other shrubbery, and the ubiquitous oleanders.

140

DEPARTMENT OF STATE
AGENCY FOR INTERNATIONAL DEVELOPMENT

OFFICE OF
THE DIRECTOR

TAIZ, YEMEN

October 8, 1963

Dear John:

I am deeply grateful and indebted for your assistance and cooperation while I was in Aden this week. I am very happy to have had the opportunity to meet with the High Commissioner and other important British officials in Aden. Carole asked that I also extend her thanks for your cooperation and to Josephine for the many courtesies we were extended.

In accordance with your request I am enclosing the most recent copies of the Mission's staff meeting reports. Also you will find enclosed the new edition of the Yemen post report. I hope these documents will be informative and broadening in your outlook on the Yemen situation.

Carole and I send our very best regards to you, Josephine and the family.

Sincerely yours,

James Megellas
Director

Enclosures - 6
  1. Staff Rept for 7Sept63 - UNCL
  2. Staff Rept for 14Sept63 - UNCL Section
  3.   do   CONFIDENTIAL Section
  4. Staff Rept for 21Sept63 - UNCL
  5. Staff Rept for 28Sept63 - UNCL
  6. Yemen Post Report

Mr. John D. Tinny
  American Consul
    Aden

Aden, October 8, 1963. Letter of thanks for services rendered from James Megellas, director of the AID/BPR Mission in the Yemen. Megellas was a decorated Army officer in World War II, and this job was part of his reward for his leadership and accomplishments in Normandy after the 1944 D-Day landings.

John Tinny at Dhala, "up country," a principality on the frontier with the Yemen, 1964. I noted at the time we spent 2 and ½ hours on those "fool camels." No stirrups and, to the disappointment of the tribesmen, I did not fall off.

Benghazi, Libya, 1964–66. The American Consulate in Benghazi. It was built in the 1930s to be the Italian army engineers officers' club. My office is behind the three large windows over the entrance.

Front door to the
Benghazi Consulate
Residence, 1964.
The room behind
the Mussolini-type
balcony over the door
is where my three
sons were when the
bomb blasted the
front door. The lamps
on either side of the
door were blown off
in the 1965 attack and
were forever crooked
when put back.

March 1965. After the
bomb the right-hand door
was rehung. Both doors
are solid oak.

Cyrene, Libya, May, 1965. Grave of Herbert Fletcher De Cou, an archeologist from Ann Arbor, Michigan, working in the ruins of Cyrene, murdered by Arab tribesmen in 1910 because they thought he had found gold.

Benghazi, Libya, October 17, 1965. Cyrenaica Express Railway cars we chartered for an all-day outing up the escarpment to Al Merj.

The Great Sand Sea of Calancio, Libya, January 1966.
The borrowed Chevrolet carryall had four-wheel drive,
two gas tanks, and 900x15 sand tires with straight airplane type tread.
The woman in white is Josephine Tinny.

Benghazi, September 1966. Italian packet, SS *Città di Livorno*,
departing Benghazi for Naples via Malta, Sicily, and Stromboli.
After Stromboli she turned west into a golden sunset.

7

Beirut

Hundreds of shouting, gesticulating, overheated travelers coming and going filled the waiting room of Beirut's Khalde International Airport when we arrived January 20, 1960. Most men and women were in western dress, but a generous sprinkling of men wore red and white *kufiahs*, traditional Arab headdress, and some women were swathed in black. The egg shaped white porcelain chamber pot, with lid, I had carried onto the plane in Cairo was still clasped to my breast with both arms. No one noticed and it rammed my way through knots of families to the tight little windows guarded with stout iron bars.

Thanks to Edward H. Springer, student and now colleague from the FSI Language School, detailed to meet us, we officially cleared customs, immigration, police (*securité*), and were properly introduced to Lebanon. Josephine watched our three active young boys who were always good in airports for fear of being left. If you can't beat them, join them, so with typical Lebanese *sangfroid* (cold blood), we were soon on our way on heaps of luggage in a long, wide Plymouth sedan with fins, *cum taxi*. Temporary lodging had been arranged at the modest, comfortable Hotel La Residence, a European style *pension*.

Unlike the dramatic midnight entrance into Cairo, our introduction to Beirut in broad daylight was fitting because here what you see is what you get. Despite riches in classical antiquities and medieval history—for example St. George fought the Dragon here; Dog River rocks record the passage of Roman Legions—Beirut's life focuses on becoming the commercial and financial center of the

Near East. The efforts were evident from the hustle and bustle of the shopping and business streets, the full house, and busy scramble at the airport. Lebanon is not driven by Nasser's Third World politics, the bitter, eternal bloodletting Palestinian/Israeli conflict, or the Super Powers' Cold War, but by the making and spending of more and more other peoples' money.

Still, the black storm cloud of Nasser's abrasive Arab politics creates an atmosphere of volatile tension and anger. Dismal, degrading camps of angry Palestinian refugees and their belligerent offspring breed hatred and violence. The beleaguered Lebanese Christian ruling elite is in a life or death struggle with Islam. Within the Moslem world mass reproducing Shi'as battle brother Sunnis for dominance. Beset from without and within, Lebanon forever teeters on the brink of destroying itself.

Driving north from the airport we entered Beirut through Ras Beirut's forest of shiny, new skyscraper apartment houses, office and "spite" buildings; useless structures which block another's view. They top the cliffs overlooking the dramatic, towering Pigeon Rocks standing tall offshore. Glistening Rolls Royces danced around donkey carts, seeking the right of way. In true Lebanese style neither would yield until, in the end, the donkey won over the fear of a scratch or dent. Our driver, who over the next two years would take our boys to school and us around town, this day took us past the American university, founded in 1866, and hospital, on *Rue Bliss*—the street named for the university's founder. We cruised along the *corniche*, the four-lane sea front boulevard, which begins at the nondescript but large, nine story American Embassy, a converted apartment building; and, finally, to the *La Residence*.

At the *pension* the boys began to explore, Josephine checked out schools and apartment rentals, and I walked the short distance back to the embassy. The language school occupied part of the fourth floor and there I met Dr. Ernest McCarus, the director. He was unimpressed with my two words of Arabic and my guttural Egyptian accent. He said his surname had an Arabic root, which, as I recall, may have been *mukarras*, which means dedicated. As language students we have the title and rank of *attaché*. Our main official embassy chore is to serve as duty officers on weekends and holidays.

Without getting too technical, Dr. McCarus told me that in the written form, the school concentrated on what is known as "news-paper Arabic," a modernized, generic version of Classical Arabic, the language of the Koran. The Arab countries try to keep this style uniform from the Arab west, Morocco, to the Arab east, Muscat and Oman. The spoken dialect the school teaches is, "Levantine," the accent of the countries in the Eastern littoral of the Mediterranean: Lebanon, Syria, and Jordan. Egypt, Libya, Iraq, and Saudi Arabia have their own accents and colloquialisms. With typical Arab con-trariness each country claims to speak the purest "Classical" Ara-bic, closest to the language of the Koran.

Meanwhile, Josephine had found a three bedroom apartment close by in a new building owned by the Nsouli brothers, members of a revered Maronite Christian family. During the post World War I French Mandate for Lebanon and Syria, after suppressing a rebel-lion, the French hung the Lebanese rebels downtown in what is now Beirut's "Martyrs' Square." Two of the "martyrs" were Nsou-lis.

The Nsouli building had an unsightly, unfinished lobby. The lobby would never be finished because taxes are not levied on new buildings until finished. Indeed, the day we left, two years later, the lobby looked as it had the day we first saw it. The elevator and telephones worked; there was a garbage chute and a dry, roomy, underground garage. Set midway between the U.S. Embassy and Saint George Hotel on *Rue 'Ain al-Mreissie*, it was the only apart-ment house in Beirut with a private beach. On the wintry January day we looked at it, a chilly breeze blew off the Mediterranean, and Josephine had a cold.

She vetoed the apartment. Two weeks later, after looking at much less desirable apartments, a two bed room unit in the Nsouli Building became available. In my chagrin I can hear myself saying that we really didn't need a third bedroom and if we did without a live-in nanny I could use the servant's room as a study. We hungrily snatched it up.

At the end of October the first three-bedroom apartment be-came available and that time we did not hesitate. In the nine month hiatus all three boys had grown bigger and stronger. They divided two bedrooms into sleeping and play areas, Josephine and I had the third. Each boy had his own bed, toy box, desk, and chair. David had started school in September and gloried in it. Clay had trouble reading—not his fault—and especially needed privacy. Gregory always needed more room; the world is not nearly enough.

At the same time Josephine had been busy seeking a school for Clayton and had exhausted the possibilities at the American, British, and German schools. They were all woefully overcrowded. The American school was the "oil" school, supported by ARAMCO (Arab American Oil Company,) its owners, and associated companies. It was apolitical and since the U.S. Government put little or no money into it; embassy children were at the bottom of the waiting list. The principal's name was Knox, so, naturally, the school is called the school of "Hard Knocks." In keeping with American liberalism the students were undisciplined and gregarious but the curriculum was American. After much argument, Clay and David did get into the American School for the 1960–61 term starting in the fall.

In the interim Clay attended the Italian school run by the Salesian Frères. Clay got off to a bad start because the first day the bus driver forgot where he had picked up Clay. Josephine, pacing the sidewalk, finally spotted Clay sitting alone and forlorn in the meandering bus.

At the language school all six students in my class were now on board, making thirty students in all. Students starting together were considered a class. The faculty numbered ten instructors and staff. Unfortunately, I have no roster and remember only a few names of classmates at the school.

James A. May was the senior man in my class. Robert Rogero and Kenneth Whitehead were the same rank as me. Later on Jim's wife Barney, and Carla, the wife of Charles Henebry (in a later class,) and both good students, became regular members of our class. Pompous but likable Charles Marthinsen and Kate (not a student), his pretty vivacious red haired wife, were a happy and popular couple.

Although Carla Henebry did well in Arabic her husband Charles had trouble. Before Beirut the Henebrys had enjoyed postings in Munich, Frankfort, and Hamburg. Beirut was not fun. After

Beirut he was sent to Tripoli, then Basra but then left the Foreign Service. Charles and I met later in Washington in 1969 and he was a disgruntled, unhappy man soon to die. Carla was pregnant at that time and refused to let me see her. The Foreign Service is a demanding taskmaster and Henebry failed to make the cut.

Charles (never Chuck) Marthinsen became one of two in my class to become an ambassador when he was given the post in Qatar. His final assignment was advisor at the U.S. Army War College. Josephine and I visited them in Carlisle, Pennsylvania. He introduced us to the super smooth Ginka, a traditional dry martini made half gin and half vodka and for that I am forever grateful to him. He was also one of the few of my State Department colleagues who knew my son, Clayton, had been killed in 1979 and commiserated with me. Charles retired in Carlisle in 1987 and died there in mid 2007.

Terrence Todman, our other ambassador, was a black man from the Virgin Islands. With his wife Doris, Todman was the best student in my class and one of the better language school students. By eighteen months in a two-year course, he considered himself fluent enough in Arabic to ask to be transferred to a duty post. His "secret" was running faster and studying harder than anyone else. He held five posts as ambassador, including in such diverse countries as Costa Rica, Denmark, and Argentina, plus Chad and Guinea in Africa. He served as an assistant secretary of state for Africa. He also knew and remembered that my son had been killed. Keeping active in international affairs, the Todmans have retired to the Virgin Islands.

In the class just prior to mine Morris Draper was outstanding. While in language school he and I explored both sides of the line in old and new Jerusalem for several days. Twenty years later he was prominent in the news. He helped write President Carter's Camp David Peace Accords between Israel and Egypt. He served as a deputy assistant secretary of state and then as consul general in Jerusalem.

In 1981 President Reagan gave him the rank of ambassador when he became deputy to special emissary Philip Habib for the withdrawal of the Israeli Army from Lebanon. Two years later Draper led the U.S. effort to force withdrawal of all foreign forces from Beirut, including the removal of Yasir Arafat's Palestine Liberation Organization (PLO) from Palestine to Tunisia. In the 1970s, after being captured in Jordan by Palestinian terrorists and held hostage for several days, he talked them into releasing him. He retired in 1990 and died in the spring of 2005.

On my class' first day of study the whole school visited former Lebanese President Camille Chamoun, leader of the Phalange party. He was a Maronite Christian as are all Lebanese presidents. Handsome as a movie star, he lived in a house resembling a Hollywood setting ten miles south of Beirut and was studiously pro-American. He commended Eisenhower for stopping the British, French, and Israeli Suez "aggression," Nasser's name for the 1956 "Suez Crisis" (our name). Eisenhower also landed 15,000 Marines on the beaches of Lebanon to save Chamoun's regime from the 1958 mid-summer, bloody, Palestinian-inspired, abortive civil war. Just as quickly the marines packed up and sailed away.

In fact, the 1950s saw Arab revolutionaries and militarists successfully seizing power beginning with Nasser in Cairo in 1952, to Serraj, in Syria, and 'Abd al-Kareem al-Kassim, who massacred the Hashemite royal family in Baghdad in 1958. Jordan's Hashemite King Hussein saved his crown and his life in 1956 by taking refuge with Jordan's twenty indigenous *bedu* tribes, mainly the Banu-Sakhr and the Huwaytat, no friends of the arrogant, arbitrary Palestinians. From these 350,000 tribesmen Hussein recruited the men and officers of the *Arab Legion*, the smallest but best of the Arab armies. Palestinians were denied officer rank in the Legion. Likewise, top officials in Hussein's government came from the sheikhs and chieftains of these *bedu* tribes.

Chamoun spoke in English and French so while we got an introduction to Byzantine Lebanese politics—no Arabic on this visit. We did eventually meet all Lebanese sectarian, meaning political leaders. Henri Pharaon, the most revered of Lebanon's cultural leaders, later gave us a tour of his residence; a veritable museum of Lebanese history and culture. During the wantonly destructive civil wars of the 1970s and 1980s his house was spared while the American Embassy was almost destroyed.

From the American university faculty members we had lectures on the history and culture of the Near East, Arabs in particular, and important religious sects. Experienced Richard Murphy, a senior at the school, (we overlapped a few weeks,) invited me to accompany him to sessions of the Parliament. Years later, then Ambassador Murphy, had a long tour as assistant secretary for Near Eastern affairs.

These lectures and activities were instructive and valuable for in depth area familiarization but the hardest and most important subject was the language. The Nsouli Building apartment would have been my "ace-in-the-hole," had I been smarter. Near home, I could have studied word lists and verbs, visited with my voluble neighbors who were always willing to talk, and practiced colloquial Levantine Arabic.

The building was advantageously situated. To the north and west were views of the "Med" in all its changeable aspects. March was stormy but some days were bright and sparkling. To the east, over the red tile rooftops of old Beirut, we saw the snow covered Sannin Mountains and to the south Mount Lebanon in all its year round beauty. I had no need to search far for scenery, just look out the window.

Our waterfront was flat rocks and large round pebbles, both suitable for walking. We had a tiny sandy cove with a sloping beach about the size of a two-car garage. Along with the up-grade to a three bedroom apartment in late October, I acquired a locally built, sliding Gunter-rigged sloop. The boat was a time consumer. I should have gotten rid of it, except, by mid 1961 all three boys had begun to relish sailing and swimming. Gregory seemed to enjoy sailing the most, although, Clay liked showing off his sailing skill to his friends. Before he could swim, David wanted to sail so badly that when the boat was anchored out and he had to swim to it, he would stand on the farthest point of rock just quivering with desire and trepidation. He finally jumped in and swam to the boat, remaining vertical, with a frantic walking motion. Twenty years later Clay would have bought his own sailboat but time ran out on him.

Our balconies, in both apartments screened with chicken wire to keep Gregory from trying to fly, were in speaking distance with the beach. Unfortunately, I couldn't accept what I had. Wrong priorities, too many exciting things to do, detracted from my Arabic studies. I was beguiled by scuba diving along the Mediterranean shore looking for a yet undiscovered Phoenician ship. In the end the diving let a sour taste. I should have followed Todman's example—stayed in one place and "run faster."

Our street, *'Ain al-Mreissie—Rue* in French speaking Lebanon, in Arabic: *Sharia*—an old, two lane street, a kilometer or two long, connected the embassy end of the *corniche* with the St. George Hotel and downtown. We were also in the district named *'Ain al-Mreissie,* the smallest but most ethnically polyglot political district in Beirut. Our Lebanese neighbors were Christians, both Protestants and Maronites, Turks, Armenians, Circassians, and a minority of Moslems. Elsewhere, Moslems were inundating Beirut and all of Lebanon. The fractious and prolific Moslem Shi'a, treated as a lower class, were increasing faster than orthodox Sunni and the smaller, secretive Druze, a Moslem offshoot. Though the Christian rulers of Lebanon denied it, Moslems were already a majority.

Lined with neighborhood shops and restaurants, it was a skip and a jump along our street, to the Embassy, with the Commissary and my school, or in other words my reason for being. On the street side of my building I could have participated in the noisy give and take of political argument among the shop keepers, fishermen, and the inevitable loungers; those with no visible means of support. Sometimes Tom Scoates, also a stellar student of the language school who would have been a good role model, and I, would stop in for lunch at one of the neighborhood shops. Our meal was a large crockery bowl of yogurt, for each of us half a kilo, covered by a tough skin of congealed yogurt. We peeled off the skin and topped the yogurt with a large helping of powdered sugar. Shops provided drinking water in long-necked earthenware jugs with round bottoms sitting in iron rings on the outside wall. Just below the neck was a small spout. To drink you held the jar up high and tilted it so water streamed out of the little spout into your open mouth. It took practice to keep swallowing without choking. The jugs were unfired so the evaporation of the condensate kept the water cool.

Dick Murphy, who also would have been a good role model, taught me to drink Lebanese style without drowning.

On the seaside was the quiet of a walled semiprivate beach, with my boat for recreation. In addition to a couple of embassy families—not language students, and including at least one CIA "spook," and a drilling equipment contractor. Our immediate Nsouli building American neighbors were Tom Streithorst, NBC Middle East correspondent, and his Lebanese wife, and Larry Collins, author of *Is Paris Burning?* The family of the local manager of the Swedish Airline occupied the penthouse.

Streithorst fancied scuba diving and occasionally borrowed my tank and equipment. He also liked Jaguar convertibles driven full out. Later that summer, driving back from Europe through Turkey, his car overturned and his wife was killed.

The mosque next door kept me apprised of the time of day with calls to prayer. On February 29, the "Holy" fasting month of Ramadan began so the *Allahu akbar*, "God is great," calls became more insistent. In mostly Christian *'Ain al Mreissie* fasting was observed in the breach. In liberal Lebanon, unlike conservative Egypt and Iraq, this was largely also true in the Moslem quarters. I could tell when it was Sunday by the doggedly plaintive bells of the church by the brazenly French, Christian, and westernized Saint George Hotel. The young women of many nationalities poolside at the St. George in French bikinis might just as well have been naked. In the internecine war of the 1970s and 1980s the Moslem dragon destroyed the Christian Saint George, and left his namesake hotel a burnt-out shell.

For visual excitement elements of the Sixth Fleet came in periodically. In March we awoke to see the aircraft carrier *Forrestal* and its battle group anchored out "front." Josephine and I, both World War II Navy veterans, enjoyed these visits. As a welcoming attraction, bare-breasted girls would water ski from the Saint George Hotel, out to and among the ships, holding the tow-rope with one hand and twirling their brassieres in the other. Hundreds of sailors hitting "the beach" livened up downtown Beirut's nightclubs, restaurants, and *souks*. In the Lebanese *souks* the twitch of an eyebrow spoke volumes. The heavy cruiser, *Des Moines,* was the flagship. The carriers varied; in October it was the *Intrepid.* Sometimes we attended receptions on the carriers.

I arranged for the commander of the Sixth Fleet, Admiral George Anderson, to address the language school. Personable Anderson is the only admiral in my lifetime to have been considered a candidate for president. I forget his sin but in the end he was exiled as ambassador to Portugal.

One thing Beirut had in common with Cairo was the hordes of dingy, black, noisy, smoky Mercedes diesel sedans. As well as taxis, they were inexpensive and popular as *"services,"* pronounced ser-VEES, and followed the electric trolley routes, ahead of the trolleys, picking up and dropping off passengers. They were fast and dangerous and talked to each other with their duck-like sounding horns that blasted out "qua-ack, qua-ack," twenty-four hours a day. The diesels were banned from Beirut later in 1960 but that did not keep the *services* from being a source of murder and mayhem.

Sometime in 1951 two *services* were racing to get to a pedestrian waiting for a ride. The driver who thought the pedestrian was rightfully his but who had been cut off by the other driver shot the offending driver. In 1961 the now-nineteen–year-old son of the slain driver got into the *service* of his father's killer. Sitting in the front seat, the boy turned to the driver and asked if he remembered so and so and named his father. The driver recognized the name, slammed on the brakes, and jumped but it was too late. The slain driver's son shot him dead along with two of the other passengers. The law, and most everyone, condoned the boy's action. Revenge in Lebanon is not only a sacred right but a sacred duty.

In defense of the *services,* the trolleys were not much safer. In 1958 the fighting that brought in the 15,000 Marines, and was winding down when we arrived in 1960 had been started by a trolley bombing that killed many of its passengers. In Lebanon every household has guns—not a gun, guns!

On a personal note, in May the sky above Beirut, already darkened by my lagging Arabic studies, saw the birth of a small black cloud which seemed to dissipate but then returned with a vengeance. I had been warned. On Monday, May 2, 1960, I wrote home:

> Dear Folks,
> We have our first real calamity to report. Clay, who loves to climb was on a short wall Monday fronting the property and fell off. He laned on our rocky beach and broke both arms with compound fractures. Both bones in both forearms were broken and protruding. Without wasting a second, Josephine grabbed a taxi and took him to the American University Hospital. Clay is still young enough the orthopedic surgeon, Dr. Nsouli, a cousin of our landlords, was able to set his right arm immediately. The doctor kept his left arm under, "visual observation" and set it the next day. Clay stayed in the Hospital until his fever subsided on Saturday. By then he was running all over the ward and flirting with a girl in the next room. He has casts on both arms from palms to elbows. His fingers and thumbs are free but don't meet.

As a symptom of the various constant crisscrossing tensions here in Beirut, when Josephine went to get Clay from the hospital Saturday morning anti-American Lebanese were "boycotting" the United States. Here that meant the university and hospital. As luck would have it, I had a busy day as duty officer. First, our ambassador, Robert McClintock, was leaving the country, and second, an American flag freighter, grist for the boycott mill, was due. Unfazed, mother bear Josephine plowed right through a scraggly lot of lackadaisical but obnoxious demonstrators and got her cub, Clay.

We were uncertain why Clay fell off the wall. The most plausible story is that Clay and David were on the wall, which fronted our garage, when a gang of Lebanese boys came onto "our" beach. Perhaps for some reason, but more likely for no reason other than that they were Americans, they threw rocks at the two, which caused Clay to lose his balance. Clay, seven, was well coordinated and athletic so we didn't understand his loss of balance. Six months passed before we did.

National Parliamentary elections scheduled for June also increased the sectarian and political tension during May to such a dangerous level the army was mobilized. One hand grenade, of several in Beirut, killed four, and an increased nighttime volume of small arms gunfire became routine. Lebanese booby trapped new, innocent looking cigarette packs with dynamite. They did not kill but maimed the person, also Lebanese, hopefully one of other religions and opposite "sects," who picked one up.

For this election Lebanon was divided into four sections and a section would vote on one of four successive weekends. The reason for this system was that the army was big enough to police only one fourth of the country at a time. After all sections had voted the ruling Christian party was to count the votes, guaranteeing Christian majorities in contested sections. Further increasing tension was the first time granting of the vote to women and voting by secret ballot. Both innovations are traumatic, even anathema to many Lebanese. To increase Moslem misery, but not exclusively, a woman was running for Parliament.

As a sign of the times, Lebanon was the third country in three years in which I had seen women vote for the first time. The previous year, 1959, women voted in Egypt. Nothing was secret about their ballots because who would dare to not vote for Nasser. In Honduras the year before, 1958, women voted using, as the men did, paper ballots colored red for one party and blue for the other.

Beirut's Election Day was Sunday June 19—the second of the four voting days. A curfew kept people off the streets unless they were voting. Thanks to the Lebanese Army and the four-section system of voting "sectarian outrages"—a euphemism for killings—were reduced and another outright civil war was avoided.

On our home front, Clay, who had broken his arms on May 2, had the cast on his left arm finally removed on June 20, two weeks after the cast on his right arm had come off. The past seven weeks with long casts on both his arms had been a strain on all of us. Clayton, most affected, had stood the ordeal with admirable stoic composure; Clay used his casts for cracking pecans.

At first, Clay's right arm was straight as an arrow but his left arm had a definite deviation. Dr. Nsouli said he expected the bend and it would straighten. He was the head orthopedic surgeon at the American Hospital and was schooled in the United States. We watched Clay's arm carefully and years later were happy to proclaim the doctor was right. Doctors are born, not made.

In August I prepared for Phase III: the travel phase of the summer seminar which included some of us from the language school. Phases I and II were for officers stationed in Washington and were activities we had already covered. Visits of varying length were scheduled for: Ankara, Istanbul, Baghdad, Teheran, Isfahan, Kuwait, Dhahran, Cairo, Port Said, Amman, Jerusalem, and by traveling via Cyprus we were able to visit Israel without running afoul of Arab paranoia.

We flew first commercially to Ankara—a pleasant, modern city. Again, as on my first visit to Damascus last year, the downtown parts of Ankara were unexpectedly clean. Atatürk, who ruled Turkey from the end of World War I until 1938, wisely moved the capitol from Istanbul to this small, ancient, and mountainous caravan crossroads village. The modern city he ordered built was designed by American engineers and architects. As construction continues, Ankara keeps its ongoing distinctive American flavor. We saw the tourist sites from Atatürk's mountaintop mausoleum to the ruins of the capital of the thousand years Hittite Empire. Nearby, Gordium was the center of the Phrygian Kingdom. All their kings were called Midas, so which one had the golden touch is anyone's guess. Here Alexander cut the Gordian Knot, the source of Phrygia's power, and took the kingdom into his empire.

Our guide, Edward Wright, a one-time Presbyterian missionary had lived and taught in the Near East since 1930. It seemed natural to call him Dr. Wright, because he knew Arab history and culture in such exquisite detail. He demurred, saying he was just "plain Ed Wright." Since their inception he has guided these State Department tours and has found the best restaurants and hotels in a dozen cities of the Near East. We were the grateful beneficiaries of his searches.

The Turkish Air Force flew us to Istanbul, a complicated and fascinating city, where we had briefings at the consulate general. By ferry boat we cruised up the swiftly flowing dark but clear water of the Bosphorus. We stopped briefly at the Hellespont where I got my swim, to catch up to Richard Halliburton. Ed tried to stop me but it is easy if you swim downstream. When we sailed into the almost fresh water Black Sea, they put us in a delightful seaside hotel in Kilyos west of the Bosphorus while we studied Russo-Turkish politics. We took the train back to Istanbul's Yesilköy airport and took off for Iraq.

In Baghdad we stayed at the newly completed Baghdad Hotel which advertised "200 rooms – 200 baths," a real innovation; with candles in every room, a real necessity. Our Embassy here was a beautiful, but smaller, exact replica of the White House. We were briefed by the political counselor, personable Roger P. Davies. Extremely well versed on Near Eastern affairs, he was one of the much maligned but knowledgeable State Department Arabists. Had their voices been heard we might not still be fighting the Jewish-Arab war already going good in the 1930s. Fourteen years later, August 19, 1974, Greek guerillas gunned down Davies, our freshly arrived ambassador to Cyprus, in his Embassy office.

Our second most important briefing was with the Iraqi dictator called "president," General 'Abd al-Karim al-Kassem, a Soviet adherent. In July 1958, two years before our visit, General al-Kassem, an intense Arab revolutionary, had been ordered to bring his armed brigade through Baghdad en route to support King Hussein of Jordan threatened by militant Palestinians in Lebanon and Jordan. Ironically, at that moment King Hussein didn't need help. Al-Kassem saw and grasped his moment to act. King Feisal II, twenty-two, first cousin of King Hussein; the regent, his uncle, Abdulilah; and their immediate families were blown to pieces by al-Kassem's gunners. The current prime minister, Nuri es-Said, long time political activist, thirteen times prime minister of Iraq, tried to escape in women's dress but drooping pants' legs betrayed him. Shot down like a dog in the street, Nuri's body was dragged through Baghdad behind a squawking taxi belching clouds of black diesel smoke.

The direct cause of the coup was Nuri's unwise decision to allow an army brigade into Baghdad with ammunition without having prepared a counter force. Brigadier al-Kassem was swift and decisive. He seized the radio station, broadcast that the royal family and adherents had been eliminated, and then sent his troops to make it so.

Whether we or the British could have rescued the Iraqi royal family from murder, and Iraq from Soviet hegemony, is problematical. The British were crippled by their role in the Suez "Aggression" and Eisenhower was diverted by the Palestinian threat to pro-U.S. Camille Chamoun. Al-Kassem made no apologies for his murder of the royal family and hundreds of their supporters. He gaily boasted his coup was a blow by militant Arabism against Western domination and denounced the betrayal of Palestine by the "imperialists" who he said wanted to destroy "Arab freedom and unity."

Al-Kassem's bloody uniform worn in a recent assassination attempt by the Baathist Saddam Hussein was ostentatiously displayed on a mannequin in a glass case in his office. During our meeting the four ton air conditioner unit on the terrace outside the French doors to his office began to rattle noisily. With increasing visible irritation he motioned to his guards and aides to do something. When they were unable to stop the rattling al-Kassem jumped up, went outside and stopped it himself.

As a plus Al-Kassem liked things American; his automobile was a Chevrolet and he enjoyed the company of the marine guards at the embassy. For the four years of his rule he attended the marine's November 10 "birthday party."

When he appeared in public and all men sat with the soles of their shoes aimed outward, toward him—a gross insult—his days were numbered. He too, was shot dead like a dog in the street and dragged through Baghdad behind another squawking taxi belching clouds of black diesel smoke.

In Teheran our presumptive visit with the Shah did not happen, although we did go in the vault to see the Crown Jewels and the Peacock Throne. In his place we were soundly castigated by the court chamberlain for luring Iran's best youth to the United States for training in various modern fields of science and technology and then keeping them. We were creating, he said, "an Iranian 'brain drain."

Otherwise Teheran looked American from Roosevelt Boulevard to Iranian soldiers who wore regular G.I. uniforms and looked like American soldiers. We know now this was the flimsiest of façades and thinnest of veneers and evaporated with the fall of the Shah nineteen years later in January 1979. The suppressed hatred of the West generated by centuries of humiliation and subsequent defeats surfaced. Iran, the only Shi'a-dominated country, is driven to assert itself. Hatred of the United States, augmented by grandiose ambitions of making Iran a European like power, voiced by the Shah, exploded into the open.

In Israel, the last stop on our itinerary, the words I felt described that nation best then was "frontier," and the Israelis, "pioneers." The Israelis knew our sympathies, as opposed to official policies, were with the refugees. They called us "Arabists" while they tried to seduce us. If the Palestinians had been robbed to begin with and were entitled to more than they were getting, to what then, the Israeli, high-breasted tour guides asked, were the Israelis entitled? Whenever an agreement seemed to have a good chance of success the Palestinians balked. Abba Eban said it best: "Palestinians never miss a chance to miss a chance." Both sides want to get what they themselves would not give.

If that is true it is also true the Israelis never yield on anything important to the Arabs. After the Israeli victories of 1948 they felt they had nothing to fear militarily from the Arabs. This feeling was reinforced by their subsequent victories in 1967 and 1973. Of course, they had the iron clad guarantee, a self fulfilling prophecy—American military aid to the last American. Israel needs never compromise. Would it be better for the Israelis to yield on sufferable matters instead of relying on unyielding hubris?

Those who were Israeli-born, the *sabras,* all seemed young and vigorous. Pedestrians in the cities and towns wore shorts, open necked, short sleeved shirts, and carried machine guns. The young women looked like those described by Leon Uris in his novel *Exodus* as high-breasted. The girls and women who shaved neither their armpits nor legs exuded an aura of vigorous, outdoor sensuality.

During the first few days our guide, Abba Eban, wore a jacket and tie. When we went to meet with David Ben-Gurion he took them off, opened his shirt collar, and never put them on again. Ben-Gurion was charismatic and inspiring. Later on when we visited two *kibbutzim,* government-owned farms, and other work places, the same feeling of inspiration, dedication, and efficiency permeated the atmosphere. We were seduced and felt that it would be exciting to be a young Israeli in Israel. Even the New Testament sites seemed affected. As I wrote home at the time our chief recreation on this trip was swimming and that included in the Sea of Galilee. Its water was, somehow, warmer and wetter than any other place I knew.

Along the Gaza Strip we saw how vision, dedication, and enthusiasm in Israel were diametrically opposed to the misery, anger, and bitterness of the Palestinians in refugee camps. There were exceptions; these were the refugees who had escaped the hold of the Arab governments and the refugee camps. In the United States and Europe they had become "ex-refugees" and wasted no time being angry and frustrated.

September 1960 and home again in Beirut I found Clay and David anxious to begin another school year, and that I had bought a car. David, after kindergarten in Honduras, Egypt, and Lebanon was more than ready for the first grade. Both started in the Italian school but later transferred to the American school despite its annoying laxity in discipline. Clayton was having problems. He should have been in the third grade but his teacher told us he could not read first grade material. We were surprised because he had been reading aloud to us. Besides, Clay had temper tantrums in the morning. However, when at school he was a model pupil, and as he did with everything, he tried hard but it was uphill.

An astute teacher recognized the problem and it was a real bombshell: "Clay has *petit mal.*" We had to find a neurologist but either way it was bad news and explained Clay's erratic behavior. Now we knew why Clay fell off the wall in May. The stress of having rocks thrown at him probably caused a minor seizure. Epilepsy, a life sentence, can be controlled with medication—another life sentence. Clay resented taking his medication the rest of his life and his resentment and embarrassment were fatal.

The car was bought from Frank Newton, the embassy's new general services officer who I had met in Washington in 1956 and could better relate to after Cairo. Frank was possibly the only person in Washington who not only knew where San Pedro Sula was but had been there. Frank had spent a night at the consulate and for lack of better accommodations had slept on a desk in the office. When he was asked the next morning how he felt he said: "Just like a typewriter." He told me then that when he joined the Foreign Service he was one of only three from Florida. In the "Ivy League" club of the Foreign Service Florida was the wrong side of the tracks. On our commissions the state of the officer is identified, as for example: "John D. Tinny of Florida." That may be true still today; Florida gets the retirees.

Frank, who should have known better or was misinformed, had brought a car to Beirut. As staff he did not have duty free privileges and the Lebanese were after him to pay the duty. In Cairo, like Charlie, he would have had duty free privileges. He insisted I buy it for *Auld Lang Syne* and San Pedro Sula and enter it duty-free. It was a good car, a 1956 Ford with a powerful V-8 engine, and served us well until we left Beirut. At that time Joe Lill, a language school classmate assigned to Baghdad as commercial officer, wanted to arrive with an American car. His current car—and wife—were German. He came to me in December 1961 and insisted on buying my Ford. I was glad to accommodate Joe—a nice guy.

The Lebanese tried to help with my Arabic. A fisherman, who lived with his mother between us and the Embassy, invited Josephine and I and the boys to lunch one day. We had typical Lebanese fare, which we had sampled before, but this was home cooked and better. Each Lebanese family brews its own *arak,* a strong alcoholic drink which turns white mixed with water; it is akin to Greek *ouzo.* The Lebanese call it "milk of the lion." Clay and David ate heartily but, strangely, Gregory would not eat.

Part of our language school curriculum was a field trip. Each of us was given $250 to use to go anywhere, in the Arab world, of our own choosing for at least two weeks. My turn came in June and my choice was the southern littoral of the Persian Gulf, from Kuwait southeast to the Arabian Sea. The United States had no representation there and I never dreamed Foreign Service officers would ever go there. My crystal ball didn't show that ten years later, from 1969 to 1973, my family and I would live in the emirate of Umm al Qawain; since December 1971 a charter member of the United Arab Emirates (UAE). Neither did I foresee that we would put embassies in Bahrain, Qatar, the UAE, and reopen the long abandoned nineteenth century embassy in the Sultanate of Muscat and Oman; the ideal post for dedicated Arabists. My fifteen days and nights were crowded with people from sheikhs and other rulers to camel drivers, and places from Kuwait in the north to the Sultanate of Muscat and Oman in the southeast. My headquarters was the "fort" in the emirate of Sharja used by the Trucial Oman Scouts (TOS,) a semi-autonomous military force with British officers for the former Trucial States.

Originally, Sharja (correctly transliterated as Ash Shariqah,) ruled by an aggressive, ambitious emir, and with a navigable harbor, was a way station on the Imperial Airways, now British Overseas Airways Corporation (BOAC), air route to India. The British built the "fort" in the 1930s as a military strong point and base and to also serve as a stop-over hotel for itinerant passengers and air crews.

Britain's International Aeradio operated the fort; the manager was named Dench. Constructed of solid concrete it had watchtowers with thirty-six-inch searchlights for warding off raiding *bedu*, Arabs of the desert, plural, often incorrectly called *bedouin*, the dual form. Sturdy iron gates were closed at night or when under attack. When asked when the attack might be, one of the Scouts told me: "When the natives are restless."

Sharja foolishly let its harbor silt up, and Imperial Airways was lured to Dubai by its aggressively ambitious ruler, Sheikh Ahmed al Maktoom.

The Trucial Oman Scouts were very hospitable in showing me around, supplying transportation, and extending to me the courtesy of their mess. To resist the temptation to spend too much time with the Scouts, I had recourse to a letter to a merchant in Doha, Qatar from a friend of his in Beirut. The merchant introduced me to a bevy of cousins, friends, and colleagues in every town in the Gulf all known to each other. The Gulf seemed to be a big happy family home. It helped that I also had letters to the rulers of Dubai, Sharja, and Ras al Khaima, and sat in on their *majlis*, or public meetings. I passed by Ajman, Umm al Qawain, and Fujerah but did not enter.

In Abu Dhabi, the western most emirate of the seven in the United Arab Emirates and while visiting British political officer Oliver Miles, I met the ruler, Sheikh Shaqbut, at the airport on his return from Das Island—the operations heart of Abu Dhabi's nascent oil industry. On that occasion, after Shaqbut disembarked from the

DC-3, everyone—soldiers, visitors like Miles and me, tribal leaders, and tribesmen (*bedu*)—made a mad dash through the softest sand I saw anywhere in the Gulf to Shaqbut's small but very picturesque fort *cum* palace for the welcome return and *majlis* with the ruler. This is real classic, ancient Greek democracy. With motors racing, flags flying, rifle bullets zinging, all four wheels on the Land Rovers churned like paddle wheels throwing sand in great "rooster tails."

The next day I drove to the oft-contested but pleasant oasis of Buraimi, one of eight villages in the Al 'Ain area at the junction of the Abu Dhabi, Saudi Arabia, and Muscat and Oman borders. In the eighteenth century Buraimi was claimed by the Wahhabis of present-day Saudi Arabia but since 1870 it has been protected by Abu Dhabi. It was considered part of the Trucial States territory with all water and grazing rights. About eighty years later, in 1952, several oil companies, British and American, began prospecting and oil rights superseded previous rights. The oil-bearing strata extended northward to the oil fields of Abu Dhabi, still, at that time, under British protection and control by "indirect" rule.

In Buraimi I met Shaqbut's younger brother Rashid. After my visit, the British deposed Shaqbut and replaced him with Rashid. They said Shaqbut abdicated but his real fault was not spending his money fast enough, by giving contracts to British companies. Shaqbut never squawked and happy to be relieved took Rashid's place at Al 'Ain to live there quietly ever after and die likewise. In every respect my trip to the Persian Gulf was worthwhile; the Gulf was still reminiscent of centuries past.

Thanks to the TOS I visited all of the emirates and in Ras al Khaima saw the British "Huntington Experiment," an attempt to modernize vegetable farming. The most modern building in Dubai was the National Cash Register (NCR) one-story office. In Abu Dhabi, the most modern building was the residence of the British political officer. At the fort drinking water from inland wells was brought in daily by tank truck, but we bathed with local, brackish well water. The only "paved" road—outside the Arabian American Oil Company (ARAMCO) area in Saudi Arabia and the British controlled island of Bahrain—I saw was in Muscat and Oman.

Several miles of road linking the capital, Muscat, and Matrah was carved through solid rock so its flat rock surface was like paving.

When I returned to the Gulf nine years later, in 1969, the changes were sweeping. At this writing in the first decade of the twenty-first century the Persian Gulf towns, judging from photographs, would be unrecognizable to me. The forts, palaces, and towns themselves have been reduced to museum pieces.

Christmas

Christmas 1960 was holiday time with the boys and me off from our schools. The five of us plus a young girl, Alice Norris, referred to us by mutual friends in Washington, working on her master's degree, hit all the high spots in Damascus, Aleppo, Amman, Jerusalem, Bethlehem, and points in between. We saw the grotto, supposedly, where Christ was born. A Jordanian Army bagpipe band was playing *Scotland the Brave* while we toured Manger Square. We loved Jerusalem and explored Jordan's extensive, preserved Roman ruins at Jerash. We quickly bypassed by the "rose red city," Petra.

In Aleppo we toured what was is reputed to be the largest *souk* in the Arab world with ten miles of covered walkways. Dick Murphy who befriended me several ways at the language school and graduated in June the year before was stationed at consulate general Aleppo. He knew we were coming and at his request I brought him medicine and medical equipment including syringes, to treat his serious bouts with hepatitis and pneumonia. Apparently our medicine was not good enough because the next month, late January 1961, Dick was evacuated to Ainaab, a small mountain village east of Beirut. We visited the Murphy's at their *pension.* It was in a park of pines up the slopes of the Sannin Mountains, just below the deep snow line and with a view of Beirut. The pines with their strong resinous smell reminded me that T. E. Lawrence had said that the Arabs were a people of primary colors and passions. In the Arab world all is primary. The resin of the pines is more pungent, the loamy soil more fertile, the water sweeter, and the rocks and peaks harder. At Ainaab Dick recovered and went on to a long and successful career.

To finish our Christmas trip, from Aleppo we went west into

southern Turkey, past Antioch. At one point we drove faster than safe on modern Near Eastern roads for miles on a Roman road. The paving stones were only slightly disarranged at the edges. Eventually, we had to turn around, because this section of road started nowhere and ended abruptly in a scene of barren desolation. The road built in 56 A.D., in the reign of Nero, took Romans 150 miles from Antioch to Acre. The whole route, now mostly paved over, is the basis for Lebanon's modern coastal highway. Two thousand years ago this was a thriving, prosperous area, but in 1960, Anno Domini, it was a lonely steppe. There was no one here except us, on a straight road that still retained the high gloss polished by six centuries of imperial Roman traffic.

Returning south inland through Syria we watched the hundred foot tall water wheels at Hama—the *nutrias*—lift water. After Homs we joined the coastal road at Tripoli in Lebanon and so into Beirut. Not a long trip, we went about 1100 miles.

Our second year in Beirut began January 20, 1961. A whole year with so little Arabic fluency to show for it is a discouraging note. The language school had done its part; so far I had not done mine.

Clayton and David were in the American school now, and David was doing well. Clay tried hard but was not doing well, as he struggled to focus his eyes and mind on the printed word. He blundered through the lightning flashes in his head at what he was supposed to do but it was an uphill battle. Josephine was doing as much as she could to help all four of us. Clay was smart but due to the epilepsy there were some missing pieces in the mechanism for the passing of knowledge from one part of his brain to another. Still, his bittersweet poem "Springtime" was included in his school class's book of poetry.

Both Clay and I were barely coping with problems we tried to ignore and were unable or unwilling to correct. Clay's admirable and dogged determination, imparted to me, would be a help.

My mind was clear but there was no excuse for my lack of concentration; Clay simply did not understand his *petit mal*. He knew something was not right, so he had to take a powerful medicine daily, but still, thoughts he knew were there disappeared. He realized other people did not understand his problem and became angry at him. Clay was conscientious, dependable, and understood the world as well as any eight year old—better than most. He was a good big brother to David and Gregory. Clay's fine qualities and capabilities as boy and man were amply shown throughout his short life.

We found only basic neurological help for him in Beirut. Josephine and I hoped that when we returned to the States next year we could get medical attention for him. We were disappointed; even Johns Hopkins in Baltimore was no help. Clay soldiered on through another twenty years in a tortured but worthwhile life that should have been an example for all of us.

For me there was no help. For example: one Sunday, instead of studying, I drove us all up to the "Cedars of Lebanon," the finest ski and winter resort in Lebanon. It is farther from Beirut than the resorts at Lakhlouk or Faraya but in slopes and facilities worth the extra miles.

The snow that day was fresh, heavy, and deep. After some elementary ski lessons from a French speaking instructor—for all of us mostly a series of comic scenes and pratfalls, recorded on 8 mm film—I thought it would be a fitting climax of the day to ride the ski lift to the top, a trip of two miles. Josephine, David, and Gregory quickly declined but Clay gallantly said he would go with me. I grabbed a chair and took Clay on my lap. He was very brave about it but his hard muscled body was as tense as a bow string because his *petit mal* even with his medication left him unsure of himself.

The lift climbed at a stiff grade over deep gorges with nearly vertical sides. Sometimes our feet were almost scraping snow off ridges and at other times we were hundreds, or even thousands of feet in empty air. At the top, the 10,000-foot level, we got off the lift and had a good look around. One of the few remaining groves of the Cedars of Lebanon was visible below us. Of course it was a tiny remnant of the vast stands of cedars which had once covered these mountains and supplied wood for the coffins of Egyptian pharaohs. The trip down, often looking down into open space over our knee caps, was scarier than going up. That was a view real skiers miss. Clay never whimpered and it was one proud but relieved boy who jumped off my lap at the bottom. For me it was another minus day in my Arabic studies.

Time wasted on skiing didn't end there. Many of my fellow students and other embassy people skied. John E. Horner, called Jack, a senior FSO was on a special truncated language course because he was slated to be consul general in Dhahran later that year. We skied together at the Cedars and again when he took a chalet at Lakhlouk for his family he invited us to visit a weekend with them there. Jack and Trinette had two daughters and three sons. I skied more than I should have and studied Arabic less. To reciprocate, Clay and I took Jack and his youngest son Billy, Clay's age, sailing. Clay enjoyed that.

The Horners were sophisticated and friendly. He had studied at Columbia and the Sorbonne. He retired in 1967, after his tour in Dhahran. They were Quakers and in 1975-79 he served as the Quaker international affairs representative for the Near East from Cyprus. He died in April 1997.

Distractions were unceasing. When the American Repertory Theatre visited Beirut I just had to see Helen Hayes and June Havoc in *The Glass Menagerie*. Helen Hayes is the finest actress I have ever seen but she didn't teach me a word of Arabic. The better students, who worked harder than me at their Arabic, skipped the theatre. On other days life went on its merry way.

At the end of August we drove to Baalbeck for the final show of the annual Baalbeck Festival. This was a performance by the Royal Ballet of London, formerly the Sadler Wells Ballet. The *prima ballerina* was Margot Fonteyn. Roberto Arias, her husband and former president of Panama, tried to stage a coup d'état from his wheel chair in 1946 while I was in Panama. Someone put a bullet hole in the door of my truck while I was on Shore Patrol duty, but missed me. As always, Dame Margot was every bit as outstanding as she was supposed to be in a troupe of top-notch performers. Clay and David enjoyed the show and told everyone they had seen the "belly dancers." The incomparable Temple of Jupiter was the setting for the festival. Leptis Magna and Sabratha in Libya come close, but do not have the visual impact of Baalbeck's temple and its tremendous columns.

* * *

A more serious diversion came in July after meeting Dr. William Grant, an American professor of biochemistry and medical doctor at the American university. He had sailed his yacht, the thirty-foot, British-built yawl *Picotee*, to Beirut and wanted to visit Cyprus during the summer holiday. He agreed to take five from our MUREX diving club. We wanted to dive on ancient Salamis near Famagusta.

MUREX was my prime time waster throughout most of 1961, and I cannot forgive myself for participating. The name comes from a Mediterranean species of the spiny murex, a marine gastropod, the shell of which was first used by the Phoenicians to produce Tyrrhenian purple—the royal and imperial purple of classical ages. MUREX was our acronym for Mediterranean Underwater Research and Exploration. The prime mover of MUREX was George Thompson, another FSO at the language school. MUREX and George, our Fearless Fosdick–type leader, monopolized my weekends. Among the ancient Greek and Roman shipwrecks no Phoenician ship has been found. Hundreds of Phoenician ships had sailed these waters for centuries; to find one meant fame.

At the same time, Josephine had two severe bouts of flu in March which put her in bed. When she complained about MUREX I mentioned that several FSOs including Jim May and Alan Logan, both senior to me, also spent time diving with MUREX. That argument was no good as a palliative because Josephine had another bout of flu and severe coughing in August. She was run down and had, the doctor said, a "lung infection," which lasted until well into September. In October when Clay and David returned to the American school and Gregory went to a nursery school she got some rest.

One doctor said that her coughing had splintered a rib, which had then torn the lining around her heart. The tear would heal in time and cure itself if she could control the coughing. She couldn't then and now, fifty years on, still cannot. A German doctor said Americans are soft and she was homesick.

Our luck with doctors in Beirut was uneven. We were very fortunate with Dr. Nsouli, who treated Clay's arms, but not with the others. The same was true with dentists. Gregory's baby teeth were not coming out as expected, so we took him to a dentist to have them extracted. Gregory sat on my lap as his milk teeth were pulled, and after each tooth I asked how he was. He answered: "Just fine."

My experience with this dentist and a root canal he did on me was not so fine. I don't know the technicalities, but after the tooth had been capped the pain was excruciating. He gave me painkillers and sleeping pills, and sometimes the pain subsided. I wanted the tooth pulled, but he refused because the crown, he said, was so "perfect." He was a "made" doctor, not a "born" doctor.

When our time was up, we left Beirut—throbbing tooth and all—and we finally got to Washington. Days later, on a Sunday afternoon in a downpour, I went straight to the emergency room at Georgetown University Hospital. A dentist was called; he came in garbed in his raincoat and hat, and without stopping took a look. He picked up pliers, said: "Open," and out came the tooth. He turned, and with his hat still on walked out the door. I never saw his face or heard his name but I will be forever grateful to that born dentist.

After weeks of preparation including a briefing from our yachtsman ambassador, Robert McClintock on a shortcut into Famagusta harbor, we cast off Saturday afternoon, July 22. Our written crew list—plus yacht owner Grant—named George Thompson, divemaster, and his teenage son Jordan, his assistant; Raoul, a young Lebanese employee of the embassy, language tutor; and me, sailing master. Tom Scotes from the language school asked to go with us and volunteered to do the cooking. Tom was prone to serious seasickness but was named chief cook and bottle washer.

Tom was brighter than George and I put together. His spoken and written Arabic, French, German, and Persian, not forgetting English, were highly rated by the department. After Beirut and tours in Baghdad, Tunis, and Damascus he was named ambassador to the Yemen. His reports from Sana'a were preferred reading in Washington. Sadly, his wife Oriette Scotes, neé Sarides, a lovely and charming Iranian whom he had met and married in Isfahan prior to Beirut, died in the Yemen. I had met them in Isfahan on our field trip. Tom resigned from the Foreign Service after Oriette's death. She was the third Foreign Service wife I knew whose death could be connected, in some way, to the Yemen. A credit to the Foreign Service, Tom was a scholar, a gentleman, and even while miserably seasick, a damned good cook.

Determined to go even though the auxiliary engine wouldn't start, at twilight we tacked laboriously out of the harbor. Then the wind died and Sunday morning found us still within rifle range of Beirut. We heard the shots but saw no bullet splashes. Ninety six hours later we finished the one hundred and eight miles to Famagusta. In the meantime, by Tuesday, we were overdue and considered "missing" by our advance MUREX team in Famagusta. Wednesday British and American Air/Sea Rescue forces from Akotiri and Wheelus Air Base had started searching for us. Syrian and Turkish authorities had been asked also to be on the lookout. Fortunately, or otherwise, not much effort was wasted in the search because at this moment, we were upstaged by Iraq's rabid Arab revolutionary president. Al-Kassem had moved troops to Iraq's border with Kuwait, claimed it as Iraq *irredenta*, "unrecovered Iraq," and threatened to invade. The British gathered forces in Kuwait, including aircraft from Akrotiri, to resist any Iraqi move, and the U.S. Sixth Fleet was put on alert. The crisis ended in an anticlimax when the Saudis sent a twelve man squad to the border. The Iraqis withdrew but never have given up their claim to Kuwait.

During the hours we were lost we practiced with deep dives limited to 150 feet, to avoid underwater narcosis, the "rapture of the depths," led by Thompson. Some of us even inched down farther but found no rapture. Grant let me do what sail handling needed to be done when we did get a breeze. In Beirut the embassy was aware we were overdue but did not inform the wives, the Mmes. Thompson, Scotes and Tinny, until Wednesday afternoon. Thursday morning a cable from Cyprus told the embassy in Beirut we had arrived. Peculiarly, it said three Americans were in good condition. This created consternation among the wives because there were five Americans on the boat (three had wives.)

Saturday we sailed jauntily back into Beirut harbor. We were greeted by three peevish wives and I still haven't heard the end of it. The eight lost days could have been made up with eight days of solid conversation with my *'Ain al Mreissie* neighbors, but like the Palestinians I too missed that opportunity.

Some slight good may have come of this misbegotten episode. Dr. Grant's girlfriend was Clayton's teacher at the American school. She was the one who had taken an interest in Clayton and first recognized his problem. Dr. Grant helped in her diagnosis.

As for the rest of us, George Thompson and I may have been great scuba divers, but we got no points for that in the Foreign Service. A newspaper obituary reported George's death some years ago from long-standing natural causes, with no mention of the Foreign Service. There was no word on his son, Jordan. I can't blame George for leading me down MUREX's primrose path. I knew better and hoped against hope that I would somehow make it in the end. (Never hope against hope!)

A second corollary benefit from MUREX was that it attracted into our midst a weird, but talented and likeable vagabond and pederast: Bruce A. de Bourbon Condé. Bruce had been born an American and had served in the army air corps during World War II, part of the time in North Africa. One of his talents was writing travel articles. He did well and after the war moved farther and farther eastward. Bruce was a captivating story teller and sweet talked "patrons" into financing his travels. H. St. John Philby, the British Arabist and father of Kim, the British double agent, was one man Bruce claimed had vouchsafed for him. Philby died one night after a meeting with Condé and me at the Normandy Hotel in Beirut.

Bruce passed through the Sudan, across the Red Sea, onto the Arabian Peninsula. He discovered that beautiful mountainous, green, and fertile area at the southwestern tip of Arabia, *al yemiin*, to the right, of Mecca, that we call the Yemen. It is similar in many respects to the mountains of Lebanon. Venturing farther east he discovered the Persian Gulf and its congeries of little sheikhdoms, or emirates: the British controlled Trucial States. At some point he renounced his American citizenship. It was Bruce who wrote the letters of introduction for me to the rulers of the emirates of Sharja and Ras al Khaima that I carried on my field trip to the Gulf in June. He had lived there long enough to do some maps of the area. Perhaps it was a British antipathy to his perversion which involved young boys that forced him back to Lebanon and the Yemen or perhaps he picked the wrong boy as a catamite.

By 1955 Bruce had spent enough time in Lebanon to research, write, and publish a 574 page book, *See Lebanon*, on historic sites. He led MUREX to dive on remote and ancient Phoenician sites we never would have found on our own—but no ships. In fact we never found a ship of any kind.

His patrons in Beirut were Colonel William A. and Mary Eddy. The first edition of *See Lebanon* was published by the Farah G. Farah and printed by Harb Bijjani Press of Beirut. A second edition, of which I have a copy, was published in 1960.

Four generations of William Eddy's family had spent their lives in Presbyterian missions in Syria, which in those days meant Lebanon, and he grew up in that environment. A U.S. Marine in World War II he had been a star in the Office of Strategic Services (OSS). He interpreted for President Roosevelt, returning from Yalta, and Saudi King Ibn Saud in their Red Sea meeting. Eddy, later our ambassador to Saudi Arabia, was considered the great friend of the Arabs—which to the Arab mind, and his, did not include Lebanon's Maronite Christians. Eddy resigned his post to protest President Truman's pro-Jewish policy in Palestine and retired to Lebanon. He was a principal supporter of Bruce during the years he was working on his book. Eddy, missionary, soldier, and diplomat, died in 1962 and is buried under a tombstone in Lebanon inscribed "U.S. Marines."

It is paradoxical that a man of Eddy's background and understanding, and his wife, equally capable, would support, or even tolerate, Condé, with a sexual perversion so revolting he had been deported from countries time and again. After 1955 Condé returned to the Yemen and was a second time deported for pederasty. For weeks he was a *cause célèbre* because no country would take him. He shuttled between Near East airports until Lebanon, perhaps at the behest of Eddy, let him enter.

Condé knew Lebanon thoroughly and showed MUREX new dive sites. He was a thoroughly nasty person but never let it show. Neither did I ever let him use my mask, snorkel, or scuba tank.

In mid-October my long anticipated orders came for home leave starting in February and then we were off to Aden. In the meantime my language training was not finished. The following month I would get my "family week"—a flexible period during which each student lives in an Arab environment. I had made arrangements through the United Nations to stay in a Palestinian refugee camp near Jericho.

The UNRWA (United Nations Relief and Works Agency) office in Jericho, headed by Mr. Antranig "Tony" Bakerjian, was my base but I would live in the *'Ein el-Sultaan,* the Sultan's Spring, Refugee Camp. The camp was near an ancient spring, *'ain.* In the camp they gave me a new typical house, referred to as a shelter in refugee jargon, intended for the camp leader. The walls were mud brick, the floor was cement and the bath local style. The kitchen consisted of a primus stove on a wooden table and shelves protected by mosquito netting. The bed, table, and stools were made in the camp. Some residents had lent eating and cooking utensils. A pretty young girl, Amnii, daughter of Ramadan, a one-armed handyman, whose house was close by, had been assigned to me. This meant light cleaning, on occasion bringing me a meal prepared by her mother—but most days only morning coffee and breakfast since I ate out a lot—and personal laundry. On day one I was greeted by Abu Ghasaan, the officer in charge of the police post in the camp, Ramadan, and other men I saw on most days. The prepared lunch consisted of roast pigeon, cheese, olives, and bread. The pigeons, which abounded around the camp were caught live then augmented the 1500–calorie-per-day UN allowance for each refugee.

The pattern established the second day was that bright and early Amnii brought me hot tea, and bread and cheese for breakfast. She was already dressed in her blue and white vertically striped dress with a white collar—school uniform—ready to be picked up by the bus. She was a good student and a good teacher. As we talked she solemnly corrected my Arabic. After breakfast it was over to the police post for coffee, thence to the mosque to begin that day's program. I was taken to visit the three neighboring camps, to Jericho, and to sightsee. The day usually ended with a late night "bull session" at my shelter.

A partial answer to the Palestinian refugee problem might be in channeling the children away. From the local school Amnii would go to a high school in Amman. From there a scholarship would take her to a university or trade school. Continuing the exodus she would take employment beyond Palestine. Unfortunately Arab governments want to hold the Palestinians, in effect, hostage. That practice would have to be changed. One day, Abu Dahuud, camp leader of the *Nuweimi* Camp, smallest of the four, showed me his camp then took me to Jericho to see the festivities celebrating the king's birthday. These were mostly young men prancing around in a circle, dancing the *"dabke,"* in the town square. Gangs of ur-chins roamed the streets demanding *baksheesh,* tips,—money from shopkeepers—rather like Halloween but more vicious. I was also shown the most ancient of Jericho's ruins; estimated to show over 7,000 years of continuous human habitation. The physical remains of ancient history, like Jericho's mud brick walls and deep, dusty trenches, are of interest for what they were. They also showed me the *'Ein el-Sultan* spring. The next day Abu Al Riish, which means Father of Feathers, a no-nonsense type who wore a pistol, camp leader of *Aqabat Jaber,* gave me a tour of his camp. With 40,000 refu-gees, it was the largest in the area. En route we stopped in Jericho to call on the mayor, the district governor and the police comman-dant. These were my official calls. These officials are not refugees but *bedu* tribesmen of Jordan. At the police barracks we were served *saada,* Bedouin-style refreshment. *Aqabat Jaber* had both the boys' and the girls' schools for the area with a total of 4,000 students. The major refugee clinics, with three doctors, were also there. Lunch was the *mansaf* mutton and rice on a large tray, placed on the floor, eaten with the fingers.

One day, Abu Ghasaan, the policeman, and Abu Youssef, camp leader of *'Ein el-Sultan,* took me to the monastery called by Chris-tians the Mount of Temptation, where Christ was tempted by the Devil. High on a mountainside reached by a footpath inches wide it was a series of caves augmented by stone walls. I saw only two monks and doubt there were many more. The monastery was old, perhaps fourth century.

One night we went to the shelter, the camp home of Moham-med Sultan, one of the men who followed me around. Again we had the *mansaf,* mutton and rice, served on a large tray while we sat on rugs and cushions. The inside walls had been whitewashed and so were more pleasing than the outside, which was mud brick. Afterward, for coffee, we went to the "shelter" of Sheikh Khaliil who had been, they said, the wealthiest man in Palestine. In any case, just enough of his wealth remained for him to present me a grapefruit. In return I gave him a fresh pack of American cigarettes. I wrote at the time: "both gifts were gratefully received."

The next day I was taken to the Essene ruins at Qumran, to the cave where the Dead Sea scrolls were found. We drove through the *Karami* Refugee Camp, different from the other camps, which were haphazard collections of mud brick "shelters," and was more akin to an organized town, with a defined business district. Nearby, the Moussa Alardi Project—part of which was known as "Boys Town"—was just what the name implies, and was a thriving community. Alardi, a wealthy Palestinian who lived in the United States was financing various endeavors for the refugees. A Florida cattle ranch exported the hybrid Brahma cattle to Jordan in the hope they would adapt to the Palestinian environment. On my penultimate day the Jordanian government held a national census and most everyone was ordered to stay in their homes. However, Tony, who could move about, took me to his home in the Armenian Quarter of Jerusalem, in a large old building which overlooked the Dung Gate. After a pleasant and plentiful dinner served by his wife and teenage daughter we retired to a spacious living room, furnished with comfortable easy chairs, for coffee and drinks. A baby grand sat in the center of the room. Beyond the piano, in the far corner from where we were sitting, a large jagged hole had been blown in the adjoining walls and part of the roof. The hole had been made by artillery fire in 1948 when Jordan's *Arab Legion* fought the Israelis to a standstill and took control of the West Bank and Jerusalem. Through the hole I saw a full moon above the roof tops of the Old City. Tony's daughter—in a low cut dress which emphasized her smooth bare arms and shoulders—brought in a candelabra, sat down at the piano, and began to play. I forget most of the pieces she played except one: Claude Debussy's "Claire de Lune."

It was a magical moment, sitting comfortably in a secluded, almost forgotten corner of ancient Jerusalem, with candlelight glowing on the long, lustrous black hair and smoothly rounded, soft, white arms and shoulders of the young girl. She played beautiful music under a brilliant full moon shining through the jagged war torn wall—a counterpoint reminder of the war around us. Good conversation, strong, black Arabic coffee, and a bottomless snifter of Courvoisier helped. Late the next day I was on my way to Beirut with a feeling of accomplishment; of having used and learned Arabic. This total immersion would have helped more had it come earlier.

An unanswered question left in 'Ain El Sultan was: what should I have done about Amnii, my sweet, compliant pre-teenage housekeeper. From almost the first moment we met, Ramadan, her father who had lost an arm to an Israeli bomb, insisted that I take Amnii. He meant for me to adopt her, take her to the States, educate and make her my own. "You may never," I told him, "see her again." I wondered if Ramadan knew that a few weeks earlier the State Department had ruled that adoption of Palestinian refugee children would be facilitated (Tony Bakerjian, who had good relations with our embassies in Beirut and Amman knew that and may have told Ramadan). After Ramadan had again mentioned taking Amnii, I asked her if she would like that. Her eyes never left my face and without blinking said, "Na'am." Yes.

The last day Amnii brought her mother to my house to plead the case for taking her. Her mother was dressed in a plain long dress, with perhaps a headscarf round her neck. She had four or five other children and she insisted I take Amnii, but it was hopeless. The only telephone in the camp was in the police station, and there was no good way to talk to Josephine. In any case, she could not see and meet Amnii. It would have been interesting to bring our three boys the sister they wanted, and Josephine a daughter, but in the end I "chickened out" and left Amnii to her fate in 'Ain El Sultan.

Continuing with the improvement in my Arabic from my time in the refugee camp I practically moved in with one of the instructors, Sari Ansari, of the language school. He was single and lived with his mother and sister who were away for a few days. He was also leaving for Europe soon so we spent afternoons and evenings making his farewell visits to relatives and friends. The time spent helped.

In mid December John Wellington Stevens, single and currently vice consul in Aden, came to Beirut on local leave and we had several hours of useful talk. Aden was John's first post and he had a jaundiced view of Foreign Service life. Aden is a hard post, especially a first one—rather like San Pedro Sula. After Aden John married Tony Hanlon, daughter of a Royal Air Force group captain and retired.

We lost touch with John and Tony for ten years but then John and I met at a business conference in New York. He had become a consultant of overseas investments and was doing well. They had two sons and as families we visited with each other for several years. John died while jogging, September 11, 1981.

In January I wrote home using my Arabic skill at cursive Arabic script for the date which transliterates to *Kanoon Al Thani 10*, January 15, to prove I could do numbers and dates. The good news is that I had been promoted from FSO-6 to FSO-5. The lowest officer grade is FSO-8—the highest, FSO-1.

Tentative plans for leaving Beirut and getting to Aden included flying to London, then boarding the SS *America* in Southampton. After a short visit in New York we took the train to Washington for departmental debriefings on Beirut, briefings on our next post, Aden, and medical examinations for all of us (important to me to get my tooth pulled as described earlier.)

For Clay it was especially important to get an expert neurology diagnosis and a long-term prognosis on what we could expect. Also, we needed to find out what Josephine's heart condition was and whether her long bouts of serious coughing throughout the past two years had damaged her heart, as one doctor suggested. With all our ailments, real or imagined, I wanted an electrocardiogram too. Despite all our worries, nothing was changed. Clay's arms had mended perfectly, but he was doomed by his *petit mal*, as we knew. Josephine, David, Gregory, and I, with normal wear and tear, got clean bills of health.

To get to Aden we would fly to New York and board the SS *Independence*, which with her sister ship, SS *Constitution*, were the American Export Lines' two finest combination passenger/cargo liners and successors to the "four Aces." En route to Naples we made stops in Gibraltar, Morocco, Spain, and Majorca. From Naples we flew to Cairo and thence to Aden.

But before we embarked, Beirut still had one more thrill to offer. New Year's Eve morning, Sunday December 31, 1961, some dissident military units made a miserable attempt at a coup d'état by taking over the Ministry of Defense. Amidst the New Year's celebrations, it was hard to tell who was celebrating and who was revolting. Honking cars blocked all main thoroughfares. Cars fresh from the mountains had piles of snow on their hoods or trunks, a general custom. The coup went nowhere.

In the aftermath of the *coup,* with restrictions on travel, the tanks and machine-gun nests that sat at busy corners lingered on as we made our preparations for departure. Furniture had to be packed and shipped, the car and boat sold. At the embassy I was the oncoming duty officer when a new ambassador, Armin Meyer, arrived amid a flurry of activity. Staff meetings and other embassy chores ate into my cramming time. At home Josephine and the boys had requirements to be looked after. At last, on Thursday, February 1, 1962, we headed for the Khalde International Airport in the same taxi that had taken us into town two years and one week earlier. With all my other worries, I barely had time to wonder what had happened to the chamber pot with lid that I had clutched to my chest when we arrived. At that moment, I didn't know and didn't care. Beirut probably smashed it. I should at least have learned the Arabic word for chamber pot.

At the language school I was immersed in final exams. Despite gallons of midnight oil and cramming, my Arabic was only passing, not good enough. We like to think that with most things anyone gets three strikes before being called out. Now, embarked on the "sand dune circuit," San Pedro Sula and Cairo count for naught; this is strike one. Maybe Aden will be an easy pitch. Time will tell.

8

Aden

From the air Aden looms up as a forbidding egg-shaped mound of black rock; five miles on its longer east-west axis, half that on a north-south line and a third of a mile high at its peak. An inverted triangular sand bar, an isthmus, stretching northward at the eastern end saves it from being an island and connects it to the sandy shore of the Arabian Peninsula. As the plane circles, you can see the steep-sided cone of a long dead volcano on the egg's eastern, bigger end. The bright, sunlit blue of the Arabian Sea offsets the unrelieved blackness of the barren Mount Shamsan, *Jebel Shamsan*. You see on the western end and northern side, on a gradual slope, low buildings, residential and industrial, clustered together near the water and sprawling up the mountainside. This is the city, the heart of the 75-square-mile Crown Colony of Aden. Citizens of a crown colony may claim British passports and many do.

If the traveler is at all knowledgeable, as a new consular officer must be, the most impressive sight is Aden's extensive, protected deep-water harbor. From Steamer Point at the western end of Aden to Slave Island in the east it is crowded with dozens of ships, either at anchor or underway. Between ships the harbor is alive with Arab *bumboats*, small launches ferrying goods and people to buy those goods.

Our crossing from New York and our passage through the western Mediterranean was made on one of the new "Four Aces," the SS *Independence*. Regardless of how an FSO travels, or where, he is never far from the "exigencies of the service;" the State Department's unequivocal reason for anything. East of the Balearic Islands and west of Naples, our next port of call, I was found. With the radiogram from the consulate in hand, pressing me to make haste, all I could do was to ask the captain to add on a few knots. He thought that was funny but, as a good captain should, promised he would look into it. Once, in Rome, as a good FSO should, I looked into making haste by taking a Central African Airways flight to Khartoum with connections for Aden but to no avail. I did find a BOAC flight nonstop to Aden, eliminating a time consuming change of planes in Cairo. One must ask why they didn't ask for haste earlier.

Our plane was a British *Comet* and this may have been the first jet flight for my family and me. The *Comets* were soon taken out of service after crashes allegedly caused by an inherent tendency to metal fatigue. Too bad; they were a delight to fly in with huge round windows. We set down at 10:00am, Sunday, April 29, 1962, Aden time. From the air-conditioned luxury of the *Comet*, we plunged, gasping for breath, into the sopping wet, fiendish heat of number seven of *National Geographic's* ten certified hottest, most humid cities on the planet. In Washington they knew at least where Aden is.

British author James Morris expressed in his travel books, *Markets of Selukia* and *Cities*, a cynical, perverse view of Aden and the British role there. He says this ancient fortress and port—a well known outpost of empire in the time of Roman Emperor Constantine—was now in the opinion of his world traveling, jet set friends the "most repellent city" they had ever seen and they saw it only once.

The books of Morris—who later changed his name from James to Jan and his sex from male to female—are critical, useful reading for Foreign Service personnel assigned to the Near East. However, after his perverse sex flip-flop I took all his opinions *cum grano salis*. Had he seen San Pedro Sula, as I had, he might have added that God-forsaken hole to his list of "most repellent" cities.

Morris notes with his peevish, cynical sense of humor that in a hundred and thirty three years of prosperous rule Britain had not brought one thing of beauty to the place—the statue of good Queen Victoria notwithstanding. W. Somerset Maugham, another Englishman, wrote that cynicism is the plain, unvarnished truth. Aden, Morris wrote bitterly, huddles there: "...blasted and despondent, as if life had become one long, awful hangover. Its streets are cracked and rubbish-blown; its buildings drab, its shops slatternly...infused with savage force Aden has no sense of majesty or power in vast rambling installations which announce the fading British Raj."

Morris finds Aden grubbily commercial at heart and that only the welcome, restless ships, coming in thirsty and going out satiated with black oil, give it a sense of purpose. He finds none of the charm and spice of a truly Arabian city. Aden has no dignified mosque; no old city with mysterious, cool alleys and scented courtyards where fountains splash. The populace is a hodge-podge of Yemenis, Somalis, Hindus, Parsees, Jews, Egyptians, Syrians, Persians, Baluchis, Chinese, British, and now — God Save the Queen — Americans. The hillocks of dusty coal which dominated the waterfront for decades have been replaced by stinking, squat, rusty tanks, bereft of paint, which pollute Aden's waters with lustrous iridescent streaks of oil. The past is not stone dead and though Winston Churchill converted the Royal Navy, and others, to oil in World War I, one Aden coal supplier survived, selling to the Russians.

Here is no ostentatious display of wealth or vice although Aden is a goose laying golden eggs and there are avaricious, venal sultans, emirs, and sharifs to spare. One, Sir Ali Abdul Karim, Sultan of Lahej, had actually been knighted. Hermann F. Eilts, American consul in Aden in 1951–53, had this to say in "Along the Storied Incense Roads of Aden" (*National Geographic, February 1957)*: "I passed through Lahej often and came to know very well its sultan, Sir Ali. Few rulers of the protectorates possess so vigorous, versatile a personality, fewer still, an intelligence so nimble."

In the late 1950s Sir Ali, contrary to all undertakings he had with the British on their position on Arab nationalism, surreptitiously and "nimbly" allied himself with Egypt's Nasser. The British put Sir Ali on a plane which took him to Bahrain and installed his uncle, plain Fadl bin Ali, as the new sultan. In the Aden Protectorates the sultans of Lahej in the western and of Quai'ti in the eastern are the only rulers styled "His Highness" by the British. So, "uncle" Fadl bin Ali, not knighted, had that compensation.

Why, one could ask, is there no sense of aristocracy, no pride of place or blood one would expect in a significant bastion of the British Empire? The wife of one British Army officer I had known in Beirut was entitled to the title of Lady. Was that it? Where is Lord

Belhaven, a proud exponent of Aden a generation past, when you need him? The governor goes about in an Austin Princess. The only Rolls I knew belonged to the Sultan of Muscat and Oman and was parked 1140 miles due east. Aden's vices were squalid enough to be kept out of sight and its virtues simply bores.

The original ancient settlement of Aden is called Crater, because it is in the crater of a dead volcano; situated on the eastern slope of *Jebel Shamsan*, facing the open sea. It is home to the local *souks* for vegetables and fish and most other necessities. Isolated from the rest of Aden by its location, a narrow, heavily used access road had been chiseled by hand through the volcano's wall.

Morris fires a final shot on his way out at the ancient tanks of Aden, still full of water, covered by a layer of hundreds of discarded Japanese rubber flip-flops:

> "...built in the millennium before Christ for the storage of rainwater, so important are they, and so fresh a light do they throw on the prehistory of Aden, they must be seen. Of all archeological remains, of all unrecognizable ruins, bits of chariots, and headbands from tombs of Bronze Age chieftains, of such scholarly phenomena, the tanks of Aden are the dullest ruins in all antiquity."

Based on my knowledge of ruins in the Near East, with that I will not argue.

So, "why Aden, why me?" Is it pointless for a junior Foreign Service officer to try to directly influence his destiny? He lands in Aden, San Pedro Sula, or both, with no ifs, ands, or buts. Exigencies of the service are small comfort, make no waves, and, as I shall discover too late, above all as a minor bureaucrat and civil servant: be civil and servile.

The airport, run British colonial style, was as was everything important in Aden busy, efficient, and Spartan. Serving commercial traffic and as a major Royal Air Force base, even as our *Comet* landed, Royal Air Force *Hawker Hunter* fighter-bombers took off. They were probably going "up country" —local jargon for the hinterland of the Aden Protectorates—to bomb an unruly Arab village into compliance, but we didn't know about that yet.

Located on the isthmus, called by its Arabic name, Khormaksar, the airport's east-west runways extended from shore to shore. A plane touching down too late, or one unable to stop, going either way, may wind up in the drink. That may be better than hitting a mountain and Aden has the highest one close by. On the other hand, these waters are so rich with starving sharks they are a major local resource. Our touch-down was perfect. As usual we were met; today by the officer I was replacing, Willard B. Devlin.

Devlin seemed deliriously happy to see me and was, I guessed, anxious to get to his next post, embassy Baghdad. There he would be chief of the consular section, a good job. He had done what I had wanted to do on my transfer from Beirut. That is, pack and ship his household effects—no furniture, our quarters were government furnished—and send his wife on home leave. Now all Devlin had to do was pack personal things in a suitcase and go. Two days later, after the briefest of briefings, he went.

Devlin had long been ready to go and had instigated the request for me to expedite my travel. No one ever wants to linger in Aden. With degrees from Tufts and the Fletcher School of Law and Diplomacy he had integrated into the Foreign service through the Information Service (USIS). After Baghdad he had several departmental assignments. In 1976 he was consul in Hong Kong, then Santo Domingo.

Leaving the airport in the consulate's Chevrolet sedan, Devlin explained that to the north—at the end of the isthmus, on the border between Aden Colony and the Aden Protectorates—lay the Arab village of Sheikh Othman, in the Sultanate of Lahej. Here are the acres of saltpans where sea water is pumped into shallow pans by dozens of short, squatty, Dutch type windmills and allowed to evaporate. In the past but not now, salt was a major export. To the west on the mainland, connected by the coast road, lay the peninsula of Little Aden; home of a new and expanding, 100,000 barrels per day, British Petroleum refinery and ship terminal. Aden and Little Aden, southward projecting peninsulas enclosed, like the claw of a crab, the large bay and harbor of Aden. Except for the Aden enclave, this southwestern tip of the Arabian Peninsula was the Sultanate of Lahej: one of the protectorates three major tribal states.

Devlin turned south toward Aden, saying we could explore

those peripheral areas, and the site of the capital, *Al Ittihad,* Union, of the nascent Federation of South Arabia, on our own. I did that later, all the way to Perim Island, one hundred miles west of Aden, in the *Bab el Mandab,* door to the Red Sea.

In Aden, we first got a quick look at the outside of the six year old, two story Consulate building containing the offices, a large, upstairs apartment for the principal officer, and two smaller first floor apartments for staff. The walled grounds had a lawn, trees, and shrubbery. It was located in a built up area, called Ma'alla, which runs west into Tawahi, ends at the western tip with Steamer Point, covers two miles or so of water front and climbs the western slope of 1808-foot-high *Jebel Shamsan.* The Consulate faced Aden's deepwater roadstead with a close-up look at the impressive, ship filled, oil bunkering harbor—its role in today's world of commerce. Aden received more than five thousand ships a year, an average of fourteen a day. This passing parade of ships, often of gleaming new liners such as Italy's *Leonardo da Vinci* and Britain's *Canberra,* had residents wistfully wishing they were on board and going, just going and getting away. The east, or dead end, of the harbor was reserved for local *dhow,* Arab sailing boats, and traffic serving coastal areas. Slave Island was once a major African slave *entrepôt,* trading center; now, who knows? In any case, Slave Island also accommodated *dhow* building, and repair yards.

From the Consulate we drove the short distance to the P. & O. Building where we would live. Directly across a large sports field we got a passing look at Aden's best, the Crescent Hotel, to be our temporary quarters. Without stopping we drove through town to the stone Prince of Wales Pier, jutting out into the harbor. Passengers land here watched over by the familiar statue of the seated, plump Queen Victoria. The main streets were crowded today with some of the 300,000 immigrants and other travelers who shop here each year. Retail businesses in Aden, a well-stocked, wide open free port, are open seven days a week for long hours. Religious holidays are covered by three teams of clerks: Christian, Moslem, and Hindu. Today, Sunday, Christians had the day off.

Along with *Scotland the Brave,* the *Barren Rocks of Aden* must surely be in the repertoire of every bagpipe band in the world. Shop, yes, but Aden was not where tourists wished to linger. On the commercial side Aden was all business and the same was true of the military. For over a century Aden existed in the shadow of British Bombay and the Indian influence was strong here. Now, in the 1960s, the loss of India and the Arab revolts of the 1950s in Egypt, Iraq, Jordan, and Lebanon had transformed Aden into a key base in Britain's army, navy, and air force Middle East military structure.

Aden may have earned a warm spot in the heart of the pretty young queen crowned in 1837. In 1839 Aden became the first addition to the British Empire during her long reign. Ostensibly to curb pirating of British ships, the real reason for persuading the Sultan of Lahej to cede Aden to Britain was to secure the only viable port in 3500 miles of south Arabian coastline. Commanding the entrance to the Red Sea, Aden was a vital link in the line of communication with India—Crown Jewel of her Empire. The opening of the Suez Canal in 1869 made Aden a vital coaling station and now an oil bunkering port. The first port ships touched after the Suez Canal, Kipling may have had Aden in mind as he wrote *Mandalay*: "*Ship me somewhere east of Suez, where the best is like the worst.*"

Threats to Britain's new colony first came from the Turks who, after a three hundred year absence, reoccupied the Yemen in 1872. Although World War I eliminated the Ottoman Empire and Turkish threat, the local ruler of the Yemen, the redoubtable Imam Yahya, stayed. He claimed the whole of South Arabia he, and his successors, called the "Occupied South."

The British ruled "indirectly" by a system that left local rulers in place to provide most government services while dependent on British financial subsidies. Threats of military force kept the noisy defiant in line. A bomb, often wooden, dropped by the Royal Air Force (RAF) near a village made the point.

Conversely, Yemeni threats were a running sore; backed by raids, skirmishing and posturing. While the congeries of two dozen tribal entities were feuding among themselves and with each other, Aden stood aloof. Neither the "upcountry," nor the port was viable alone. Adenese, marginally civilized by decades of beneficent colonial rule, distrusted the fanatically Moslem, "wild and woolly" tribesmen and used bombings and assassinations as arguments in unity negotiations.

I first met two of these "wild" tribesmen early on while driving northeast of Aden in the "up country," chauffeuring our regional agricultural attaché to the Abyan cotton-growing region. One generous flooding of the fields before planting provides water for the crop. Two gaunt tribesmen, wearing wide grins and not much else, appeared out of nowhere in the road before us. Brandishing their rifles they signaled me to stop. I assumed, that is, hoped, they just wanted a ride. Here, as elsewhere in the Third World, locals without wheels expect vehicles to pick them up on demand without qualms.

This was tribal land and these were warriors. What branded them as "wild tribesmen" was that their torsos were covered with a thick coating of deep blue indigo and odoriferous woad, which serves to keep them warm in the chill of night and to ward off the most harmful of the sun's rays. The leaves, or berries—the recipes differ—of the indigo plant are pounded by the women to a dark blue or purplish paste which is applied liberally. One British army officer told me it now could be bought in "tins" —we say "cans." This was the "wild" part. The "woolly" part describes unkempt, unshorn halos of hair.

I put them on the tailgate. At a place, which looked like all the desert scrub, they moved as if to jump off, so I stopped. With a wave they scampered away like they knew where they were going. Our encounter was fortunate, but I sensed that these men would stop grinning and brook no disagreement with their myopic view of the world. No wonder the Adenese distrust tribesmen and achieving unification is so difficult.

Deeper sectarian differences between the Sunni's of South Arabia and the fanatical puritan Shi'a Zaydis of the Yemen, that is, between intolerant tribesmen and prejudiced townsmen further complicated the long negotiations toward unity. Nevertheless, by our arrival in 1962 the British had cobbled together regional tribes into a Western and an Eastern federation. The time was ripe to unite them, and Aden, into one, being The Federation of South Arabia. Another problem was the literally explosive tentacles of fanatic Arab revolutionary zeal espoused by Nasser, Kassem, Palestinians, and radical Arab demagogues who had already made their bloody handiwork felt in South Arabia.

After this bit of sightseeing Devlin returned us to the Crescent

Hotel, a broad imposing building of deep verandas, which the Victorian colonists of the last century and the first half of this one would have remembered. We unloaded our luggage and ourselves, who after a day which had begun in Rome the night before, were beginning to weary. The boys were fidgety and Josephine was worn out.

As he prepared to drive off, a relaxed Devlin, relieved I was here, called out: "See you in the office tomorrow morning, John, as early as you can make it." After two more days in Aden he was gone.

Reasonably early Monday morning I enjoyed a full Victorian British breakfast in the dignified dining room at the Crescent, attended by haughty, barely civil, but well-trained, black Somali waiters. Then, as eager to get started as was Devlin, I took the five-minute walk to the Consulate. The Crescent was expertly managed by the gracious and accommodating Mr. and Mrs. Volpi and her mother-in-law from northern Italy. The Volpis were born *hôteliers*, and the Crescent is second only to Claridge's in London as the best-managed hotel I have ever known. With comings and goings from our huge AID program in the Yemen, we were their best customer. The second hotel in Aden, the Rock Hotel, British owned and managed, took the constant overflow from the Crescent.

Devlin introduced me to the principal officer and consul, debonair Stephen J. Campbell. Steve was nine years older than I, about my size, and wore a Clark Gable moustache. He had been an army officer from 1942 until 1948. In 1949 while still in France he joined the Economic Cooperation Administration (ECA), which administered the Marshall Plan. As had Devlin, he had come into the Foreign Service through the Information Service (USIS). After a posting in Teheran as a press officer he was assigned to Aden in June 1960. While in Paris, he married a well-known heroine of the World War II *maquis*, the French Resistance. When they came to Aden in 1960, she was in poor health from torture suffered under the Nazis and soon returned to France. She came back briefly after we arrived in 1962. I met her once, for a few minutes. She returned to France and died soon afterwards; Steve remarried. After Aden Steve was named consul general in Jerusalem, which accorded him the title of "The Honorable" He ended a successful career as a Foreign Service inspector at the top grade, FSO-1.

Aden's extensive consular district included the Sultanate of Muscat and Oman, on the southeastern corner of the peninsula, one of the United States' first treaty partners. We signed with Muscat a still valid treaty of comity and commerce in 1833. Also included were Abdul Quri, Perim Island, Socotra, Kamaran Island, British Somaliland, and Dhofar.

In 1880, a year after the first American consul arrived in Aden, the Sultan of Muscat and Oman invited the United States to send a consul and we did. The consulate in Muscat was closed about the time of World War I. It is said that when one of the last consuls steamed in with his wife he left her at the pier and went to arrange accommodations. On his return he found a note on their luggage, which read: "Do you see our ship leaving the harbor? The woman waving the white handkerchief is me..."

In the 1930s the probability of oil in the sultanate was the source of serious friction between Muscat, ruled by Sultan Sir Sayyid Sa'id ibn Taimur, and Oman, home of the Ibadi tribesmen. The best prospects were in the territory around the Buraimi Oasis, also called Al-'Ain, which was contested by Muscat, Oman, the Saudis, and Abu Dhabi. By 1956 the British and American oil companies had delineated their concessionary territories. The villages of Al'Ain, including Buraimi, were set aside as a "neutral zone." I visited Buraimi as described on my field trip to the Gulf in 1960 and again in 1970 when we lived in Umm al Qaywayn: one of the United Arab Emirates (UAE).

Devlin left on May 2 after three harried, stressful days, ameliorated by the fact that he was going, filled with tying up loose ends. After Devlin left, the P. & O. apartment was painted and some small changes were made to fit the needs of Josephine, me, and our three boys. In any case the Crescent Hotel with its large, high ceiling rooms, wide halls, efficient and sophisticated Italian management, and trained but temperamental staff was comfortable. I almost felt like author and world traveler W. Somerset Maugham on one of his story gathering jaunts he describes so well.

On a personal level getting acquainted was taken care of on the job since the British military, civil, and commercial communities sustained a daily whirl of social activities. Many of the affairs, hosted by British military or government officials, were official. The

British military presence included Middle East commands for the army, Royal Navy and RAF. RAF. Air Marshall Sir Charles Elworthy was head of the entire British Middle East Command.

The RAF base here has offensive and defensive responsibilities for everything "east of Suez" and the Arabian Sea. The Royal Navy's Flag Officer Middle East (FOME), Rear Admiral (RADM) Scotland, covered the same area with ships at his beck and call. The British pronounced it "FOAM." I pronounced it "FOAMY." Middle East Land Forces included one battalion of a regular British Army regiment on station,…plus numerous smaller army units. For quick and dirty work, two companies of Commando Royal Marines, the fortieth and forty-second, were there. Lieutenant General Harrington was the army commander.

At the same time the RAF commander was Air Vice Marshall Fred Rozier; a friendly and unassuming survivor of the 1940 "Battle of Britain" and the rest of the war. Most RAF pilots who survived are immediately recognizable by burns on the parts of their faces not protected by goggles. Hot gases from flaming engine exhausts, overheating machine guns, and cannons left marks. Rozier's face bore the honorable scars of glorious combat and personal courage, belying his soft spoken and studious demeanor. He was impressed by Joseph Heller's *Catch 22* and gave me a page-by-page review of the book.

Rozier was replaced in 1964 by Air Vice Marshall John E. Johnson, also a veteran of the "Battle of Britain" and the war on the Western Front. With thirty-eight confirmed victories, "Johnnie" Johnson was the top-scoring Allied fighter pilot in Europe. In addition to Britain's DSO (Distinguished Service Order) and DFC (Distinguished Flying Cross), he wore the French Croix de Guerre and the American DFC and Legion of Merit. A comparison with the Luftwaffe's top ace, Adolf Galland's score of ninety-four confirmed kills helps explain why the war was so hard to win. Johnson was more outspoken and gregarious than Rozier. With his affinity for chomping cigars he was the image of a "hell-for-leather," high-scoring fighter pilot. He offered me a ride in his favorite personal aircraft, the two-seater jet fighter-bomber, the *Canberra*. It was a thrill. In January of 1992 he came to Ponte Vedra on a book-signing tour and we reminisced about our days together in Aden.[7]

***

Local forces, with cadres of British officers, were the Desert Guards, a border patrol; the Federal Guards; the Hadhrami Bedouin Legion (HBL,) in the Hadhramaut; and the Aden Protectorate Levies. The levies were created in 1928 under the direction of the Air Ministry with officers on loan from the British Army. After several changes of responsibility at the top, at the end of November 1961, the Levies were reconstituted as the Federal Regular Army (FRA). The FRA maintained internal security, kept the roads open, pacified unruly tribes, and guarded the border with the Yemen and frontier areas.

Military hosted social functions, and those of the other diplomatic and consular missions, were where you learned what was going on. The French and Italians had active consular missions. The Indian commissioner, because of Aden's long role as a dependency of the Bombay government, took an avuncular proprietary attitude. Ethiopia had a consul general as did Somalia.

The large Somali expatriate community was the most voluble and troublesome in Aden after the Yemenis. The Ethiopian and Somali consul generals were perennially at odds with each other as to which was dean of the consular corps in Aden. Traditionally the officer with the longest service at a particular post was dean. The conundrum came about because one was assigned here first while the other actually arrived here first. The question will only be resolved when one goes or they kill each other.

Greece, Lebanon, Sweden, Denmark, Norway, Belgium, Portugal, the Netherlands, and the German Federal Republic maintained honorary consuls. These latter are resident businessmen and traditionally concerned with shipping and seamen problems. Some were active politically, especially the Germans. They paid dearly when the German Consulate was bombed and the consul, doing his laundry, lost an arm.

Thanks to the long tenure of the British, Aden had many good features and advantages for us, such as social clubs and schools for the boys. David did well in school, but Clay with his *petit mal* had inherent problems. In addition, our transfers had cost Clay a year of school. Gregory, who was very fond of Clay, followed Clay's lead without understanding Clay's problems. On the positive side, the apartment was roomy; it had air conditioning of sorts, ceiling fans, and terraces; and it was convenient to everything.

As deputy principal officer I did economic reporting. The principal officer handled political affairs and this established the priorities. Thus, in my job I noted the influx of American oil companies. Marketing companies such as Caltex and Mobil (still Standard Vacuum) were coming on strong. British Petroleum was well entrenched as was Royal Dutch and Shell in the United States. First to begin exploration was Pan American International with its eye on the island of Socotra as well as the mainland.

To establish their concessionary rights on Socotra, Pan American chartered the Aden Airways aircraft and flew a seismic party to the island. Since it was in our consular district I went along. In WWII the RAF had a small base on the island but litter was all that remained.

Socotra has two claims to fame. First, Socotra has been identified as the Panchaia of Virgil; birthplace of the mythical Phoenix which lived hundreds of years in a perfumed nest of cinnamon and frankincense twigs. It was said to be a large bird, always male, the only one of its kind, with gorgeous plumage and a sweet voice. The Phoenix lived a long time, some versions of its story say from 500 to 1,461 years. When death approached it set its nest afire and was incinerated. From its ashes a new Phoenix arose.

Second, Socotra is the source of the frankincense tree, a leafless, twisted, lichen-covered grotesque caricature of an undersea coral formation, which when pierced leaks a gum resin that becomes a semisolid. This resin was known to the earliest Egyptian Kingdoms, and was used in embalming for its inexplicable qualities and its fragrance. Today, the tree, *Boswellia sacra,* also grows in Oman. The magi brought frankincense to the Christ child. In Biblical days, it was worth its weight in gold; today, even more.

On Socotra I looked for the Phoenix and frankincense trees. The ugliest tree I have ever seen, the frankincense was easily found. The Phoenix was not to be seen.

The most sought-after concessionary areas were along the protectorate–Saudi border. This is the huge area known as the Empty Quarter, or the al Rub' al Khali. John Mecom, an independent oilman from New Orleans, had taken over the Cities Service concession in

Dhofar in the Sultanate of Muscat. This is the aggressively contested area around Buraimi and the Al'Ain oasis.

In June our consular officer, Vice Consul John Stevens, was transferred. The position had been abolished, "exigencies of the service," but we were assured Stevens would finish his tour. No such luck; Stevens left. Almost exactly a year later the position was reestablished with a vice consul, George Mercer, coming to his first post. Meanwhile, our local consular clerk, Mohammed Al Gallas, was efficient.

The post did have some staff positions; all-important. Dean Miller was administrative officer. Olga Lukasuvich was budget and fiscal officer when I arrived but was ready for transfer. In a lucky break for us her job would be taken over by Helen Miller, Dean's wife and experienced in Foreign Service finance. Helen had also been secretary for Steve and myself; more for Steve than me but that is logical. A new secretary, Mary Flood, was en route. Jackie Rubinec was a combined communications and file clerk. We had electronic encryption capability and as a constituent post communicated with our supervisory post, London. We did have the unusual authority for a constituent post to go directly to the department.

With John Stevens gone, his collateral duties as naval liaison fell to me. On July 24, 1962, the new commander of our Middle Eastern Force—in navy jargon, COMIDEASTFOR, also constituted as the Navy's Third Fleet—Vice Admiral B. J. Semmes, Jr., came over from his headquarters in Bahrain for a three day orientation visit. Steve and I did a lot of visiting, from Governor Sir Charles Johnston on down, introducing the admiral. Lunch at our apartment for twenty-four heavy with British and American admirals, generals, and British air marshals, marked the end of my first visit from COMIDEASTFOR.

Admiral Semmes was a very pleasant, congenial man. Previously, he had been the navy's legendary chief of personnel so I, and all navy officers, knew his name. The Third Fleet consisted of six ships. Three seaplane tenders, stylish, destroyer sized ships, painted white: the *Duxbury Bay*, *Greenwich Bay* and *Valcour*, rotated as flagship so one was always on station. Never in one place long, they carried the Third Fleet commander to ports, large and small, from Suez to Singapore. Three destroyers on loan from the Sixth Fleet stayed three months and when one was arriving another was leaving.

Destroyer visits, which had slackened earlier in the year, picked up after Admiral Semmes' visit in July. My notes are sketchy so here are only some of the ships and their skippers visiting in 1962–1963.[8,9] In September a destroyer came in, and my memory is no help. Not only do I not know the name of the ship—home ported at Mayport, Florida—but the name of the captain, who was my class-mate at Northwestern University Midshipman School in 1944, is forgotten. The consulate made quite an affair of the visit. John and Anne Wheelock took their three boys out to the ship, as well as the three women from the consulate. Olga and Jackie were attractive, single, and enjoyed meeting the sailors. Mrs. Miller was not single.

I took Clayton and Gregory. On this Gregory's first visit to a U.S. Navy destroyer, he behaved himself and thoroughly enjoyed the experience. The reason for all of us going was that we were given access to the ship's store to buy things unavailable here. If I had stayed in the navy, as I once contemplated doing, I too might command a destroyer. To paraphrase myself, I would rather be an American consul than the captain of a destroyer.

Almost a year later, in April 1963 as his tour of duty here was ending, Admiral Semmes in his flagship and a couple of his de-stroyers sat off the west coast of the Yemen, just north of the Bab al Mandab, near Perim Island, watching developments in the Yemen as elements of the Egyptian Army off loaded at the Soviet-built port of Hodeida. I flew to Perim Island to deliver new staff members to Semmes. In return I got, the Admiral said, "Cold beer, grilled camel steaks, and thanks."

Visits by U.S. Navy ships continued on a frequent schedule. COMIDEASTFOR tours were short. Admiral Semmes' relief and new Third Fleet commander, RADM A. F. Schade, came through in early August 1963. In September we had destroyers *Waller*, *Robert A. Owens*, *Noa*, and *Cone*. The *Noa* had picked up John Glenn after a splashdown had ended his 1962 space flight. White footprints on the deck marked where he walked. I took my three sons out to see Glenn's footprints.

The *Cone* was named for a cousin of Josephine's, Admiral Hutch I. Cone. Gregory's middle name is Cone. Josephine's mother was a Cone. The Cones settled in Lake City, Florida, in the early 1800s—"Florida pioneers," as Josephine called those progenitors.

Another of my collateral duties was to carry the diplomatic pouch to neighboring posts with mail for them that, mistakenly or otherwise, had come to Aden. My favorite post to visit was Khartoum, a sprawling, ugly, dusty desert town, but fun. Arthur L. Lowrie, another language school alumnus, was there; and since I always had to wait days for a return flight, he took care of me. The hotel was comfortable, with good food and good service. Throughout the Near East, Sudanese, vastly different from the Somalis, are sought after as cooks and house servants. We had Sudanese cooks in Cairo and Aden. Khartoum is as hot as Aden, 100 to 120 degrees Fahrenheit, but with no humidity, except in October when the Nile is in flood.

Posts are what you make them. Art Lowrie was a fine FSO, but his tour in Khartoum was unremarkable, like mine in San Pedro Sula, and he retired early. Hume Horan was ambassador there twenty years later. Hume had an exciting tour, described later, which sent him soaring to fame and glory.

Asmara, an important navy communications facility and another pouch run in eastern Ethiopia, formerly Italian Eritrea, part of Mussolini's "new Roman Empire," has near-perfect weather. The latitude of Asmara is a degree or two further north of the equator than that of Aden, which, combined with an altitude of 5,600 feet, gives Asmara an equitable climate year round. Its seaport of Massawa, at sea level, has a fiendish climate like Aden's. The Italian built road from Asmara to Massawa down the 5,600-foot escarpment is a beautiful example of excellent road engineering, reminiscent of Italy's Amalfi coast road. Italian road builders—and drivers—relish hairpin curves.

British friends in Aden, the Dunlops, had a teenage daughter in the American school there, and they asked me to take her some things. Massawa, hot and sticky, was saved from utter misery by a seaside club with good wine and a welcoming, relaxed Italian ambiance.

Djibouti, just across the mouth of the Red Sea from Aden was

French but unmemorable. Hargeisa in British Somaliland retained some benefits of British colonialism like Aden but had no ocean.

Meanwhile life went on, the boys were all in school until afternoon when Josephine took them to the civilian beach club, Gold Mohur, named for an Indian coin. The military officers' beach club was called Tarshyne, which we were also "invited" to join, but both have the same amenities — different clientele.

The boys had their own agenda and stayed healthy. Fair skinned and blond Gregory had skin problems, a rash and blisters, called "monsoon blisters;" an aggravated form of prickly heat. He had suffered in Alexandria. In August, when the building's air conditioner went out, David also was affected by the heat and had a rash. In the P. & O. Building the air conditioning was set to keep the inside temperature ten degrees cooler than that outside. So with the outside temperature at its usual 100 degrees, the inside temperature was 90 degrees. We had ceiling fans installed in the living and dining rooms for such an eventuality, and the boys slept there on pallets. We were told the building had air conditioning problems and it certainly did. Josephine and I were affected but to a much lesser degree than the boys.

While Josephine and I were busy during the day with our respective responsibilities the evenings were filled with cocktail parties first, then it was on to dinner. Perverse as it may seem, rough and dismal Aden prided itself on its formality. Perhaps it is a rule of colonial pseudo-exile that the more distant the post from home and its customary conventions, the more formal it becomes. Aden, basically a military base, was a man's world and for social functions protocol and proper dress were prescribed in military order. Likewise, seating charts, place cards, R.S.V.P. responses, and thank you notes were *de rigueur*. At one elegant *soirée* we were regaled by a clear view of an American satellite in orbit passing overhead. Our hostess claimed credit, saying: "When I give a party I go all the way!"

For daytime formal affairs men wore lightweight, light-colored summer suits — Haspel cord was popular. For outdoor, daytime military reviews, parades, and the races, a Panama or "Trilby" hat was not only usual but a good idea. At fifteen degrees above the Equator in Aden's cloudless skies the sun is hot enough to burn rocks black. Americans, adverse to hats, appeared for days afterward with parboiled noses and foreheads. One of us from the consulate calling on American warships had to wear a hat. Partly in keeping with the navy rule not to salute unless covered. When calling on any ship, whether tramp freighter or cruise ship, a hat was proper and usual. Dark suits were usual for outdoor nighttime parties and military tattoos. For official, formal occasions the familiar "black tie," or tuxedo—dark or white jacket—was required dress uniforms for the military. For less formal occasions "black tie" could be modified into the "Red Sea Kit" or "Persian Gulf Rig." Common to both were dark trousers with satin stripe, black patent leather shoes, and cummerbund. Popular cummerbunds were the long, narrow pieces of brilliantly colored and patterned material used by the tribesmen to make their turbans. The Kathiri and the larger Qai'iti Sultanate in the Eastern Protectorate and Lahej in the West provided the best choices. A tie, jacket, and shirt—sleeve length, long or short as specified—varied almost by hostess's whim.

Once, hurrying to get dressed for the evening's fun and games when the telephone rang, David answered. When the caller asked for me David replied that I was in the shower. When the caller asked for his mother, Josephine, David replied that she was in the shower too. That story lost nothing in the telling.

For the women fancy cocktail dresses were popular, but full length evening gowns were often seen. Wearing jewelry is, I suspect, a competitive sport among the women. Short and long white gloves, cotton or kid, were not uncommon. Women wore hats with brims, such as sunhats, at outdoor affairs for the same reason men do; I always did. Outdoors on a devilishly bright day decorative parasols were welcome. Indoors women wore hats and gloves, long or short, depending on the occasion and certainly to church.

Sundays were not immune from the social whirl and often featured a "curry lunch." The best were hosted by one of the military units whose British officers and noncoms had served in "Injia's sunny clime," as Kipling described it. Lunch started after church and went on until late. I described one in a letter home this way:

Sunday, August 26, 1962

Dear Folks,

Today we had an enjoyable time because the commanding officer of the Fourth Battalion of the Federal Regular
Army (FRA), Lieut. Colonel W.B. Thomas, DSO, MC (Military Cross),[10] invited Josephine and me to their encamp-
ment for a "curry lunch." Curry, you know well as an Indian
spice served with three main meat dishes and thirty or more
meat, fish, vegetable or fruit side dishes. Much of it is spicy
hot. Here a "curry lunch" is an all day social gathering. The
(officers') "mess" at the F.R.A. Bir Fuqum rest camp, across
the bay from Aden, is an open tent on the beach with huge
oriental rugs and mats for flooring. The battalion is in reserve after a year on the frontier. Josephine and I and our
three boys were the only Americans but other youngsters
were present. Clay and Gregory went swimming but David
had to stay dry because of his "monsoon blisters."

One afternoon in early August while at the office catching up
and writing a letter home I had this to tell them:

Dear Folks,

I just looked out the window and we are having a terrific
sandstorm! It has come up very suddenly although we have
been having high winds all day. The view we have from
here, across the open water of the harbor, is cut down to a
few yards. The closest ships are reduced to dark blotches in
the dun colored fog of sand. We are in the monsoon season,
when sandstorms often occur but this is our first really bad
one.

Every day is hazy and sandy, especially towards the north
and the mainland, but a real sandstorm is unmistakable. Once,
unsuccessfully attempting a round of golf at Aden's only course
at the Khormaksar Club, north of the airport, we spied a huge,
silent black cloud, churning and boiling, rolling across the desert
from the north towards us. We barely had time to take refuge in

the clubhouse—a one story concrete block structure. The sand blew in under the doors and eaves, around the windows, and through previously undiscovered cracks. Inside the storm the roar was deafening. Still roaring it rolled on to Aden and out to sea. Sand was piled up on the floor in front of doors and on the window sills. In the parking lot cars had sand up to the door sills and high around the wheels. Under their hoods the engines were covered with sand. A golfer and car owner with windows left open will not forget this day.

The consulate was scheduled for an inspection to start August 13 and last three or four days. Steve, chomping at the bit to get away, was staying for the inspection since it covered his tour. The inspectors' recommendations would be implemented by the new Principal Officer, John Wheelock, due August 16.

The inspection of the post began as scheduled and lasted a week. An inspection is mostly agony but puts people on their toes. This was my fourth inspection—after San Pedro Sula, Cairo, and Beirut. The inspectors take over, commandeer the principal officer's office and give orders, and their frowns rock us poor FSO types whose careers hang by their smiles. They look not so much at what we do but the way we do it. For example, in my economic reporting, was I covering all the factors required by the Comprehensive Economic Reporting Program (CERP)? Hauling Department of Agriculture regional attachés didn't count, unless they had complained. In order to keep a tight control on our foreign representation, State had to bend over backward to keep the other federal departments and agencies happy. This was brought forcibly to my attention in March 1963.

In the past many federal departments had had their own foreign representatives and wanted back in the game. President John F. Kennedy had to reinforce the rule that the State Department in the person of the ambassador was in charge in our foreign posts. This often fragmented an otherwise unified approach to a problem. The man from Agriculture was personable and we got along but every time he wanted something I had to jump or he could say we were not giving him, that is, the Department of Agriculture, support. The Aulaqi tribesmen we met "up country" kept him quiet. He was nonplussed when I told him a British hundredweight was one hundred and twelve pounds. He had to redo his calculations on cotton production but took it well. If I hadn't told him we would not have known Aden's true cotton production.

John Wheelock arrived the morning of August 16 and Steve Campbell left that evening, an even shorter briefing than mine. Anne, John's wife, and their three boys arrived Aug. 18.[11] On the political front the big news was that the ministers of Aden Colony, the ministers of the Federation of South Arabia, and the British Government had agreed on the procedure for admitting Aden Colony into the federation. Talks in London had been secret but the proposed constitutional amendments were made public and sent to the Legislative Council. I think most of the citizens of the colony favored joining the federation but a large, well organized trades union was opposed. The ultra nationalists and the Arab nationalists wanted immediate independence for Aden and its right to make its own decision. We didn't anticipate any violence but the diehards were prone to set off a few bombs. I thought the plans for Aden and the federation would be approved by the council; the Adenese do not like supporting the tribal "entities."

Oil exploration had been proceeding apace in the Eastern Protectorate, especially the Qait'iti Sultanate. Preliminary seismic reports predicted large commercial sized fields. If they were true producers, the Sultanate may have become economically viable and opted for independence. Why not? The UN and New Yorkers love these *opéra-bouffe* "nations" ruled by gorgeously clothed "sultans" with Oxford accents. Farther east, oil fields were producing now in the Sultanate of Muscat and Oman.

I celebrated my thirty-eighth birthday September 14—not because it was my birthday, but because mid-September seemed an auspicious time, for the ten-hour drive up into beautiful mountains and highlands of the land the ancient Greeks and Romans named *Arabia Felix*, Happy Yemen. Medieval scholars erroneously, or maliciously, translated the Arabic root YMN as the word *yumn* (happiness), instead of *yamin* (to the right). This meant to the right of Mecca facing east. We have paid for their blunder ever since. I was headed for Ta'izz, the provisional capital and site of our legation and American activities. You don't make the trip "by road," because there is no road. The best driving is in the stream beds, skirting the truck sized boulders left by floods and ice age glaciers.

North out of Aden the forty mile wide coastal plain with broad stretches of sand dunes soon gives way to the mountainous plateau, or *johl*, of the Haushabi tribal lands. On the gravel plains rocks are burned black by the sun on top but remain pink underneath. The rocks clang metallically when struck, especially two rocks banged together. Approaching the frontier border we turned west near Dhala. This territory has a known history dating to times before the Queen of Sheba, as attested to by the ruins of the Marib dam and of the city of Ma'an.

The beginning and end for most local traffic out of and into Aden was the equivalent of a classic caravanserai, near the Arab town of Sheikh Othman. Any such place, like a busy truck stop, is at best scruffy and so was this one but it had one redeeming feature; camel caravans with dozens of animals coming from the fertile valleys to the north and the Yemen, bearing produce, dates, and spices, announced their arrival through the dunes and across the gravel plains by their chiming camel bells. Audible at a distance the music of the bells rises as the caravan mounts dunes and falls as they descend into gullies. Arabs can tell the distance away, speed, and number of camels from the clanging of the bells. When a caravan is approaching, even the Arabs, and certainly Josephine and I,[12] cannot but pause and listen. The melodious chimes of camel bells call across the desert heralding the mystery and majesty of thousand year old empires now long dead and long forgotten.

Animals, camels and donkeys, were loaded and unloaded here, as were many lorries and a great number of motorcycles. The latter, cheap and fast, carrying one passenger and his duffel bag, are long range taxis, to the Yemen and other states of the Protectorates. The motorcycle drivers are daredevils and coming and going in the mountains, passed us with almost the agility of mountain goats. They didn't all make it. Broken and rusting pieces of their motorcycles marked the route.

Before reaching the presumptive Yemen border we were up 5,000 to 6,000 feet. On a large-scale map this border is sanctioned by the Anglo-Turkish Boundary Convention of 1914. Accepted by no one else, the line is a series of alternating straight lines with lines which follow natural features. They say the straight lines were drawn when the surveyors were attacked by tribesmen and took flight. When the firing ceased the surveyors resumed drawing a realistic border following natural features. In the Yemen Imam Yahya ended the bloodiest of the merciless sectarian guerilla fighting between the Zaydis and the Ismalias.

The Yemeni mountains are rugged, sharp edged, green, and beautifully terraced far up the slopes. *Qat,* a narcotic plant of which the leaves are chewed, is the chief money crop. Yemen's choicest coffee, Dhämar, is grown just north of Ta'izz, around Ibb, at the 6,000 to 8,000 foot level, and exported from Mocha, which gives it a name. Civilian traffic with the Yemen is heavy because Yemenis are Aden's largest minority. Many are skilled artisans, carpenters, brick layers, and stone masons. These obstreperous Yemenis are a fifth column "in-being" with an announced and uncompromising object of uniting Aden Colony and the Protectorates with the Yemen. The second largest group of outsiders consists of Somalis and they are friends with no one—not even each other.

Robert M. Stookey[13] was the chargé d'affaires of our legation in Ta'izz, a much sought after post among Arabists. I once requested Ta'izz. Now, two years after the post was opened and dependents were permitted, he was accompanied by Louise, his wife. As a good Foreign Service wife should be, Louise was businesslike and protective. Stookey was a classical pianist and miraculously his grand piano made the journey into the eight-nine thousand foot high mountains of Ta'izz unscathed. It is a transcendental experience to come upon the legation residence, teetering on the side of a mountain, overlooking Ta'izz, to the strains of Chopin resounding over the valley.

The legation was authorized ten employees counting an ambassador, USIS public affairs officer, and an army attaché. The Agency for International Development mission had fifty eight employees. Since dependents are allowed those numbers may be almost doubled. The logistics for supporting this large number of Americans in a barely accessible location are considerable. The many local employees also have requirements.

Stookey didn't like to wear a hat so the day I arrived he was suffering from a painfully sunburned face, nose, and high forehead received facing the sun, waiting for the Imam to appear for a military parade. The Imam was late and as we now know very soon was the late Imam.

The Agency for International Development and Bureau of Public Roads' (BPR) American contingent in the Yemen guided a diverse development program, chief of which was building roads. Thanks to BPR, a modern hard surfaced road across the barren Tihamah coastal plain now connected Ta'izz to the ancient Red Sea port of Mocha. They were now building a road northward to join Ta'izz and Sana'a. The port at Mocha in the *al-Tihamah* — the flat, hot and often muddy Red Sea coastal plain — is an unimproved open roadstead. In a Cold War coup the Russians, invited by the Imam's son, al Badr, built a modern port at Hodeida, a hundred miles to the north, close to the traditional capital of Sana'a. The Yemeni need only one port, so we had to be content with the open roadstead of Mocha and use little barges called lighters and mobile cargo-handling equipment.

Robert Brown, deputy principal officer in Ta'izz, was my opposite number. We overlapped at the language school. The Information Agency public affairs officer was Robert T. Curran, a career Foreign Service reserve officer. Stookey, Brown, and Curran in Ta'izz answered to "Bob" while Wheelock, Tinny, and Stevens in Aden answered to "John."

To vary the monotony of names, Harry F. Weber represented the other "agency." Harry was left alone in the Legation building a short time after the September military coup d'état and revolution, when a howling mob materialized at the front gate. Keeping calm, Harry asked the leaders to wait until he got his camera to take their photo. When he returned the mob had dematerialized. Weber was replaced as political officer by Henry S. Sizer,[14] a classmate from Beirut, not from the "agency," but called "Harry."

It was inevitable that classmates from Beirut met and served together frequently on the "Sand Dune Circuit." It was no surprise when Richard C. Blalock, another Beirut classmate, was named chief of the consular section in Ta'izz. James R. Fees, vice consul, whom I did not know, worked for Dick.

Ta'izz had an administrative officer, John A. Hollingsworth—

not an Arabist—who had the unenviable task of paying the Yemeni employees—not only for the legation but also the gangs of local workers for AID and the BPR. They demanded payment in Maria Theresa thalers, the solid silver coin named for the eighteenth-century Austrian queen.[15] The thaler, slightly larger than an American silver dollar, was about 99 percent pure silver. Receiving bags containing hundreds of thalers in Aden and taking them to Ta'izz usually involved two or three American officers. Security was a matter of timing, secrecy, and weight.

Many of the AID and BPR Americans wore pistols on the job but I never heard of one drawing his weapon. Americans would be loath to deliberately point a gun at a Yemeni because then he would have to shoot him. The hard eyed, unsmiling, machine gun toting, teenaged, Yemeni guards at road blocks have an opposite mind set; diametrically opposed to American values and experiences. They are easily capable of shooting other Yemenis, or Americans, with equal equanimity. The Yemenis, like other South Arabians, carry their rifles on one shoulder and point the muzzle end of the barrel forward.

The danger was emphasized when an officer at the British embassy in Ta'izz, who answered a knock at the door, was fatally stabbed. The British are the enemy but they and we are equally foreign.

Our legation, not quite an embassy, occupied an office building in the city and had a variety of U.S. leased and furnished housing outside the city walls. The *chargé's* residence, was large and comfortable as was most of the other housing, and was located behind Ta'izz. The town could be charming and from a distance appeared so. Up close it loses its charm and has not the Spanish colonial architecture as in Latin America. The palace in Sana'a is mud brick lacking even the stonework at which Yemenis are adept.

The old city of Ta'izz is completely encircled by a stone wall with gates that are closed and barred at night. Inside the city, in a large area paved with flagstones, is an open market place (a *souk*) with small stalls and shops. Outside the walls are new, larger parts of the city guarded by manned road blocks.

At the guard post near the AID guesthouse a soldier in typical Yemeni dress, rifle over his shoulder, held in Yemeni fashion, greeted me with a smile. Between his turban and his sandals, he wore a cotton shirt, a *futa,* sort of wrap-around knee length kilt, common to South Arabia; broad leather belt with his sheathed *jambiya,* dagger, with broad curved blade; and crossed bullet loaded bandoliers over both shoulders. A typical Yemeni, I thought, but why the smile? He gave me the answer when he broke out in fluent idiomatic and recognizable Brooklyn accented English. Obscenities he had learned in New York blended in euphoniously with other adjectives and verbs. He had driven a taxi in New York City for seventeen years. A number of other Yemenis with similar experiences worked for us.

Yemenis are adventurers and have lived and worked in the New York, Detroit, Michigan and Lodi, California. The monthly distribution of Social Security and other retirement checks from the legation in Ta'izz, as in so many Third World countries, numbers in the hundreds but don't make them love us.

Yemenis and other indigenous natives of this south western corner of the Arabian Peninsula are a race apart. Some anthropologists claim that the brown skinned, long headed people that have become identified as Arabs first appeared here a few dozen millennia before Christ. They proliferated and as the pressure of population growth increased migrated northward.

After two days in Ta'izz I was offered a ride to Ibb, the farthest point of progress on the Ta'izz to Sana'a road, and a bed at the surveyors' camp. Clinging to a mountainside, defended by a beautifully fitted stone wall with gates that work, Ibb exists as if it still belonged to an age before gunpowder. Scavenging the materials of earlier and better builders the current inhabitants have taken for their use the ancient paving stones from the original highway up to the city gate. Stone paving on streets and markets exist inside the city. Asphalt won't last as long or, which amounts to the same thing, get stolen.

The "king" of the Yemen, *Imam* in local parlance, also called "Ahmed the Devil," son of Yahya, died in bed on September 19 of natural causes. In 1948 Ahmed had moved the capital to Ta'izz from Sana'a, because of its changeable climate. His oppressive fourteen-year reign had become increasingly murderous, making equally murderous enemies who would have much preferred to slit his throat. Authoritarian governments react to such news by closing the borders. The Imam's American doctor managed to get out in one piece. My place was Aden. After a quick briefing with Stookey in Ta'izz I made a dash for the border before those hard eyed, teenaged guards cradling their submachine guns slammed down the barriers. I made it.

Ahmed's 36-year-old-son, Seif al-Islam (Sword of Islam) al Badr, "the Crown Prince," claimed the throne. He promised to join the Yemen to the "caravan of world progress." His first near-fatal act was to name Col. Abdullah Sallal, captain of the Soviet built port of Hodeida, to command his palace guard.

Colonel Sallal was notorious for his abortive plots against Imam Ahmed. Sallal was a Soviet admirer and a stooge of Egypt's Nasser. Militant Arab nationalism and revolutionary fervor had come to the Yemen. Col. Sallal easily switched his open secret conspiracy from father to son. On the night of September 26, 1962, the "Sword of Islam" was reported to be dead and buried in the rubble of his mud brick palace in Ta'izz blasted by the artillery of his palace guard. At midnight Radio Sana'a proclaimed the birth of the Yemen Arab Republic. The Soviet Union recognized the YAR with Khrushchev's bombast; "Any aggression against the Yemen is an act of aggression against the Soviet Union!"

From New York, Badr's uncle, Prince Hassan, chief Yemeni delegate to the United Nations, headed home to reestablish the monarchy. The Yemen was an early member of the UN, having joined in 1947. Thus began a long running civil war exacerbating traditional tribal and sectarian bloodletting.[16]

It is a mystery to me why al Badr made the same fatal mistake in 1962 that King Farouk in Egypt had made in 1951. Nuri al-Said and King Faisal of Iraq did the same thing in 1958. Hussein of Jordan, forced by the nationalists to fire his British military advisers in 1956, was saved two years later by his *bedu* tribesmen. By some quirk of the Arab mentality, in a moment of crisis each entrusted crucial roles to ambitious, revolutionary fanatic army officers in direct command of armed troops.

The new YAR made life difficult for us by keeping the frontier unsafe and uneasy by renewing its tenacious claims to Aden and all of South Arabia. The Yemenis would often refuse to admit our AID and BPR people for no good reason. In mid-November we had thirteen AID folks, who had arrived without notice, stashed in hotels while we and the legation in Ta'izz negotiated their entry. Newcomers think they are the first and only people to discover Aden but all hotels stayed full. Beached merchant marine sailors didn't help. The AID types ran out of money and patience, and the hotels out of rooms. After the Yemenis had made their point, they let these imperialists, who were making roads for them, enter.

Aden's Legislative Council, "Legco," convened Monday, September 24, 1962, to debate Aden's accession to the Federation of South Arabia. Members of the council were the sultans, emirs, other tribal leaders, and a representative for Aden. President of the council was unassuming Sir Arthur Charles, a British civil servant. His wife Mary, unlike many of the British wives, was warm and friendly to Josephine. The council met in a handsome stone building, a former church, on a hill in town. This was two days before Col. Sallal launched his successful military strike in Sana'a. The shopping streets encircling the base of the hill would be a great place for a riot by the opposition. John Wheelock and I went to watch.

Aden had two opposition groups; the largest opposed accession and wanted union with the Yemen, the second wanted independence. They equally opposed each other, the British, and the Federation. Both opposition groups threatened dire consequences to everyone in general if they were opposed.

The Trades Union Congress led by an Aden Airways ticket clerk, Abdullah Asnag, was the larger, more dangerous group. Their slogan was: "One People, One Yemen, God is Great." With the tacit approval of the British Steve Campbell had introduced me to Asnag at the union's headquarters up on the slopes of *Jebel Shamsan*. Asnag was personable but brusque and did not waste a lot of time with me, the Deputy Principal Officer. After Wheelock's arrival the British did not want the Americans too friendly with the opposition so I never got the opportunity to introduce Wheelock to Asnag. The United States is in an enviable and unusual position by not getting embroiled, omnipotent, respected, and acceptable to all sides.

Asnag got a year is prison for sedition; the price of his rioting but didn't serve the whole year. Actions of thousands of protesters, mostly Yemenis rampaging through downtown, were predict-able. They ransacked a pro-federation newspaper office, smashed automobiles, burned piles of tires, and looted Indian owned shops. Police shot dead three rioters and wounded another six.

As preordained, the council approved joining Aden Colony to the Federation of South Arabia. The plan had to be approved by the British Parliament with debate in London scheduled for the follow-ing March.

The British were not surprised by the riots and reacted with impunity. From headquarters, Middle East Command, with com-bined forces of 40,000 troops, Air Marshall Sir Charles Elworthy, C-in-C, said: "This command is on twelve-hour alert for action any-where, and it can operate regardless of any misguided campaign here. Aden is the only rampart from the Mediterranean to Singa-pore, and ours the only force defending Western interests in the Middle East."

Much as I admired Sir Charles, and we talked a number of times, he was disregarding the U.S. Third Fleet. With global radio communications facilities at Asmara in Ethiopia and Jufair in Bah-rain, three modernized destroyers always on station or available, we had a heavy trip-wire force.[17] Even the three yacht-like flagships had two five inch thirty-eight dual purpose guns. These are accu-rate, powerful weapons. The appearance of one of these handsome, gleaming white ships in a small Middle East harbor bespoke of be-nign power and authority. Admiral Beecher, predecessor of Admi-ral Semmes, was proud of being a descendent of Harriet Beecher Stowe. He noted once that the rattle of the anchor chain through the hawse pipe of his flagship *Duxbury Bay* in Khor Fakkan, part of Sharja on the Gulf of Oman, resounded across the water like a "clash of cymbals."

Aden quieted down in mid-October, so I took an official "familiarization" trip (State Department jargon) to the major frontier town of Mukeiras. Mukeiras is 6,000 feet in elevation, on the edge of Audhali plateau; it is the capital of the Audhali Sultanate. Aden Airways had regular service and a small hotel there, not a BOAC Bluebird but adequate, caters to the British. I knew the commander of the first battalion of the Federal Regular Army currently based there. He had offered to look after me "up country."

Aden Airways had only one aircraft, a Douglas DC-3, or more likely a military C-47 "Dakota." When going "up country," they carried a mounted spare tire in the passenger compartment. Otherwise, if they had a flat it would be difficult to get a replacement to the disabled aircraft. The hostess checked all rifles to be sure there was not a round in the breech. The FRA helped by running an armored car down the runway a couple of times before a plane took off or landed to detonate any recently planted land mines.

The sultan, Saleh bin Hussein, was the minister of internal security in the federal government, and enlightened to the extent of having a shiny, new Mercedes-Benz four door sedan, the only such vehicle in the sultanate. He was in Aden now but I had an introduction to his brother Ja'bil, the *Naib*, deputy, or governor, depending. Ja'bil kept neighboring Yemen at arm's length while another brother, Nasser, administered the half of the sultanate below the escarpment.

This was rugged and difficult country although the valleys were fertile and grew fruit, corn, and vegetables. Mukeiras is an ancient market town and lies on a trade route used from prehistoric times. The men were respectably dressed in kilt-like *futas*, shirts, and blue turbans. The women were coy but went unveiled and wore flowing voluminous gowns, which accentuated their figures. They sprinkled their faces with a reddish powder; a relic of the ancient Himyar rulers of the Yemen. This was entirely different from the men's blue indigo woad. The women tended the crops and fetched water in large earthen jars balanced on their heads with a graceful undulating walk. Men sometimes carried things on their heads but not so gracefully.

One morning *Naib* Ja'bil and I with seven of his armed retainers made a foray for reconnaissance—I called it "familiarization," in my report—into the Yemen. We went on foot about three miles to one of Ja'bil's favorite observation posts overlooking al-Beidah, the most important town in that corner of the Yemen. Later, as the three week old Yemeni revolution escalated, Mukeiras and the Audhali sultanate would be on the front line, much to the detriment of its peace, stability, and economy.

Not to be outdone, my friend at the FRA provided horses for a guided tour. To avoid an "incident" for the United States, and me, we stayed well clear of the border. The British and *Naib* Ja'bil knew weapons and explosives brought in from the Yemen were stored in houses in remote and almost inaccessible valleys.

My views of the Yemen covered only the southeast—adjacent to the protectorates and the Red Sea coast, the *Tihamah* from Ta'izz to Mocha—but I know that the rugged mountains, with green slopes and valleys rising to 9,000 feet, extend northward parallel to the coast through the 'Asir region now part of Saudi Arabia. Most impressive are the thousands of terraces on the slopes, the oldest of which must themselves in turn be thousands of years old. They are reminiscent of the terraced mountains of Lebanon. My visual impression of the Yemen made clear to me the fate of the columns of Soviet built tanks sent by Nasser to aid the republicans. Higher up the royalists loosened tank sized boulders to roll down the mountainside onto the tanks and troops with predictable results.

A popular story in Aden was that—taking a page from the American foreign aid book—Nasser sent fifty Egyptian school teachers to the Yemen. After several weeks with no news from Sallal, Nasser wired him. "How are teachers?" Sallal answered: "Teachers fine, send five hundred students."

Naval visits picked up in back November, 1962, as a result of the civil war in the Yemen. Admiral Semmes in the *Greenwich Bay* was in port. We were also meeting one destroyer and a submarine.

The three boys and I toured the submarine; for them a fascinating experience. Coincidentally one of the sub's officers had served on my minesweeper, the USS *Dextrous*, during the Korean War. As with my WWII classmate from Northwestern now commanding a destroyer I have forgotten this man's name.

My economic reporting suffered from a surfeit of consular chores which devolved onto me when John Stevens left and our visa clerk Mohammed al-Gallas had taken a long planned leave. In addition to issuing visas to foreigners, I catered to Americans who had either lost their passports or faced other calamities. Fortunately our attractive receptionist, a true Adenii, was adept on the typewriter.

She arrived in the morning in a fancy Japanese car driven by a young man and accompanied by two women; all three women were swathed in black. As the car left our receptionist came up the sidewalk shedding her black gown on the way. In the office she was ready for work, dressed fit to kill in a low cut dress, usually red, and her hair stylishly coifed. She greeted people this way all day. In the evening she reversed the process and got back in the car fully covered.

The regional agricultural attaché was back. We went to the Central Produce Market and watched the auctioning of vegetables, all grown in the surprisingly fertile *wadis* "up country." He got the weight right.

Despite the workload, there was time for a picnic in the desert where the boys could run around and chase eagles. Enticing desert pools of water, which harbored the bilharzias flukes so prevalent in the Nile, had to be avoided at all costs. Once we drove east along the coast as far as Shuqra—home to a gaggle of fishermen. Shuqra boasted a dozen or so date palm trees and the fishermen's grass shacks. A muddy hole in the ground, the well, with a wooden A-frame over it produced brackish water. Close by, amidst desert dunes, squat the black tents of *bedu* and their flocks; wary of the meager comforts of such a poor oasis.

However, Shuqra is memorable to me as the site of two incidents told by G. Wyman Bury, a British political officer here sixty years ago, in his book *Land of Uz*. In one an old woman fell into the well, broke her neck, lay there dead and soured the water. No one would do anything until Bury came along and pulled her out. After that the tea tasted better, or as Bury says: "it could have been worse."

In the second, smokeless powder in rifle cartridges got its Arabian baptism of fire nearby. Attacked by tribesmen, Bury fired at one with his new ammunition and steel jacketed projectile, but the man kept coming. After the tribesman behind the first one fell dead the first finally fell. It was determined that the powerful new powder had driven the projectile clean through both men and would have felled a third. Then tribesmen had spears; now they too have rifles, smokeless powder, and steel jacketed projectiles.

After the September riots a general strike in November was

rather tame. Fighting in the Yemen was in the north but people here stayed agitated. The United States recognized the YAR on December 19, 1962, on the condition the Egyptians removed their troops and any equipment they could save. I'm sure the troops were happy to see the last of the Yemen, its mountains and valleys. In a saber-rattling gesture the Saudis announced they were mobilizing. At best they could secure the Saudi-Yemeni border.

Aden became part of the Federation of South Arabia January 19, 1963. In celebration the fighting went on, but we had a twenty-eight-day hiatus: Ramadan.[18]

By the Moslem calendar we were in the holy month of Ramadan when all true believers fast during daylight hours. Smart Moslems take their vacations at this time. Businesses, governments, and demonstrators go home early and little work of any substance is accomplished. Ramadan, whenever it comes in the year, is a slack time. Over in Ma'alla an opposition group, unidentified but certainly Yemeni, planted three grenade sized bombs. Bombs are Aden's favorite way of showing displeasure.

One Sunday we all climbed the trail to the peak of the 1,808-foot *Jebel Shamsan*; me, Josephine in a silk dress, and five-year-old Gregory. The Turks once had a signal station on the peak. The round trip climb took four hours. Ruins of the seventeenth-century Turkish fortifications on the *Jebel* were even less remarkable than the ridiculous "tanks" of Aden.

It was Christmas time, 1962, and the boys were on holiday from school. Clayton had difficulty with his studies because of the *petite mal* despite his valiant efforts. David was doing well, especially in math. Gregory had a new expression, "naughty boy," which he said he heard from his teacher. Gregory was not really naughty—more like Dennis, the Menace. We still went swimming, although the weather had moderated. January temperatures could dip to 76 degrees Fahrenheit. The dress was now "black tie, with jacket" for the endless rounds of dinners and cocktails. We hosted our share. We had had a rain, not quite a downpour. The radio station interrupted its regular programming to describe the rain. A year later, January 1964, we did have a downpour. This time of year it was just gloomy and cloudy.

In talking with the British wives at Gold Mohur while the boys were swimming, Josephine had become interested in putting them in an English public school. They would avoid moving at inopportune times. At the end of terms and holidays they would come to where we were. We had written to boarding schools, and it was discouraging to learn that boys Clay's age were doing algebra, geometry, Latin, and French. Here he was getting the most rigorous schooling available and had been put into a smaller class. If put back again he would have backed into David's grade. We were seeking a prep school for Clay in the United Kingdom, moving to a British-type "public school."

Clay and I went to the Khormaksar Club when we could for horseback riding for him and polo for me. Clay and Gregory enjoyed riding—with jodhpurs and black British style hard hats— more than swimming, which they loved in Beirut. I'm no judge of horseflesh but the club's horses gave us plenty of excitement. Although Lord Belhaven's wild stallion *Centurion* is gone to glory his progeny and spirit live on. David missed the sailing but we could not afford the time or money for a boat. I was always a day late and a dollar short. David was developing a good swimming style while Gregory enjoyed splashing at the Gold Mohur Club. British army officers took us sailing at the Forces Yacht Club. Sir Charles Elworthy sails and often wins the Sunday races. When I complimented him he said: "It's not the first." As Air Chief Marshall of the RAF, Sir Charles was one of the four service chiefs who guarded Churchill's casket in Westminster.

Two Americans—a man and a woman—cruising the world sailed their 35 foot ketch in, and took a group of us out for a sail. I took David along, his first experience sailing a bigger boat than our daysailer. Beyond the harbor entrance it was breezy and rough enough to be exciting. David loved it.

The ketch's owner had been an army dentist. On the last day of World War II, at the Elbe River, a diehard Nazi sniper shot him in the face taking out all of his teeth and leaving a wound that will never heal. On this round the world cruise during a stop in the Philippines some natives carved him a set of two beautiful dentures from mahogany, ironwood, and ivory. An inset brass plaque gives the date.

Admiral Semmes was moving his flag from *Greenwich Bay*, after four months, back to *Duxbury Bay* on February 6. The Admiral stirred up a hornets' nest in January by wanting to exchange salutes with the British. The British demurred until they remembered that February 6 is the Queen's Accession Day so they wanted lots of salutes. Naval vessels would be full-dressed and fire twenty one gun salutes at noon. The consulate was hosting a galaxy of star clusters on the shoulders of generals, admirals, and air marshals.

The Legislative Council convened March 1 and we went to hear the "Speech from the Throne." Here, the "throne" is the High Commissioner Sir Charles Johnston. They put on a good show, lots of ceremony, brilliant uniforms, guards of honor, and a seventeen-gun salute.

A correspondent for *Time* magazine, George de Carvalho, who had been "lost" in the royalist held mountains of northern Yemen for three weeks turned up on our doorstep. His itinerary had planned ten days there so *Time's* New York and London offices were hounding us to find George. He said he wanted two things right away: a hot meal and a finger nail brush. Josephine fixed him a cheese casserole (in Ramadan we had no cook) hot enough to burn his tongue. I didn't own a fingernail brush; one out of two.

Carvalho left, dirty fingernails and all, and now we had Tom Abercrombie and Robert Sissons, both photographer-writers from the *National Geographic Magazine*. Tom was doing a story on the Yemen but would base himself here. He had foot lockers full of film and beautiful equipment. He left me his sleeping bag, which the boys and I used for years. His story was upstaged by Kennedy's assassination.

Sissons was doing a story on the Indian Ocean, and to start off he joined an oceanographic ship scheduled to arrive that day or the next, or sometime. This survey was a three-year project, and Sissons' articles appeared over the years. He chartered a *dhow* for a day trip photographing the sail handling. He let Clay, David, and I come along provided we stay out of his pictures. The trip was a wonderful experience for all three of us.

Meeting these men was a pleasure and privilege for me. They were cosmopolitan in the best sense of the word. When they come into a place like Aden, in ten minutes they know their jobs and the way around.

In addition to the navy we had the U.S. Merchant Marine and the A. H. Bull Steamship Company was bankrupt leaving 27 ships stranded around the world. Two, the *Inez* and the *Elizabeth* with a hundred seamen, were in Aden. Bull was bought by a Greek, Kulukundis, who was prepaid for cargoes and freight and pocketed the money. Now they needed $100,000 for each ship for wages, fuel costs, and Suez Canal fees. One seaman wanted special treatment because he was, he said, a grandson of President Calvin Coolidge. The machinists and engineers worried about losing their personal tools. I arranged a plane charter for $30,000, the company paid and flew them out, president's grandson and all—except one troublemaker.

Live merchant seamen can often be a problem—dead ones even more so. Two dead ones arrived on separate ships several weeks apart and according to the ships' captains their final requests were to be buried at sea. If they had done that before *rigor mortis* set in it would have been simpler. Instead they put "the deceased" on ice and brought their request to me when I visited the ships. I was the American consul, wasn't I? One captain, to be certain I got the message, had called me at midnight New Year's Eve on the radiotelephone to say he was coming, what he was bringing, and what he wanted done.

There were forms: "Death of an American Citizen," death certificates, cause of death, disposal, and local requirements. Unscheduled deaths are routine in Aden. The military and civilian authorities keep five open graves always ready with coffins or other covers. This time I had to find a boat ready, willing, and able to take us out to a suitable spot beyond the 300 fathom curve, and not in the harbor or the traffic lanes. Time was important because the captain was anxious to sail and once he got rid of the body he did. The civilian Anglican priest agreed to officiate. He also wondered about the chance to "wet a line."

Actually for us, the living, it was almost enjoyable; the first burial was easy, the second easier. I found a suitable, small, clean tugboat with a three man crew. With a canvas bag from the ship, planks, sawhorses, some links of heavy chain, and a flag from the ship we were ready. Not needed this time were the five open graves; when they fill one they dig another. We got underway after an early breakfast and were back by lunchtime. The tug was seaworthy, the crew serious, and the Anglican brief—no eulogy or fishing. He gave the Burial of the Dead: Rite One, and the Committal, substituting "the deep," similar to that in the Episcopalian Book of Common Prayer. It is a pity consuls don't often have this opportunity. I arranged another burial at sea two years later in Benghazi. It is not an unpleasant experience.

Early in 1963 we had a Soviet Merchant Marine defector from a Russian coal burner. I don't know how he got ashore, but occasionally Soviet sailors are allowed off their ships and one now sat in my office. The admiral was not in port but with our Third Fleet, the Royal Navy, and together we got him into a hotel with no one else the wiser. The British Army was involved but I don't think the civil authorities were. Regardless of how much many foreigners claim to hate America, when defectors have a choice they head for the first place they see the Stars and Stripes. Like the man in San Pedro Sula, as his first point of contact, this one referred his questions to me to find the answers.

There it was, in writing. On March 3, 1963, Adrian Middleton, executive director, Bureau of Near Eastern and South Asian Affairs, wrote a scathing two-page letter to John Wheelock castigating me, complaining about my reception of three AID employees—Charles Flinner, Donald Richardson, and Vaughan—en route to Ta'izz. Here was something else to worry about. Middleton wrote:

> I was quite disturbed by the things they told about John Tinny....
>
> Although the group was obviously hot, tired and completely exhausted, neither Tinny nor his wife offered any of the usual courtesies that one would expect under the circumstances. Oh yes, in the course of saying the group did not have reservations, Tinny also said he did not want to call some of the hotels because he wasn't on very good terms with the management....True or not, it has created a lot of heartburn with the high-level AID people.... If correctly stated, John Tinny, for his own welfare and that of

the Service…should be given the facts of life as to common courtesy.

John Tinny just happened to be at the airport when they arrived. [This was at 6:45 a.m.] He [Tinny] referred to other "AID-types."

[The three and Middleton] found this phrase particularly offensive and "uncalled for."

He suggested they use the phone at the Consulate but did not offer any other assistance. The tired travelers then proceeded to find their own reservations after a lot of fruitless chasing and harassment.

I answered the allegations to Wheelock. For reasons I forget, he had not been present but had been in Aden over six months and knew our situation. We did not normally handle the AID people. As always Carlos Crabbe, assistant supply advisor to the AID mission, had come down to meet them, take care of their needs, and take them to Ta'izz. Large numbers of American personnel transit Aden. As I remember it, my confrontation with the three was a tense moment. I think I was more helpful than Middleton says, but not helpful enough. Wheelock gave me a copy of the letter, to which I responded with a five-page defense of my actions. Use of the offensive word "types" is a British affectation and I should have known not to use a British colloquialism with Americans unless they also were familiar with the term. Wheelock, who as my supervisor was also on the block, answered Middleton. I have no idea what he said.

I don't understand Middleton's remark about my wife; Josephine was not involved. The crack about being on bad terms with the hotels is untrue. These facts don't change anything. The three men had accosted me in the consulate garage where Clay and I were trying to get my car running.

There was nothing much Wheelock could say on my behalf; he wanted to "protect his back," take care of himself. He probably said he would look into the matter, insure that nothing similar would happen again, and reiterate his concern for AID personnel coming and going. Middleton killed himself soon after in a careless car crash on the beltway in Washington. I didn't know him and he didn't know me.

No matter what I say, the fault is mine. These three men were "constituents" and should have been treated with kid gloves, as I treated the agricultural attaché. They were more important to my life than all the sultans of South Arabia put together. I grind my teeth as this episode haunts me yet.

Finally, well into March we all drove to Mukalla, capital of the Quai'iti sultanate, three hundred miles east up the coast from Aden, the biggest and richest state in the Eastern Aden Protectorate. Sitting at the water's edge and backed up against steep mountains, Mukulla with its whitewashed buildings and minarets is a picture perfect Arab town. Cynical James Morris who found Aden "repellent" described Mukulla as one of the prettiest of Arab towns. So it is, from a distance. We stayed with Arthur and Mrs. Watts. He was the British resident advisor to Sultan Awadh bin Salih bin Ghalib, the Quai'ti ruler. For me this was another "familiarization" trip and I wanted to explore the area. Mukulla is the door to the Hadhramaut, the one hundred mile long, north-south-west tortuous valley, which with its tributary *wadis* is the South Arabian version of our Grand Canyon. Our first night the Watts took us to the palace to meet His Highness the Sultan, and watch tribal dancing. Faint shadows and echoes of former glories may be seen today of the past in their dress and heard in their speech. Then the Quai'ti Sultanate ruled enclaves in India and the east coast of Africa. The sultans have close ties to the court of the Nizam of Hyderabad to whom they once provided a praetorian guard. This guard is much as is the Swiss guard in the Vatican.

The fifteen miles west of Mukulla is beautiful white sand beach and the Arabian Sea a clear and brilliant blue—the Watts' favorite swimming spot. East, the coast is rocky, good for snorkeling.

The Watts were very hospitable but we were a burden. They lived in one of the tall, multistoried, mud buildings unique to South Arabia. In Mukulla they reach six floors, in the Hadhramaut twelve floors, seventy or eighty feet high. The toilet facilities are commensurately primitive and are called "the long drop." Holes in an overhang on a sunny side of the building give the urine and fecal matter a long drop.

The wealth displayed here is accumulated in the East Indies and brought home. Like so many émigrés, Hadramis do well in business overseas.

Hermann Eilts—later a stellar Foreign Service officer and, as mentioned before, ambassador—knew Watts, then political advisor to Sir Ali Abdul Karim, sultan of Lahej. Ten years later, Watts's pet project was building a road where none existed into the Wadi Hadhramaut. His road was modeled on ancient Roman roads with a deep rock-filled foundation topped by a large flat rock surface, with camber and curbing. He estimated his cost at $4,000 a mile, using local labor and materials. Watts was an accomplished violinist, and we heard him play here and in Aden. He and Bob Stookey had music in common but never knew each other.

We had hoped to stay in Mukulla another day or two but Wheelock telegraphed me to return to handle the stranded ex-Bull Line merchant seamen. They had wrecked one hotel with their drunken behavior. Besides, a British aircraft carrier in port increased our naval and social responsibilities.

On another trip into the Hadramaut, I passed by but did not enter Tarim—the garden city reputed to have many gardens and a mosque for every day of the year. Shibam, the "skyscraper" city, is an amazing sight. Infidels are not welcome in the cities and I didn't push my luck. The British resident Ted Ayres put me up in a Hollywood type oasis "guest house" with palm trees, babbling brooks, being irrigation canals, and a swimming pool. No dancing girls, in fact, no girls were to be seen at all.

My good friend (I like to think so) and self-sufficient Tom Abercrombie from the *National Geographic Magazine* was in and out, and sometimes I could be a help.[19] His article "Behind the Veil of Troubled Yemen" appeared a year later in March 1964. Tom did another article, twenty years later, in October 1985, called "Arabia's Frankincense Trail." His wife, Lynn, accompanied him that time. Winston Burdett from CBS (Columbia Broadcasting System) had just filmed a story on the Yemeni war. *Time* magazine had reporters in—not de Carvalho, however—and *U.S News and World Report* sent John Law, who was fun. Dana Adams Schmidt of the *New York Times* stopped by briefly but was more interested in Muscat.

When Lowell Thomas filmed a travelogue on the "frontier" area of the Aden Protectorates he had them remove all the Kodak Film and Goodyear Tire signs hanging over shop doors. He thought he could pay in U.S. dollars but they were refused. Adenis wanted only East African Shillings, the local currency.

Admiral Semmes, in port on his flagship *Duxbury Bay*, invited Josephine and the boys out for a visit and sent his Admiral's barge for them. I was making sure the captain of a U.S. flag ship in port took, as he had promised me, our last beached Bull Line seaman, drunk or sober, if I had to have him shanghaied. He hadn't left with the others because of his paranoid fear of flying. He would work his way home. The two Bull Line ships, *Inez* and *Elizabeth*, becoming derelict, are still stranded here.

Josephine had written to dozens of British prep schools to find one for Clay and David and had finally succeeded. We wanted to avoid interrupting Clay's school year. I could be transferred in the middle of the term and Clay would come on holiday to wherever we are. He would return, and this is most important, to the same school. She had good help and advice from the British families here with boys in school in England, especially the Dunlops. He was the local general manager of Mitchell Cotts, a British import-export firm. Their son Bruce, same age as Clay was here on holiday, and the boys became good friends.

Bruce went to St. Bede's School in Eastbourne, Sussex county, due south of London, on the English Channel. It is in a beautiful setting next to the Downs, rolling plains atop high chalk cliffs focusing on Beachy Head, a headland with a well-known lighthouse standing offshore. They raved about the school and especially the Headmaster, John Keeling. At first St. Bede's balked at taking Clayton because he would be eleven this year—too old for his class—but were quite happy to have David. We had befriended Bruce and another student at St. Bede's, who were here on holiday because his parents were stationed here. If Clayton went to St. Bede's he would already have two friends there. The boys also noted that screen and TV actor, Roger Moore, lived in an apartment across the street from the school. We took these boys and Clay to visit the new oceanographic survey ship, *Atlantis II*, from Woods Hole.

Jacques Cousteau's ship, the *Calypso*, had been in for emergency repairs. It seems one of the stainless steel tanks holding their wine had sprung a leak. On the *Calypso*, at least, that constituted a real emergency.

The space program became a factor in our lives in May. In anticipation that the Mercury shot, scheduled for May 24, might land in the Indian Ocean a recovery team from Wheelus Air Base in Libya was present here in Aden and ready. This required a lot of coordinating with the British. However, Scott Carpenter landed *Aurora 7* on target in the Atlantic.

The Sultanate of Muscat and Oman was the object of my next "familiarization" tour and on May 23 I flew across the Arabian Peninsula to Bahrain in the Persian Gulf. The Arabs refer to the peninsula as the "Island of the Arabs," *Jezirat al Arab*, and as noted before consider it their primeval home. From Bahrain I flew to Dhahran in Saudi Arabia, a fifteen minute flight in a twin engine BOAC Lark, to "consult" at the consulate general. Jack Horner, who I knew in Lebanon was consul general and had a crew of our classmates from the FSI language school. Jim May was Jack's deputy, while Eugene Bird, Pierce Bullen, and three others did consular work.

Gene Bird was accompanying me to Muscat but did not have a visa. On our arrival there it took some fancy footwork, but with the help of the British consulate general we got him admitted. Our host in Muscat was the Dutch Reformed Church's American Mission with its hospital. We were met by Dr. and Mrs. Nykerk, who were there only temporarily, filling in for the director, Mr. D. T. Bosch and his wife, Eloise, who were on leave. We were entertained at a "tea" by Miss Jeannette Boersma, the head nurse. All of the hospital staff were of Dutch ancestry, and all came from the little town of Holland, Wisconsin.

A UN delegation led by Ambassador De Ribbing, Swedish ambassador to Spain, representing U Thant, had also just arrived. De Ribbing was investigating Omani demands for independence.

The new British Consul General Jock Duncan gave a soirée for the UN delegation and included Bird and me. It was a grand affair with top officials of the Muscat government, members of the sultan's immediate family—except for the sultan who was away—senior officers of the Muscat military forces, and their British advisors. The men (except Bird and me) were in evening dress or dress uniforms, with medals. The ladies including those from the mission were lovely in evening gowns—although not so *décolleté* as those worn by the beauties of La Ceiba—and jewels. A brilliant crescent moon above the perfectly maintained Portuguese fort, constructed in 1508, adjacent to the consulate added the right touch.

De Ribbing went on to Salalah to meet with the sultan while Bird and I stayed in the twin towns of Muscat and Matrah. The mission hospital here, established in 1895, was connected to the missions in Kuwait, Bahrain, and Sharja. Bigger than the others, it is self contained with hospital, church, residences, and power station. We drove along the Batinah coast, south east of the straits of Hormuz, and inland as far as the Jebel Akhdar, or Green Mountain — the Omani stronghold of the independence- minded Ibadi tribe.

The town of Muscat is walled and pedestrians at night must carry an oil lantern. In the courtyard of the British consulate general stands a tall flagpole with a large stone base. A slave who can reach that point and clasp the base of the flagpole is manumitted. I also visited the garage where the sultan houses his Rolls. Another attraction is the sultan's "autograph book" a stone faced hill inscribed with names of ships and officers calling there from the earliest times. Still barely legible is "Horatio Nelson, Midshipman," written there by himself.

The official report of the parliamentary debates of the British Parliament is known as Hansard —the name of its first printer. It is printed daily and is very similar in form and purpose to our Congressional Record. On 26 June 1963, Hansard carried the following paragraph introduced by Joint Under-Secretary of State for Foreign Affairs Peter Thomas:

THE YEMEN (BRITISH SERVICE PERSONNEL)
The United States Vice Consul in Aden has also been assisting a British Political Officer in negotiations on the frontier.

The vice consul, of course, was me, although not named, and was news in Aden. The British military, including Major-General John H. Cubbon, C.B., C.B.E., general officer commanding Middle East forces, and civilian officials, including Sir Charles Johnston, the high commissioner, and others who usually read Hansard, mentioned it to me. Being in Hansard is rather like "being mentioned in dispatches," another British term. Several more times, until the captives were freed, Hansard referred to activities of the U.S. FSOs in Ta'izz and Aden and former Prime Minister Mr. Edward Heath, now Lord Privy Seal, "paid tribute" to them.

The story was that on June 22 an "adventure party" of 44 service men and service women, officers and enlisted, set out in the Sultanate of Lahej, for an exercise which was part of their "adventure training." These were office and clerical workers who in the course of their duties never get into the field. Once a year they are sent on a sort of extended camping trip, usually unarmed, guided by experienced, armed soldiers and in safe territory. Their planned line of march kept them well away from the Yemeni border but they got lost. About 9:00pm this night, moving along a desert track they took a wrong turn and drove, I think they were mostly in Land Rovers, right into the most violently fought over area of the frontier. They were fired upon by alert Yemeni tribesmen who probably thought they were being raided. The British party split and 18, including four women, escaped back into Federation territory. Twenty six others pinned down by fire surrendered and were taken captive. One royal marine and three army enlisted men were shot dead and two other men were wounded in the exchange of fire. The bodies of the four dead and four more women were returned. Eighteen men, including the two wounded, were held captive in a nearby Yemeni border fort in the vicinity of Tor al-Baha.

Parliament was considerably exercised not only by how this could have happened but why these unskilled service members were sent into an area so close to a hostile country with which Britain had no diplomatic relations. Shooting scrapes occur often along this volatile, hostile frontier. The British asked the United States, since we represented British interests in the Yemen and had recognized the Yemen Arab Republic, to request the return of the 18 men. Our chargé d'affaires, the personable and gregarious Jim (James N.) Cortada, who had replaced Bob Stookey in Ta'izz swung into action. Cortada and I had served in Cairo together and I knew this was a situation in which he — a physically large man, bold and boisterous — could really utilize his energy and while quite serious, if I may use the term, enjoy himself.

The British captives were being held at the border and we wanted to get them returned before they were moved to Ta'izz or even Sana'a. Also involved were the tribal leaders of the tribesmen who had started the fracas. Yemeni tribesmen are as ornery as the tribes in the Federation and want their due. None of the tribesmen had been wounded or killed or we would have heard; their "injuries" would surface later. By keeping the captives at the border they could be attended by a British doctor and supplied with British army rations. The political officer cited in the report, Michael Crouch, was in charge at the border.[20]

The British on their part, in a show of force, had moved the 40 Royal Commando Marines with their armored cars up to a Federation border fort. The Federal Regular Army (FRA) had also bivouacked troops outside the fort. I was "bivouacked" inside the fort. The Yemenis were now represented by an army officer. Crouch fastidiously arranged our daily negotiation meetings in detail—especially the seating. He also arranged for the two wounded men to be brought out on stretchers by Land Rover.

A week into the confrontation, on July 4, Cortada in Ta'izz negotiated the release of the last sixteen men with the delivery of a diplomatic note to the Yemeni Government. The note said in part: "Her Majesty's Government regrets the incident...and will pay 150,000 East African shillings (equivalent to £7,500) for casualties incurred by the Yemenis and damage to property." It was a ransom. The British had given Cortada discretion in the amount, and as a born negotiator, he got a good deal.

In any case, the British soldiers walked out of Yemen unscathed. Mr. Peter Thomas sent a telegram to Secretary of State Dean Rusk expressing the thanks of "HMG" for the devoted work of Mr. Cortada and other members of the Foreign Service. As quickly as it had begun twelve days earlier, it was almost over. Later, a member of Parliament asked if they had recovered the adventure party's vehicles. A Bedford truck was used, and Land Rovers. There was a subsequent Court of Inquiry but I did not see its report.

John and Anne Wheelock, with their three sons, left for home leave on July 6 and were due back at the end of October. That meant that

I was in charge of the consulate, and I made my own mistakes. One of the biggest was to move the consular clerk's desk into an empty office—that is to say, I should have left it where it was.

In July we were still trying to get rid of our two bankrupt Bull Line freighters which were on the verge of becoming derelict. One got out of port with a skeleton crew but broke down and had to return. One caught fire, had no potable water, and no food. The drunken homesick crews sobered up in jail.

For months the brutal Yemeni civil war had waxed and waned and was now waxing. Egyptian war planes had devastated royalist held villages in the north with heavy casualties but wanted to extricate themselves from a no win war. In the south, Ethiopian Airlines had resumed direct flights from Addis Ababa to Ta'izz. UN efforts to separate the Yemeni royalist and Saudi forces from the Yemeni republican forces with their Egyptian allies are dilatory. Both the Saudis and the Egyptians are out of their element in the high mountains of the Yemen. I was involved because the UN was using Canadian aircraft and personnel. Canada depended on us to represent them. It is hard to get armies disengaged without, to use a WWII Japanese sophistry, "losing face."

Josephine was frantic trying to get Clay into a prep school in England. He was now two years behind his age group and most prep schools said he would not be able to pass the common entrance examination to get into a public school. He was the anchorman in his class. That doesn't mean he was the bottom one that passed—it means he was the bottom one. Five schools in Sussex, easily accessible from London, would take Clay. Josephine and Clay flew to London on September 7 to visit St. Bede's.

Josephine had worked a year on getting Clay into a prep school. First, we narrowed down the 680 U.S. boarding schools listed in the *Porter Sargent, Handbook of Private Schools, Forty Sixth Edition*, to those convenient to the DC area, our current home base; or Florida, convenient to Clay's grandparents. These schools were quickly eliminated. Our preference was for a school convenient to London so we could get to him easily and *vice versa*. For that Josephine had the latest U.K. *1963 Public and Preparatory Schools Yearbook*. We narrowed it to St. Bede's, Tyttenhanger, Normandale, and two others.

The Aden wives who knew about putting boys into schools

were helpful. All clothes, towels, and the like had to have a special type of name tag sewn on. These were available here as were winter clothes—big sellers to immigrants headed to England and Europe. For uniforms and other particular items each school had its "supplier." Clay had to bring a trunk to serve as a locker. Clay already had a cedar lined footlocker. In the trunk he had to at least have a dictionary, a Bible, and a Church of England hymnal.

Apart from cost, money arrangements were a problem. We used the Chartered Bank, West End Branch, London, which had branches in Aden and throughout the Near East. Cost was a big worry, but we discovered that the English schools charged much less than the quasi-American schools in England or Switzerland. All three of our boys went to English prep and boarding schools for a combined total of almost ten years for the amount it would have cost to put one through an overseas American school.

Josephine and Clay had to get their immunizations renewed. The British Army helped there.

In mid July, the long-time high commissioner Sir Charles Johnston left and his departure was celebrated with all the ceremony this unpretentious outpost of empire and the British Raj could cobble together.[21] A military parade featured columns of *Saladin*—armored cars, no tanks here—companies of camel mounted troops, both British and FRA; and infantry in their vehicles. A flyover by the RAF featured *Hawker Hunter* fighter-bombers. A demonstration of a slow speed landing by a troop carrier was remarkable. The plane, a huge Bristol, seemed to land flying backwards.

The King's Own Scottish Borderers (KOSB) liked twilight Tattoos, with parades and pipers, usually climaxed by a spotlighted lone piper playing a Scottish lament. The *Barren Rocks of Aden, Scotland the Brave,* and *Amazing Grace* were perennial favorites. Gregory was so much impressed by these displays that once when asked what he wanted to be when he grew up he said: "A Scottish soldier."

We had been introduced to the KOSB at one of their monumental curry lunches. As I recall, this was the first battalion of the regiment and had a long record of service in India. Their curry was excellent.

The Camel Troop of the FRA, revitalized by the FRA Force

Commander Brigadier James Lunt, performed their graceful dance routine to the strains of *Bonnie Dundee*. The troopers carried lances with steel tipped heads and the Troop's pennants flying. When the sixteen circling camels turned inward and passed between each other at a fast trot with leveled lances everyone gasped and held their breath. A camel skewered by a lance at a similar recent event had died on the spot.

Major-General Lunt recounts his service in the Aden Protectorates in his book *The Barren Rocks of Aden*, published in 1966. He tries to analyze why British, French, and Americans are so fascinated by Arabia. A clue might be found in Wilfred Thesiger's book *Arabian Sands*, which Lunt found so enthralling.

The governor in a white uniform bedecked with medals, sword, and a balaclava sun helmet adorned with white feathers, looked the part. It was a scene to make Kipling proud. When all was done and his excellency, usually referred to as "H.E." had shaken our hands, he marched out to a RAF transport command *comet*, (never mind the metal fatigue) followed by two KOSB pipers playing *Barren Rocks of Aden*—a nineteenth century lament by Pipe-Major MacKellar of the seventy-eight Highlanders. The door thudded shut, the Rolls Royce engines whined into life, and he was history, as he had made it.

August 26, 1963, the day Sir Kennedy Travaskis ("call me Ken") officially became high commissioner, was the same day RADM A. F. Schade who had replaced our old friend, RADM B. J. Semmes, Jr., accompanied by Mrs. Schade, made his maiden visit to Aden. When it rains, it pours, even in Aden: two "must attend" events on the same day, though at different hours.

In August I visited an outpost of the empire in one of my familiarization trips. Kamaran Island, *Two Moon Island*, even more forlorn than Aden but not completely insignificant, sits off the coast of Yemen and commands the entrance to a fine harbor at Salif—a potential hotspot. Until WWII, Kamaran was a major quarantine station for entrance into Saudi Arabia for the pilgrimage to Mecca— the *Haj*. Long rows of tiny rooms called "coolie lines," which housed the pilgrims awaiting clearance, and the long concrete

piers where ships from distant Moslem countries, especially the
Far East, brought the tens and hundreds of thousands of pilgrims,
are all fallen into ruin. Even the British commissioner's residence
has been vandalized out of existence. However, thanks to the whim
of a navigator on one of His Majesty's ships in 1933, we know the
exact location of the commissioner's tennis court. Fastened to a
broken fragment of the court's wall is a brass plaque which says it is
located at latitude 15 degrees 20 minutes 20.59 seconds North and
longitude 42 degrees 36 minutes 51.52 seconds East. In addition the
commissioner had his own wood-fired water desalinization plant.
Still in operation it is the island's source of fresh water. I don't know
the source of the wood but they use it sparingly.

The inhabitants of Kamaran are wards of Britain but some had
gone to Saudi Arabia to seek work and had illegally obtained Yemeni passports. In the ongoing civil war in the Yemen, the Saudi
support of the royalists has soured relations with the Yemen Arab
Republic, so the Saudis deported these Yemeni passport holders.
Back on Kamaran they were dissatisfied with the dole and had seen
enough of the world to learn to riot and that is what they did. The
Aden government sent a squad of armed police, and a political ad-
viser, Jimmy Lloyd, to calm things. He invited me to come along.
The police knocked a few heads together and Jimmy promised
them enough so they went back to netting sharks.

Piles of sharks higher than my head were brought in weekly
to the old piers. Parts of the sharks—tails, livers, skins—were exported to Saudi Arabia and elsewhere and some parts were eaten
locally. Centuries of brisk shark harvesting worldwide attests to the
fecundity of sharks.

By mid September Josephine wrote that St. Bede's had accepted
Clay, starting in the 1963 term. and that David and Gregory would
start in succeeding years, 1964 and 1965. She was impressed by
the headmaster, Mr. Candlin, as was everyone who knew him.
Unfortunately, he died soon after the term began and John Keeling
took over temporarily. Clay soon established a bond with his
permanent successor, Rex Lord. Putting the boys in public schools
in England and keeping them there for the next six years was one

of the best things we ever did for them. After Clay was killed in November 1979, I wrote to the new, young headmaster at St. Bede's, Peter Pyemont:

> Clayton's fondest school memories were of St. Bede's. He often spoke of his masters, especially Mr. Lord, for whom he had the highest regard. During Clay's first term President Kennedy was assassinated.... The school lowered its colors for one week in respect for our President. Clay, the only American at St. Bede's, was very impressed. When they sang "God Save the Queen," Clay was allowed to substitute, "President" for "Queen."
>
> Clay loved the Downs and spoke enthusiastically of seeing Sir Francis Chichester sail past on his triumphant return from around the world.
>
> All three boys remember you, Mrs. Pyemont, and Mrs. Wise fondly.
>
> Please use this money (£200) for something on-going in Clayton's name.
>
> Clayton's St. Bede's necktie was buried with him.

Mr. Pyemont replied: "Words fail me.... I was saddened by the death of Clayton. We will purchase a snooker table so the older boys can play snooker and billiards. We will place a plaque on the table engraved, "The Clayton Tinny Snooker Table."

In early October the Wheelocks were still on leave but I had managed, no more AID debacles. Cortada had been a regular commuter from Ta'izz since the legation got a *Piper Aztec,* a small single engine airplane, and was often in Aden. He and I had lunch together until Wheelock asked me to stop. When Admiral Crowe, pronounced "craw," former commander of the Sixth Fleet was in Aden en route to Ta'izz, I asked Cortada how he preferred I transport the admiral. Cortada replied: "Let Crowe fly."

Since Mary Flood, our secretary, abruptly left for the States to see her ailing mother and with our communications clerk Jackie Rubenbic still on leave, Josephine had been helping with the typing and filing. She had also been supervising the remodeling of the kitchen in the Wheelock's apartment on instructions from Anne. This was an unrewarding chore for Josephine with poor, untrained help.

Both civilian government and private sectors in Aden had gone on a Moslem workweek with Friday the day of rest. At the consulate we still closed on Sunday, so I used that day to call on officials — a workday for them — and do other business outside the office. As for telegraphic traffic, the vice consul did our deciphering; the administrative officer did the enciphering; I helped with both and did the drafting. We filed everything chronologically, by color. The color was determined by the multilayered forms with carbon paper interleaved between the pages. Each page was a different color denoting its use. This particular Sunday we received five telegrams to be acknowledged; each a thousand words of mostly "boiler plate." My office hours started at 6:00am and finished at 9:00pm. Sunday was not a workday.

Four star General Paul D. Adams, head of the new central command based at MacDill Air Force Base in Tampa flew in Wednesday, November 13, in his "flying submarine" — a huge jet with no windows. We arranged for our Third Fleet Admiral Schade (Arnold F., "call me Arnie") and General Adams to confer with the heads of the three British commands. The commander-in-chief was still Major General Cubbon; the Royal Navy's flag officer, Middle East, was Vice Admiral Scotland; and Air Vice Marshall J. E. Johnson (Britain's ace fighter pilot, "call me Johnny") had replaced Fred Rozier as RAF commander.[22]

The assassination of President Kennedy shocked everyone here, "friend and foe alike." The British, of course, were with us on this. The Arabs, not strangers to assassination, readily kill each other in the name of a religion they invented; and were not surprised. We heard the news going into a dinner party and immediately took our leave. We went to see the Wheelocks who were back from their long holiday in Australia. They had heard the news. The consulate began a thirty day period of mourning. The BBC picked up and rebroadcast the funeral live and we followed it to graveside.

Tuesday, Dec. 10, High Commissioner Sir Kennedy Trevaskis, "H.E.," and a few federal ministers en route to London to discuss Aden's voting lists were the target of a hand grenade thrown into a group of them at the airport. I had offered to go to the airport but Wheelock, contrary to all tradition, insisted I need not go. He probably saved my life since I would certainly have been standing close to Trevaskis. One woman bystander was killed and George Henderson, a popular and efficient political officer standing next to H.E., received a wound which proved fatal a week later. He was awarded a second George Medal. This grenade was a harbinger of more attacks on civilians and the military. Likeable, diminutive Sir Arthur Charles, speaker of the Legislative Council, was machine gunned leaving the tennis club. The German honorary consul, a German citizen, lost an arm to a bomb thrown into his home. The pretty, red haired, freckle faced daughter—home from school—only child of a British Army officer, was killed by a bomb thrown onto their terrace at her welcoming home party. Yemenis were blamed for these murders.

Two officers serving with the FRA were killed "up country" in the line of duty by a landmine. A third officer, a South African veteran of the desert war in WWII, serving with HBL, was shot from ambush. He liked desert service and had served successfully with Arab soldiers for over twenty years.

The weekend outing planned for the family in Dhala on invitation from the Emir of Dhala in January 1964 was cancelled because of tribal unrest and I went alone. An operation in the adjacent Radfan province to quell the "dissident tribesmen" involved two battalions of the FRA, out of the four, plus other units. Some patrols were cut off and it took several days fighting to pull things together. Political Officer Michael Crouch was there with wife Lynette, who was still working on her tan. Major George Bowden and his wife Elizabeth helped take care of me.

In the open we could hear rifle bullets passing overhead ripping the air so distinctly it seemed we could almost see them. As George Washington said about the tearing noise of bullets passing overhead, "there is something charming in the sound." Charming is an eighteenth century word and not one I would use. Still, the unique sound of a high flying rifle bullet makes you look up and hunch down. They say you never hear the bullet that kills you—but how do they know?

In Dhala, between rifle fires, I did get some camel riding. The tribesmen urged I not use stirrups—their idea of a joke. I agreed because I ride; sometimes we play polo without stirrups, and my balance is good enough. I had ridden camels on the beach at Bir Fuqum where I also learned you never ride a camel into the surf.

Without warming a camel will flop down in the water and either drown the rider or crush him to death. So no stirrups, but if they had expected to watch me to fall off, the joke was on them.

In April 1963 the remaining peace corps volunteers sent in last year were brought out of Somalia to Aden for physical exams and debriefings. It had been a rough nine months for them. The previous fall the peace corps sent fifty twenty year old volunteers—and two others, an older married couple—to Somalia. They were the first or second peace corps unit to actually arrive in Africa. We staged them through Aden, first to Hargeisa, capital of the former British Somaliland, and they deployed from there. The unit director, a forty-year-old former California state legislator, was a sick man when he arrived but vowed to see it through. He succeeded but killed himself in the process. He was in and out of Aden; visibly physically deteriorating from a ravishing skin disease. He died just before we pulled his volunteers out.

At the end, twenty-five of the fifty two volunteers were left. Two had died in Somaliland; the other twenty-five had just flown the coop. The first to die was a young man from a disease poorly diagnosed as cholera. We don't know what it really was. The second was a pretty, bright, young woman who had drunk something toxic in a wine bottle at a late night session. I think it was kerosene for lamps, Josephine thinks it was a cleaning solution. An American doctor and nurse went to help bring her to Aden. Josephine and I stayed with her before she left for the States. Continuous coughing brought up bits of bloody matter the nurse called pieces of her stomach lining. She made it home to the States and died in her mother's arms.

Our oldest volunteers, the married couple in their early fifties, were also our most successful. Neither was a large or imposing person but both were thirty year veteran school teachers and able to better manage the arrogant and unruly Somalis. The Somali girls were worse than the boys and when errors were pointed out to them they flew into a rage, snapped their pencils in two, and ripped apart their notebooks. Being older, married, and experienced this couple did not participate in outside activities with the young and immature volunteers. I don't know if more volunteers were sent into Somalia after I left Aden. I hope not—their efforts would have been equally fruitless and dangerous.

April 1964 and orders to my next post as principal officer, consul, at the consulate in Benghazi, Libya had come. Josephine and I were happy at the prospect. It would be an easier commute to England where all three boys would be in school. We would leave here July 3 and spend three weeks in England waiting for Clay to finish his third and final term for the year at St. Bede's. We were all praying he passed. He did. We would leave England for New York on the new *United States*. Our first crossing was on the old *America*.

Meanwhile we stayed busy. In April eight navy ships, including an aircraft carrier, entered in six days. All were dying of thirst for tons of black oil. They got it. We had the carrier's skipper Captain Morrison for dinner. The Wheelock's had the task force's commander RADM Moore. It was old home week for us. Morrison was from Leesburg, Florida but now called Clearwater, Florida home. The admiral's wife was a Tampa girl, Jo Ann McDaniel—unfamiliar to me.

In May I again visited the Hadhramaut on a farewell swing through the Eastern Protectorates. Money in the Hadhramaut brought by Hadhrami entrepreneurs financed education and agriculture. In the years since I left Aden returning immigrants prospered in Aden's business and government.

In June the courier missed a flight so I again carried the pouch to Khartoum and Asmara.

Due to the usual end of the fiscal year budget shortfall we had to do all of our packing. My orders stated that no funds could be spent on my transfer until after the new fiscal year began July 1. However, we were scheduled to leave July 3. At the same time my salary had reached the lofty heights of five figures—a one followed by four zeros ($10,000.)

I had run afoul of the State Department bureaucracy. We arrived in Aden under a cloud, the Consulate wired us to "expedite" our travel. We are leaving under a cloud, scurrying around with no funds for packing and travel. The problem is largely due to my own ignorance of the rules and then not knowing who to ask and what the question should be. The fact my *béte noire*, Adrian Middleton, is executive director of the Near Eastern and South Asian Affairs, is a strike against me. Our Administrator, James R. Scott, did only what he must as did our Budget & Fiscal Officer, Ted R. Barlow. They abided strictly by the letter of the rules. For shipments of excess personal effects to Aden and Benghazi, in part due to my amateurish packing, I was charged $342.72 and left on my own.

At the same time I wrote Dr. Lewis K. Woodward, Jr. Chief of the Medical Division at State to ask if Clay could get a physical examination to verify the state of his *petit mal*. I also asked that Josephine be examined for her anemia. I can find no record of answers to either requests.

I have received a nice form letter from the Honorable E. Allan Lightner, Jr. ambassador to Libya, who is, "...pleased to learn of my assignment to...Benghazi." He doesn't know me. A letter from J. H. Lennon, executive director, Bureau of African Affairs, welcomed me to that bureau. He added this: "If I can be of assistance to you in your transfer, please let me know." Had I been smarter I might have been able to solicit his, "assistance " when most needed, which was at that very moment.

Robert W. Chase, a personnel officer in Lennon's Bureau enlightened me, rather apologetically, as to why I am going to Benghazi as the second, or worse, choice. Dick Blalock had been first choice for Benghazi but declined and asked to extend a year in Ta'izz, trumping my request for Ta'izz. At the Language School in Beirut, Blalock had often, loudly proclaimed that he did not join the Foreign Service to do grubby consular work, issuing visas and stamping passports. He was only going to do, "significant," political reporting. Now in Ta'izz, Blalock, head of the Consular Section, had persuaded Harry Sizer, a Political Officer, to switch jobs and that was his rationale for staying. The rumor mill said Ta'izz was to become an Embassy, with Blalock the Political Officer. Benghazi was only a Consulate.

Chase found me, although I am a grade lower, O-5 instead of O-4 specified for Benghazi. That would have been a plus had I been smarter. I was euphoric, "fools rush in..." at the prospect of Benghazi. (Like the Curtis C-46 World War II troop carriers of Honduras' national airline I have a second, "design flaw," besides my speech impediment, which causes me to crash and burn.)

A blow of bad news came a month or so after we had left Aden and were on home leave. Robert B. Houghton, Chief of Political Career Management, wrote that he noted Wheelock's last Efficiency Report on me had not been discussed with me as recommended and contained critical comments. He advised I come to Washington to read the Report and respond. Mr. Edwin Adams, in Houghton's office, read the adverse portions to me on the telephone and agreed I could say nothing to counteract Wheelock's opinion. Is one fatal misstep is more "fatal" than another? I made another by not heeding Houghton's advice. Like the helicopter pilot in Honduras, how many "fatal" missteps does one need?

In all the gory mess of our departure from Aden there had to be one bright spot. The two and a half weeks the four of us spent in England waiting for Clay to finish the term at St. Bede's were a happy time. After the Fourth in London we rented an Austin, four door sedan and drove to Eastbourne. Clay was in good spirits, I was pleased with St. Bede's and the faculty. David and Gregory were thrilled at the prospect of going there. We stayed several nights in Alfriston, at the Star Inn, the second oldest inn extant in England. We decided to drive around England and discovered, "Bed and Breakfasts." "B & B." At a fraction of the cost of inns, for a bed in the spare room and a breakfast with the family, they are perfect for one night stays. We tried the little "tea rooms" and carried snack food to eat in the "Lay-Bys," rest stops on the main roads. We headed west through Devon and Cornwall while David assured us Nelson's *HMS Victory* was in Plymouth. When we got there I asked the first "Bobby" I saw how to get to the *Victory*. He said, "Turn around, go to the bottom of the hill, turn east and go 200 miles, it's in Portsmouth."

Instead, we decided to go by way of Scotland, up the west coast, down the east coast. We turned north through the Dartmoor moors, across the River Severn, through Somerset, Wiltshire, Cardiff, into Wales. Through the Cambrian Mountains we headed straight to Chester, bypassing Liverpool and Manchester. From Lancashire we entered Westmorland, the Lake District, and Lake Windemere in particular. Cumberland and Carlisle, the Solway Firth, were the gateway to Hadrian's Wall. If we had let him, David would have walked the entire length of the Wall. We couldn't decide whether to go west to Glasgow or east to Edinburgh so we spent our first night in Scotland at a memorable B & B, a working potato farm in Sterling. David and Gregory shared a huge double bed with snow-white comforters, spreads, and pillows. We were aghast when our hostess brought the boys cups of hot chocolate. They did not spill a single drop.

In the Grampians we skirted Ben Nevis and skidded to a stop at Loch Ness. We stayed long enough for David to say he "thought" he saw "something." Was it the monster we asked, or Nelson's *Victory?*

We came out at the top of Scotland at Tongue and went east to John O'Groats. This was mid July and it had been cold and rainy but here at our northern most point, almost 59 degrees north latitude, about 47 degrees north of Aden, we had beautiful, sunny warm weather. The fields were full of brightly colored tents, a boy and a girl to each tent. David and Gregory thought they were Boy and Girl Scouts and maybe they were. We headed down the east coast.

The "Tattoo" in Edinburgh, the Castle and Princess Street were worth seeing. We passed through Peeples, the home of George Kyd, our banker in Aden. We zipped through Yorkshire and Lincoln. Cambridge and Stratford-on-Avon were places we had to see and we did.

At Oxford we hit our second memorable B & B. It was already dark when I spotted a B&B sign off on a narrow dirt road. We were getting anxious so turned in. The house was a 350-year-old farmhouse whose most notable occupant was a huge boxer dog, and for it and David it was love at first sight. We met other farm animals, including a sow with her 99 piglets. David would have stayed if we had let him.

At Kent we by-passed London and stopped at Hastings. Finally, at last, to David's great relief and pleasure we got to Nelson's *Victory*. It is a beautiful ship. Next stop Eastbourne to pick up Clay.

On July 23 we boarded the *SS United States* and the crossing was an enjoyable continuation of our holiday. This ship was new and faster than the old *America*. In compensation the staterooms were not as spacious nor as opulent and the service not nearly so sophisticated.

In Beirut, I had fanned the air, strike one. The call on Aden was still out but left much to be desired, thanks to AID The State Department gave me the benefit of the doubt, or so said Robert Chase, who was thereby off the hook. Benghazi had all the earmarks of an important and decisive post. Living in the Foreign Service is akin to riding a wild tiger. Once you get on, you can't get off.

9

Benghazi

Four of us, Josephine, David, Gregory and I, flew out of Aden on July 3, 1964; Clayton was finishing the term at St. Bede's in Eastbourne. We left almost as we had arrived, but not in the air conditioned luxury of a BOAC *Comet*. We now flew in a Canadian *North Star* seated facing the rear. Flying backward, gooney-bird style, like looking backward at your life, may not always be bad, you know what you see, like it or not. Our odd departure date avoided a redundancy of the farewells we had enjoyed the past weeks in the raucous social life in the Crown Colony. The biggest shock in London was the forty-degree temperature drop from Aden's 100 degrees Fahrenheit, with humidity to match. In England's dry windy sixty degrees we shivered.

On our second day we did rouse ourselves to attend the Fourth celebration in the Embassy garden and that was exciting. The two political officers responsible for reporting on North Africa, had asked me to visit them and were very gracious. David Dunlap Newsom was senior and both he and Hermann Frederick Eilts were to come to Libya a year or so later as ambassador and deputy chief of mission respectively. In the years to come, both attained high rank and each had important departmental and ambassadorial posts. Had I been more astute and attached myself to the coattail of one or the other, my tale might have had a different outcome. That is the gooney bird talking.

Our driving tour of England and Scotland and the crossing on the SS *United States*, have been described. After the required Departmental consultations and visits in Washington we spent most of August in Tampa with my parents. Then I would go to Benghazi and get started. Josephine and Gregory would join me after settling Clayton and David in at St. Bede's.

Both of us were fortunate in having good late summer flying weather. I flew from London on Libya's gold-plated airline over a welcoming, bright blue Mediterranean on September 2, 1964. Libya advertises its airline as "24 carat gold." The comely Tunisian stewardesses distributed the usual immigration forms and currency declarations and then disappeared, their work done.

Entry formalities tell much about a country. The more demanding and inquisitive the immigration card, the more onerous the politics and intrusive the police, including the hordes of "secret," police. Convoluted currency declarations proclaim a poor, over-regulated economy. Libya has begun to produce oil, but the extent of its reserves is unknown and large amounts of income from oil are still in the pipeline, so to speak. After a dozen years in a subsistence economy exporting esparto grass for paper and wreckage from World War II, the Libyans did not know how to spend money. Nominal independence, for those years ruled by an elderly, parsimonious king, had barely introduced Libya into the mid twentieth century.

The flight, which at first I had hoped would never end, now seemed to be rushing precipitously forward. Seated on the starboard side of the plane I had a clear view of the Libyan coast as we headed due east over the Gulf of Sidra (Sirte) to make a long, straight descent over Benghazi to the International Airport at Benina, twenty-two miles farther east. Still over water, peering south over my right shoulder, I could see where storms beginning with the dry, cold squalls of the French mistrals, had swept across fifteen hundred miles of open water to eat away at the Sirtic Desert. For thousands of years the sea had splashed ever deeper towards the black heart of Africa. This Sirtic Desert divides the Arab World and Libya in two halves; the east, *Mashreq,* with its oriental influence, and the west, *Magreb,* bordering Morocco, frontier of the seventh-century Arab conquest in Africa. Turning north into Spain the Arabs were finally stopped by the "Hammer," Charles Martel, at Tours in France..

From the air, Benina, with its ominous appearing but crumbling Ottoman fort and mud brick houses, balanced on the brink of an abrupt escarpment, was a dramatic picture. Eastward was the *Jebel Akhdar*, the Green Mountain. The high plateau and vast wheat fields of the perennially fertile, but earthquake prone, Barce Plain, had been the breadbasket of the Roman Empire. The area centered around the town of Barce was recovering from an earthquake when I arrived. The biggest difference today from Roman times was the strain of two-headed wheat developed by us in the last decade's Green Revolution in the Philippines and introduced here by us as part of our AID programs. From Benina westward, after the first precipitous drop, the coastal plain sloped down to Benghazi and the Mediterranean.

There is a consistency in history with the ancient fortress and modern airport sitting side by side. The Turks built the fort with rough chiseled stone four hundred years ago atop the smooth fitted stones of a first century A.D. Roman citadel. The Romans in turn had adopted the site of an outpost built a thousand years earlier for defense against the earliest Libyans. Twenty five centuries after its first known use the Italians built their airport there because the site was as strategic as ever and pragmatically because it was beyond the range of British naval guns.

The coastal plain and the high plateau with their heavy loam topsoil, the rich reddish brown color of dried blood, gave the land its sanguinary name, Barca al Hamra, Red Cyrenaica.

A battlefield since before recorded history it was reputed to be the Land Of Ulysses' Lotus Eaters. I remember well the great battles of World War II when armadas of German and British tanks swept back and forth across this desert like ships at sea. My generation thrilled at the brilliant tactics of the Desert Fox, Erwin Rommel. Outnumbered but not out-maneuvered, he routed the combined forces of the British Empire. Even Winston Churchill acknowledged that beyond the havoc of battle, Rommel was a great soldier. For over twenty years in books and stories I have fought the World War II desert war many times over and have walked on its battlefields. As the plane circled in approach I stared at the ground hoping to see a battle scared relic of such a long, sanguinary history. No such luck, only the harsh and unforgiving land, as bitter and silent as its people, survived.

The airport terminal building, trim and modern in design was drab and stark with a tired, frayed look. For years it had been blasted by *ghiblis,* the vicious sandstorms of the Sahara that race down the slopes of the high Tibesti Mountains of Chad. Gathering momentum, they charge across eight hundred miles of open desert to grind at whatever lies in their path. Inside the terminal the sands of those storms long past still lay un-swept in corners and grated underfoot.

Customs and Immigration were unreachable with knots of gesticulating, shouting men pushing up to small barred windows. Fortunately, I was spared that by Yusef Najjar, the consulate's "expediter," a knowledgeable local employee who did the necessary pushing and shoving. In the hurly-burly confusion of the main waiting room most of the men wore Western style dress, but very few neckties.

Stern-faced older men, attended by equally stern-faced sons and black-shrouded wives, wore the graceful, traditional Libyan dress. A hand-woven white woolen blanket with a geometric design, was draped in classical Roman toga style over one shoulder. Under that were a short jacket, an embroidered gabardine vest, a cotton shirt and full length, voluminous pantaloons. These were the horsemen and camel drivers of the Western desert, the *Magreb,* descendents of the indigenous Berbers and waves of fierce Arabs, the Beni Hilal and Beni Saqar who came in the ninth century, the last migration from Arabia. These tribes had ended urban life in North Africa and the *Magreb* for a thousand years. They were proud men, descendents of the Arab warriors who would conquer Spain and threaten Europe. At the western shore their General, 'Amr ibn Al'As, hurled his sword into the ocean and exclaimed, "If I knew there were lands beyond this sea I would conquer them as well!" The hubbub around these taciturn, dour men, even the airport itself, a necessary evil, were disdained in the vivid memory of their warrior heritage.

The sloping coastal plain seemed empty but it was not. To the right, north side, of the highway to Benghazi was the mythical site of the Garden of the Hesperides, the beautiful female guardians of the golden apples, one of which was given to Hera on her marriage to Zeus. The Garden, first described in the fourth century B.C., was also the location of the underground River of Lethe (Oblivion). The souls of the dead drank this water and forgot their past lives.

Although I could barely see it in the gathering dusk there are underground rivers in this area which have broken the surface causing holes or long, narrow cavities. The largest, called, *Jokh al-Kebir*, is a quarter of a mile long and thirty-five feet deep. With the plentiful underground water these spots are verdant and rich in wildlife but by of lack of interest by modern Libyans they have become overgrown and unkempt. Libyans take no cue from the ancient. Cadets of the twentieth century A.D. at the Libyan Royal Military Academy barely a mile away see no symbolism in golden apples and the lovely Hesperides. Their memories are of hard-riding desert raiders always on the move, never looking back.

From the airport I was driven to the Principal Officer's residence, a large, fully furnished house in the older suburb of Fueihat, four miles from the center of town. The streets were narrow canyons between high, stone walls stained blood red by rain-splattered mud, surrounding residences. Beginning at the harbor and nearby municipal buildings the city comprises a series of half circle, principal concentric Circular Roads on the east, to the west is the sea. The outermost "ring" road featured block houses spaced with overlapping fields of fire. With machine guns and searchlights, Mussolini's beleaguered Italian settlers and soldiers tried to keep marauding Libyan tribesmen on horseback in the night dark at bay.

My predecessor, Andrew L. Steigman, had left enough groceries to last a short while. The house, in local jargon a villa, was being painted on the inside in a surprise month-long project. The painters made me glad Josephine and the boys would miss their efforts.

All in all, I was quite happy and felt as I had almost exactly eight years ago on my arrival in San Pedro Sula. Then I was a raw Vice Consul at my first post in an unknown town. Here I was, a raw Principal Officer at my own consulate, in a major city. To myself I said as I had on that earlier occasion, "I am the American Consul, better that than the King of England." Alas, here I was to learn that a consul is no smarter than a vice consul, I have been both and know.

Plus groceries, Steigman had left me a fully functional Consulate. The Deputy Principal Officer, a Vice Consul, responsible for consular work was a bright young Ivy Leaguer, G. Henry M. Schuler, accompanied by wife Nancy. They had a villa, one of several occupied by Consulate staff, smaller but newer and more modern than mine in Belawn Farms, a housing area without the traditional high, enclosing walls. The Schulers had arrived in December 1962 and Henry had done astute political reporting. Ambassador Lightner specifically requested he continue reporting and Henry was preparing a comprehensive biographic and analytical register of the major political players in Cyrenaica.

Henry and I were competitors in the worst sense of the word, a fatal distraction. I too, wanted to do political reporting. In an underhanded move, when Henry completed his biographic study he mailed it to the Department and the Embassy on a day I was away. He properly signed it as reporting officer but then signed it as approving officer which he was not. That was my duty as Principal Officer. He made me look incompetent and widened the breach between us. He didn't care how it looked and it did nothing to save his career, which ended after Benghazi.

Not to duplicate Henry's work I wrote a report over the next six months on the members of the royal family who were active in the government. Whether or not my report contributed much to our understanding of Libya is not recorded. In any case the royal family was consigned to oblivion along with my report on it by Mo'ammar Qaddafi's September 1969 coup d'état.

We did have a real political officer, our resident "spook," from the other agency, a tall, gangly redhead, Paul Jones. Although attached to the Embassy he actually had a vice consul's commission empowering him to sign visas if need be. He had an American secretary and an American communications clerk with his own radio transmitters and receivers, both from the Agency. I was not privy to his reports either in or out.

The "Spook," his wife, and their three red headed children, lived in Belawn Farms, in practical terms an exclusive British and American enclave especially the military contingents. All of our Army personnel, assigned to the fifty man U.S. Military Assistance Advisory Group (M.A.A.G.), headed by Colonel Hannah lived there. Personnel with families took separate houses while small groups of single officers or noncoms banded together and rented a house.

The British Military Mission to Libya, (B.M.M.) headed by Brigadier E.S. (Ted) Lough, M.B.E. performed a similar role to our

Group and both were accredited to the Libyan Army, including the Royal Academy. Brigadier Lough was a battle tested and decorated survivor of World War II. He was also a fine raconteur with a stock of apocryphal stories about King George VI, referred to and pronounced as, KG6, "Kay Gee Six." I can easily sympathize with "KG6" because I too have a stutter.

The British had been here since 1943 and were well-established along with a battalion and other parts of an active duty regiment based in the renamed Wavell Barracks and the Duke D'Aosta's Barracks, both former Italian Army compounds. Stationed here when I arrived was a battalion of the KOSB I had been with in Aden.[23] They were relieved by the 1st Battalion of the Fifth Royal Inniskilling Dragoon Guards, the "Skins."

Gregarious Paul Jones and I met frequently and he was convivial, more so than Henry. That did not mean he was on my side. His usual greeting was, "What does it all mean?" Paul considered himself an outdoorsman and hunter and had an arsenal of sporting rifles and shotguns to prove it. He desperately wanted to hunt gazelle but by this time the gazelles which had survived the guns of foreign workers had been driven east and south into inaccessible areas. However, pigeons were plentiful in the large sinkholes, the underground rivers, and east of Benghazi. Later on, he, myself and others, usually from the M.A.A.G force, would place ourselves around the perimeter of one of the circular pigeon holes often facing one another and bang away with shotguns at the birds entering or leaving, hitting them high enough to not fall into the hole. I had an old, family twelve-gauge, double-barreled Remington which killed pigeons as well as Paul's modern guns. Josephine was very adept at cleaning our bag and roasting them there over an open fire while the other ladies watched. Some of the hunters were careless, firing too early or too late, aiming low as I learned from the crackle of shotgun pellets landing on the hard ground around me. Paul was chief among the careless types although he denied he was seriously trying to kill me.

George R. McCurry, the administrative officer, accompanied by his wife and children also had a villa in Belawn Farms. George was the quiet, efficient type but had bad luck with his wives. He had been married and divorced before coming to Benghazi. The wife

I knew there was a beautiful young Swiss woman who at his next post ran off with a handsome young ski instructor.

My American secretary was the conscientious and attractive Harriet Lovett, close to my age. She said her job was to make me look good and she succeeded most of the time, but not at the end.

We had an American Communication Clerks and File Clerk, a married couple, the Fons, who soon were transferred and replaced. Harriet later married our then new Communications Officer, Victor Maffei. I saw them, in the department in the 1980s. They were still happily married and had two daughters.

Our local staffs, especially drivers, receptionists, and maintenance technicians, were mostly Libyan but we had some Scottish and German third country nationals. All were satisfactory. One Libyan I caught red handed stealing money exceeded the limits and I fired him on the spot.

Libya's emergence into the modern age came between 1911 and 1914 with the ill-fated Italian dream of creating an Empire emulating the British and French colonies in Africa. Italy tried to drive out the last of the Ottomans. World War I finished the Ottomans but the rest was a nightmare for Italians and Libyans. The Italians hung on in Libya by the skin of their teeth until Mussolini came to power in 1928.

Mussolini re-energized Italy's efforts to create a Fascist Italian Empire. Wheat farms on the Barce Plain and banana plantations, pomegranate groves, and lush gardens along the coast, with sturdy, furnished houses, were ready-made oases prepared to be occupied by Italian settlers. The towns were trim, hygienic and attractive with ordered rows of white cottages, city halls, churches with huge brass bells inscribed with the town name and municipal sewage plants. Hospitals set in the midst of gardens and towns had working fountains. Concrete houses were in one of a ponderous modern style as was the mahogany, Fascist furniture. Outside walls were decorated with Mussolini's slogans, *Credere Obbedire Combatire* (to believe to obey to fight). Estimates on the high side number the Italian settlers at 150,000.

The fascists practiced genocide. As fast as they could round them up, not an easy task given the vastness and harshness of the terrain, Libyans were herded into desert camps at Mersa Brega and left to starve. In suicidal guerilla warfare the Libyans fought back. They drove the Italians into fortified villages and towns, limited Italian travel to armed convoys, but the Libyans could not win. The fascists executed guerrillas by dropping them out of airplanes over their home villages.

The most notable victim was Omar Al-Mukhtar, a school-teacher who had become a successful, beloved, guerilla fighter. He was dropped from a high-flying Italian bomber over Soluq, on the coastal plain before the escarpment, fifty miles southeast of Benghazi. There are monuments and annual celebrations in his honor. In a bit of bureaucratic ignorance, when the Peace Corps came, the Volunteer assigned to Soluq was an Italian-American. I killed that assignment before the Libyans killed the boy.

Soluq had a mountain top fort, similar to Benina dating from prehistoric times with Roman, Ottoman and Italian overlays in descending quality. An adjacent *wadi*, or watercourse, also had commensurate low *barrages* (dams) to slow and sometimes store water. I learned that the oldest, and best, was Roman. The newest, a haphazard string of boulders, was the work of American AID. In the heyday of our foreign aid programs we spent $129,000,000 in Libya.

At least our wheat was worthwhile. Libyans are unenthusiastic farmers and traditionally had planted oats or barley which their animals and they themselves, would eat, not wheat which the animals would not eat. Now the government ordered the farmers to plant a high percentage of wheat.

Had not World War II happened when it did, every Libyan in Cyrenaica, the southern province of Fezzan and the few die-hard Libyans in Tripolitania would have been annihilated. Even the Berbers were not safe from the Italians. The entry of the First Battalion of the Gordon Highlanders into Tripoli in January 1943 ended Italian authority in Libya. The British Eighth Army led by General Montgomery, that had chased the Germans and Italians from Egypt to Tunisia fought onward. On May 11 the New Zealand division and the 90th Light Division of the Afrika Korps, both elite units, broke off contact. On May 12, 1943, all organized enemy resistance in Africa ceased. General von Arnim surrendered for all Axis forces in Africa. General Hans Johann Cramer surrendered the Afrika Korps.

The British loaded the thousands of living remnants of the Italian settlers, farmers and artisans, still in Libya on hospital ships and returned them to Italy. The vengeful and angry Libyans continued to order the bodies of buried Italians exhumed and shipped back to Italy as late as the 1970's.

Postwar, the United Nations exercised political authority through Commissioner Adrian Pelt. Libya was "granted" independence on December 24, 1951, the first nation recognized under U. N. auspices.

I often wonder if it was a fortuitous happenstance or blind bureaucracy that Libyan Independence Day was Christmas Eve. Christmas Eve means nothing to Libyans, for some it may be gross blasphemy. For the Christians it was welcome to see towns and cities lighted and alive with celebrations. Government buildings were outlined with strings of lights. In the 1960s Christians were accepted in Benghazi, where a double-domed Roman Catholic cathedral dominated the skyline, especially from the sea. American sailors dubbed it, "Mae West." Catholic priests and nuns were in attendance. Enough Greek Orthodox communicants lived here to support a Church and there was a Synagogue. Christians tended to keep Christmas in house with no public displays of Santa Claus, Christmas trees or Nativity scenes. To be safe Christians privately associated the Independence Day lights and decorations with Christmas.

Mohamad Idris Al-Maadi Al-Sennusi was named King Idris under the 1951 Federal Constitution of the United Kingdom of Libya, modeled on our Constitution. Libya was composed of the provinces of Tripolitania, Cyrenaica and the Fezzan. Not surprising, the first Justices of the Supreme Court were Americans. A year earlier, the British had recognized Idris as the Emir of Cyrenaica, which Britain unilaterally declared independent. His authority as king was carried over all of Libya in December by the United Nations. Tripoli was furious at having had no voice in the selection of their king. A month after I arrived in 1964, the word "United" was dropped and the name became the Kingdom of Libya.

***

The recorded history of Libya extends back over thousands of years and the Libyans with whom I lived and worked had commensurately long memories. That was plain to see but not understood by me on arrival at the airport. Cyrenaicans are more culturally Arabized than any Arab group not excepting the Tamim and Quraish of Mecca and Medina in Saudi Arabia. In phonetic and grammatical essentials their language is the closest to that of the ninth century, Beni Hilal. In Cyrenaica no language competed with Arabic, no religion competed with Sunni Islam and no custom with Arab custom. Even the fractious Berbers had been Arabized.

Cyrenaica and the Fezzan are linked to the classical Arab world of the east, the *Mashreq*. Tripolitania, Tunis, Algeria, Morocco, are parts of the *Magreb*, the west and strongly influenced by large Jewish colonies, European contact and European immigration. Cyrenaica was first settled by Greeks and was closely linked to Egypt. In my day it still was. A Cyrenaican who wanted a wife went to Egypt, and a week or two later brought one home. My chief Libyan local assistant, Yousef Najjar, had done exactly that, and his was not an isolated case. His first wife, from Alexandria, was charming and handsome, and together they had a beautiful daughter. He went back and got a second Egyptian wife. As I was departing Benghazi Youssef told me both wives had just delivered babies within days of each other.

Cyrenaica became associated with Byzantium in the later years of the Roman Empire while Tripolitania, settled (three thousand years ago) by Phoenicians was traditionally linked with Rome and Carthage. The border had been decided in classical times by a foot race between two brothers, the Philenii, with one starting from Oea (Tripoli) and one from Bernice (Benghazi). Where they met was to be the border. The brother from Oea went much farther, Tripolitania is twice as wide, east to west, as Cyrenaica but overall smaller. When the boy from Berenice was accused of not trying he offered to be buried alive at that spot and so he was. That spot is still the border and the Italians built a tall arch there, a landmark visible for miles across the desert. British soldiers dubbed it the, "Marble Arch."

Like Mussolini's fascist Italy and empire his arch is hollow, flimsy and was crumbling when I saw it in 1964. Conversely, the desert road it stands astride, the Via Della Vittorio, is a two thousand mile link between Egypt and Tunisia, the east and the west. It is a marvel of Italian road design and construction. Stone posts mark the kilometers and stone guesthouses, with water wells are frequent. The guest houses have helpful WW II British graffiti warning of German booby traps and low level strafing by the Luftwaffe. In addition to older wells, the U.S. dug wells along the Via. For $129,000,000 in AID programs after World War II Libya got a few water wells with troughs for camels, a make shift barrage one Libyan knew was American and as a real bonanza, two headed wheat they were forced to eat.

When the Italians invaded in 1911 the Tripolitanians accepted them but the Cyrenaicans and Fezzanese fought back. Until the 1914 outbreak of World War I they were aided by the Ottomans led by Shariif, younger brother of Idris, and Mustapha Kemal, Atatürk, the future dictator and modernizer of Turkey. However, the Italians had picked the winning side. When the war dried up Ottoman aid, Shariif and Kemal were evacuated to Turkey by a German submarine while Idris went into exile in Cairo. The British in Egypt expected Cyrenaica's ferocious Sennussi tribesmen to storm out of the desert and attack.

Earlier, in the nineteenth century, the fundamentalist Sennussi religious sect took total control in Cyrenaica and the Fezzan but was rejected in Tripolitania. The tomb of the Grand Sennussi, Founder of the sect is at Al-Jaghbuub, 200 miles due south of Tobruk, close to the Egyptian border. The Sennussis built a series of religious outposts, called *zawiyas*, across the Cyrenaican desert. Part mosque, part school, they were also self-sustaining rest stops for travelers.

On one weekend foray into the desert with others interested in outlying Roman border forts, called *limes*, we came upon a *zawiya* still active. For me this was a living link to the nineteenth century. Three elderly Arab caretakers were hospitable, they gave us tea, and were surprised I recognized and knew a *zawiya*. We left them some of our supplies and money.

The 1951 Constitution stipulated in a compromise between Cyrenaica and Tripolitania that Benghazi and Tripoli were to be cocapitals. The government moved from one to the other every two years. For the king and queen the move was a lark. For the inevitably growing bureaucracy of government, even one so primitive as Libya's, by 1964, the system had become unworkable. For us, two capitals meant that embassies and other national and international organizations had to move. The consulate was an Embassy Branch Office except that when the capital was in Benghazi it became the Embassy. When I arrived the staff in Tripoli was packing, preparing to move and squeeze in. Luckily that did not happen; the Embassy stayed in Tripoli and the office in Benghazi stayed a consulate.

Britain, France, West Germany, Italy, Tunisia, Egypt and Syria, (i.e., the United Arab Republic), the Soviet Union and Greece, who also had embassies, were more phlegmatic. They settled in Tripoli and only their ambassadors traipsed back and forth across the country six times. The British ambassador drove a big Jaguar. He boasted that on the long straight stretches of the Via he could cruise at 120 miles per hour. The King had a bright idea in 1964 and decreed the establishment of an, "Administrative Capital," in Baida, in effect, a third capitol.

Baida, a small town, home of the Sennussi Islamic University of local fame, is beautifully situated at the northern tip of Cyrenaica's *Jebel Akhdar,* Green Mountain, at an altitude of almost 3,000 feet. At the same time it is inconveniently located in the middle of nowhere, halfway between bustling Benghazi and Tobruk, of World War II fame and the King's favorite residence. Adjacent to Baida are the extensive ruins of the eighth-century B.C. Greek city of Cyrene, hometown of Simon, the man who helped Jesus carry the Cross to Calvary. The village of Shahat actually sits amidst the ruins of Cyrene. In 1964, when I arrived, Benghazi had been designated a consulate and an Embassy Branch Office was opened in Baida.

The Embassy Branch Office comprised several separate buildings. In one there was an office suite for the ambassador and his staff and an office for the permanent officer-in-charge. The Italians had spent time and money exploring the ruins of Cyrene, and the director of antiquities had a spacious house which the United States used for many years as an ambassadorial summer retreat. Two residences served the officer-in-charge and a staff member. Comfortable smaller apartments housed guests and temporary embassy staff.

***

Hume Alexander Horan was the first officer-in-charge in Baida. Fresh out of Harvard in 1960, Horan joined the Foreign Service and opted for the "sand dune circuit" when he requested Baghdad. duty in Iraq, then under the bloody, dictatorial but inept and doomed rule of Abdul Qarim Kassem, it was either a challenge or a warning. Hume survived and took a Master's degree in Middle Eastern Studies from Harvard. With his lovely, charming wife Nancy and son Alexander, Horan had some trepidations about his posting to Baida but intuitively saw its unique potential. The call of the desert and the Arab world was irresistible. Horan, also unique, was happily on his way to stardom in the Foreign Service.

Horan was born, August 13, 1934, in Washington to a prominent American mother and a future Iranian foreign minister, Abdollah Entezam. His parents divorced when he was three, and his mother married Harold Horan, a *Time* magazine foreign correspondent. Hume was favorably influenced by formative years with his family in Buenos Aires. From 1954 to 1956 he served in the U.S. Army. Alexander served as a tank commander during the 1991 Gulf War.

Hume had a good ear for languages and early on became proficient in English, Spanish, and French. He began Arabic training at the FSI Language School in Beirut, arriving in 1962, after I left. In addition to the Levantine dialect the school taught, he mastered the Egyptian, Libyan, and Saudi dialects. The Libyan dialect is said to be close to the classical, and he learned it well. With his facility in languages he became the standard by which graduates of the school could be measured and the envy of us all.

He enjoyed Baida and became well known at the Islamic University as he translated Arabic texts into English. In 1964 and 1965 he and I worked back and forth between Baida and Benghazi. State toyed with the idea of again renaming Benghazi and naming me Senior American Representative for Cyrenaica. Benghazi stayed a consulate and I stayed a consul.

After Baida Hume returned to the State Department as Libyan "desk officer" and was the point man in 1969 when Mo'ammar Gaddafi ousted King Idris. Hume, destined for glory, raced ahead winning the most prestigious State Department awards. He moved to Capitol Hill as aide to Senator Edmund Muskie, later a powerful secretary of state and a helpful friend. Next he was posted to Jordan after which in a big leap upward in 1972 he served for a long five years as number two, deputy chief of mission, in Saudi Arabia. His command, not only of the Arabic idiom but also Arab history, classics and philosophy and his personal charisma gave him *entrée* into the convoluted, rigid levels of Saudi society.

As number two for five years he could be more informal as ambassadors came and went. He moved easily through the complex, paranoid Saudi hierarchy, especially the vastly extended royal family, with an estimated 10,000 royal princes. Perhaps blinded by his own brilliance some of Horan's "friends" may have led him to be innocently culpable in the machinations of discontented Saudi royals. Returning to the department in 1977 he was named a deputy assistant secretary of state. In a change of scenery he was moved to the African Bureau in 1980, as ambassador to Cameroon and Equatorial Guinea. He was, he said, "knighted." An ominous sign, it was to a dingy corner of the big, black continent. Did anyone ask:

"Just where is Yaoundé, Mr. Horan?"

A first post of your own, even in an obscure corner of Africa is a first step up; Horan was unstoppable. With cynical irony Yaoundé was named "Post of the Month" if not the year. In a new twist Ambassador Horan was pictured on the cover of the February 1983 *State Department Newsletter* as he stood beside a pygmy headhunter. One cannot but wonder what went through the minds of two such different men. The quintessential Harvard intellectual preppy in button-down shirt, smiled. The pygmy chief in cast-off shirt grasping bow and poisoned arrow with both hands was unsmiling.

In an area so remote from the familiar Near East Bureau, Hume, as always, was outstanding. For a reward he was given the embassy in turbulent Khartoum. Exercising great ingenuity, he helped reestablish Sudanese national stability amidst terrorist attacks, rescued and removed to Israel a beleaguered Jewish sect, and survived a bloody army coup d'état. In a final step up he was named ambassador to Saudi Arabia, the most important post in 1987 on the "sand dune circuit."

Alas, after a glorious few months, disaster followed disaster. His tour and his career were dramatically shot down in flames when

King Fahd declared him *persona non grata* and demanded his recall. Rumors abounded, but the king did not need to give a reason. It was popularly believed that the king was angered when Ambassador Horan, as ordered by President Reagan, "stiffly" protested the Kingdom's secret purchase of ballistic missiles from China. Horan protested he not be ordered to give the king a verbal rebuke. The king, he said, could not but be outraged. Ordered again to make the protest, he did so with the predicted blow to Hume himself and American-Saudi relations. Adding insult to injury he was stabbed in the back when, unbeknownst to him, the department delivered a much less incendiary message via the Saudi ambassador to the United States, Prince Bandar, a royal favorite. It was rumored that one of Horan's "friends" was a perceived enemy of the king. To the *Washington Post* Hume only said, "My goose was cooked." Heaping insult on insult, Secretary of State George P. Shultz ordered him to "personally" present the request to the king for approval of his successor, the ultimate humiliation. Horan was then ignominiously ordered home.

Under a black cloud and off the "sand dune circuit," Hume was exiled as ambassador, again in black Africa, this time to Côte d'Ivoire. Now the headhunters were in Washington, and he stood alone. After marking time, "walking the halls," as the expression goes, he retired in 1998.

In 2003 the "circuit" needed Hume's expertise, and he was sent to Baghdad. Designated senior counselor at the abortive Coalition Provisional Authority headed by L. Paul Bremer III, he was the resident expert on Iraq. No one was more qualified or could contribute so much to trying to understand Iraq and our tenuous pseudo success there.

As vigorous physically as he was mentally, he had crewed at Harvard and, in his free time, bicycled through France, New Zealand, and, finally, the United States. He published a fictionalized but revealing Foreign Service–based novel, *To the Happy Few*, in 1996, set in the Sudan. Keeping up his Arabic he translated Arabic novels and stories into English and wrote poetry in Arabic. His professional articles emphasized the importance of the Foreign Service. He described the Foreign Service in a *Washington Post*, article as "the infantry of American diplomacy.... Someone has to be on the scene, speak the language, know the leaders, make our arguments, report back … and say what we should do."

He and Nancy seemed an ideal Foreign Service couple, well adjusted, a pleasure to know and to be around. Rearing three children in our uncertain, dangerous, and nomadic life is not easy, as Josephine and I know from experience with our three. The Horans' later divorce was a surprise, and I cannot even speculate on the reasons.

His second wife, the beautiful high achiever Lori Shoemaker, was a Foreign Service officer with an exceptionally fine career record. A mutual friend of Hume's told me that Lori and Hume believed that together they would have superior children. Hume married Lori and together they had two children, whether superior or not I do not know.

Hume died July 22, 2004, at 69, of prostate cancer. Young by today's standards, a victim of the inadequate Foreign Service medical care we live and often die by, he was also a victim of bureaucratic intrigue and mismanagement. Not quickly forgotten, or to make amends, parts of nine pages in the *Foreign Service Journal*, issues for September and October 2004, extol Hume's life and career with accolades and testimonials from colleagues young and old, great and small.

From 1964 when he came to Baida, for a quarter century until 1988 when King Fahd declared him an unacceptable person, Hume Horan was a bright comet in the Foreign Service sky. There was something Victorian about him in his casual versatility. Not really handsome but distinctive, he was strongly built and athletic, with an effervescent combination of mental and physical prowess.

His story feels like a Greek tragedy, the hero doomed by his flawed brilliance. A role model for Foreign Service officers, I wish I had learned better. He must have made a mistake in Saudi, perhaps, revealing his superior intellect. A pernicious rumor said he had corrected someone's Arabic; the king's, perhaps? *The Middle East Quarterly* called him "the most accomplished Arabic linguist to serve in the U.S. Foreign Service." In no way abrasive, a word once used to describe me, I know no one who knew him who did not like or admire Hume. Was he too good, and set the bar too high even for himself?

***

Josephine and Gregory arrived in mid-September and quickly adjusted to Benghazi. Our personal car, a 1962 four door Chevrolet Corvair arrived from Aden about the same time but much the worse for its long sea voyage. Accessories such as the radio, air conditioning and windshield wipers were history. There was a General Motors garage in town but the manager and only employee was an Alexandrian Greek. The Greek colony in Cyrenaica was smaller and less competent than the mother lode in Alexandria.

In the Arab World many so-called experts are Alexandrian Greeks. The man in Benghazi tried hard but with little training was left to his own devices. The big loser was General Motors and the U.S. Gone are the days when Ford assembled cars in the huge assembly plant which I saw when we were in Egypt.

By contrast the Volkswagen garage had ten Germans and operated like a tank repair patrol of the Afrika Korps. Veterans of Rommel's army had returned to Cyrenaica, often in skilled trades and were very competent. The French Peugeot garage was similarly well staffed. Big-bodied Peugeot station wagons originating from Francophone Algeria and Tunisia were the long-range jitneys, across North Africa doing the job Plymouths did in the Levant and the 1937 Buicks did in Egypt. The small diesel Mercedes-Benz sedans dominated the Near East taxi market and high end model Mercedes were gaining prestige. They had excellent sales and repair facilities.

Except for the Land Rovers brought in by the British military, British vehicles were poorly represented. The American carmakers were stubbornly uninterested in these markets. The State Department 1950's experiment to use Nash Ramblers without any infrastructure to back them up had been a disaster. We had a junkyard of Ramblers parked alongside the consulate. Between Benghazi and Tripoli we managed to keep a Chevrolet running often by our own know-how. Wheelus, the U.S. Air Force base near Tripoli, was helpful to the embassy but for us in Benghazi it was 650 miles away.

At the end of October we moved to an apartment directly behind the consulate, a three or four minute walk, infinitely more convenient than Fueihat. Except for a large entry foyer and storage on the ground floor the apartment was all on the second and third floors. With sitting, drawing and dining rooms, bedrooms and a big kitchen on the second floor and a huge rooftop terrace on the third floor outside an apartment, used for guests, entertaining was simplified. A small sandy yard at the back gave Gregory a play area, a place for his pet usually a feral, "pi" dog puppy, or a rabbit. There was a small triangular city park with tall eucalyptus trees and shrubbery at the front entrance. Originally built for the Cathedral nuns and as a school before the war, our ambassador had used it in the 1950's when the capital moved to Benghazi. It was also haunted by the ghost of a murdered nun.

The life of the Italians in Libya, despite Mussolini's pretentiousness was not a happy one. In Benghazi the priests, including a bishop, and nuns at the Roman Catholic Cathedral probably had had the best of it. In two years, from January 1941 to January 1943, Benghazi changed hands five times. Each change, no matter who was winning, brought destruction from artillery and aerial bombs, British and German alike. The Cathedral, by means of interior scaffolding and planks which created floors under its twin domes, had become a hospital for both sides and was spared.

The Banco di Roma building with its ornate lobby, tile fountains and polished marble columns had served as an officers' club for both sides, and survived intact. Rank has its privileges. In 1964 it was again Banco di Roma. The consulate building had been the Italian Army Engineers Officers' Club and its beautiful tile framed windows were unscathed by the war. Unscathed, that is, until my Administrative Officer, Anthony Santiano, on the strength of inadequate Departmental instructions to put iron bars on the windows over the air conditioners tore off the tile to comply. My instructions to him to, "save the tile," were equally unclear and he framed and "saved" for me one piece of tile. We had already defaced the building with a large wooden structure shrouding the columned entrance. The ugly, unnecessary ironmongery around the air conditioners were added in the name of security.

The only real security the Consulate was provided by iron grillwork on the landing of the inside staircase and the walk-in sized safe door I had proposed for the Communications and File Room suite. The efficacy of the safe door was realized during the tour of my successor when for several days it thwarted a howling mob that had come in the front door. I don't know if my successor had a chance to use the two-way radio transceiver kept in my bottom desk drawer.

From the outset the embassy had warned me to be wary of my relations with the M.A.A.G. and careful in dealing with the officer in charge, Colonel Hannah. To establish my position before doing anything I was to wait for him to make the first move and call on me. The problem was that with my arrival on September 2, Jim May, Chief of the Political Section in Tripoli, also arrived in Benghazi. He appeared at the consulate and peremptorily demanded I introduce him to the Colonel.

Jim, James A. May, was a fine officer and we had done our two years at the Language School together. He didn't care about my situation. I had been in Benghazi only hours and protested that I was in no position to introduce him to the colonel contrary to protocol. Jim insisted, so with a guide I found our way to Colonel Hannah's office. I ushered Jim in, gave the colonel his name and backed out.

M.A.A.G.'s offices were in an adjacent building connected to the consulate by a covered walkway, close but yet so far. The M.A.A.G. officers and enlisted personnel seemed exemplary and probably were carefully selected for this duty. They and their families enjoyed a different lifestyle from State employees. Their rates for *per diem* expense money were higher than ours. Most had big American made automobiles popular in the late 1950's and early 1960's. Colonel Hannah had a huge Cadillac El Dorado convertible and even though a tall man he sat on a cushion always with the top down. Coming into town, head above the windshield, he reminded me of the chariot race in the movie *Ben Hur*. His successor, Warren Phillips had a massive Chrysler Le Baron, not a convertible. All M.A.A.G. cars were air-conditioned.

M.A.A.G. personnel, through the British Military Mission, had access to the Libyan Army Armored Corps mechanical repair facilities. Their cars ran better than ours.

The embassy did not warn me that M.A.A.G.'s every wish was my command. I learned the hard way. My run in with AID in Aden should have taught me something. The arrangement in Benghazi had worked for fifteen years, what was there to know? The colonel never called, he sent his wife, Mrs. Hannah. Seated in my office she explained in words of one syllable so I could understand that she and the colonel had never worked with State Department people and could only do things the Army way.

The Hannahs were older, closer to retirement, and more experienced than I. I could have said that I had never worked with the Army. A superficial friendliness with Col. and Mrs. Warren Phillips, Col. Hannah's replacement, led me down a primrose path of self-deception. Mrs. Phillips constantly and annoyingly hovered around Josephine. Maybe that, too, is the Army way. The fact was that Josephine always had work to do, and Carol made it difficult. With the Army you only make a mistake once.

My staff meetings in 1964 were like mini, painfully purblind Country Team meetings. Usual attendees included Colonel Hannah, Army, strictly military; Michael L. Di Legge, the U.S. Information Service "know-it-all" branch public affairs officer; our ebullient resident political officer, Paul Jones, Central Intelligence Agency; Hume Horan, officer-in-charge of the Baida Branch Embassy Office, if in town; Henry Schuler upon occasion; any visiting embassy officers and other federal department officers, for example, from Commerce and Agriculture. I am embarrassed at how blind we were.

Libya, divided down the middle at the Gulf of Sirte geographically, culturally and politically between Arab East, *Mashreq*, and Arab West, *Magreb*, gave us a lot to talk about. Three years of oil exports, growing rapidly, bringing vast sums of money in Libyan terms, created havoc in the economy. Belligerent Arab nationalism exemplified by Egypt's Nasser, upset the *status quo* with political growing pains. King Idris, the First, and the last had five years to go and already students from the Royal Military Academy on the banks of the River of Lethe, forgetfulness, were plotting his end.

In Libya as in most of the Arab world, the word "royal" was anathema to the army and, therefore, to the people. One young Libyan lieutenant, soon to be a Captain, Mo'ammar Gaddafi, was at the Royal Armored School in England. The most critical memory he took from England was not army lore but the sight of Libyan bureaucrats throwing away thousands of pounds sterling of Libya's oil revenues in gambling casinos. As Gaddafi stalked down Piccadilly Road in traditional Libyan dress he seethed with anger and his coup d'état of September 1, 1969 was conceived. On that long planned day Idris was in Egypt and never returned to Libya. Without the King to die for, his personal army, CyDef, Cyrenaican Defense Force, after a desultory resistance joined Gaddafi's coup inspired Army forces.

If Gaddafi had come in for an American visa we might have gotten a clue to the future but he didn't. Even without that, on the colonnaded sidewalk adjacent to my apartment building along a main thoroughfare, cafes with outside tables were frequented by many Army officers. I made it a practice to linger there over coffee and engage them in conversation. They knew who I was and most of them were gregarious, friendly and delighted in teasing me. If this had been Honduras with its many coups, they would have requested visas to the U.S. as an escape hatch. I was blinded by the strong public feeling that the monarchy and status quo were safe while Idris lived. My Libyan Army acquaintances gaily pandered to my myopia. Even the British Military Mission (B.M.M.) with whom I had close contact, as did our M.A.A.G., and who provided key instructors to the Academy, seemed to believe as I did. For example:

Question: Who do you think, newly returned from training in England, was adjutant of the Libyan Army Signal Corps, with his fingers on all Army communications?

Answer: An angry Mo'ammar Gaddafi, scion of the Bani Hillal and Berbers, with five years to plan and prepare. He and his Revolutionary Command Council (RCC) staged a perfect coup d'état.

With five years to go my myopia continued after a newly arrived British officer, Major Tom Todd, whom I had known in Aden, joined the B.M.M. to instruct at the academy. Tom was a charismatic, likeable fellow with a beautiful baritone singing voice who would frequently break out in the "Star Spangled Banner." He sung it in a traditional manner, the way I think it should be sung.

Tom had worked with Arabs in Jordan and Aden for years and knew all the Arabic cuss words. On his first day at the Academy while getting acquainted, in an offhand remark he referred to Israel in unacceptable terms. In an explosive demonstration of Arab nationalism in the Libyan Army, the cadets and Libyan faculty protested violently and demanded his removal. Tom remained in Benghazi a short while awaiting reassignment but never returned to the Academy. The rest of us failed to see the handwriting on the wall spotlighted by Tom's bombshell. In Libya all reference to Israel was strictly forbidden.

At this time Libya had two armies. The Libyan Army was head-quartered in Tripoli but King Idris, still mindful of his days as king of Cyrenaica, had his private army, the Cyrenaican Defense Force, CyDef, headquartered in Tobruk. This is not uncommon in the Arab world. King Hussein of Jordan had his *bedu* tribal Arab Legion, and Faisal of Saudi Arabia his Wahhabi National Guard. The rival Libyan Army, always poor mouthing, complained that CyDef was better financed and equipped. The Army's Armored Corps, six British Centurion tanks, was based in Benghazi and therefore vulnerable to a CyDef attack. (According to the B.M.M., it was a good day when they could get one tank running.)

Meanwhile, first moving in at Fueihat and then a month or two later moving into town has kept Josephine on the go. At the same time she was busy selling UNICEF Christmas cards, out in the rain, on a busy street corner. Instructions from the embassy were unequivocal. The department leaned on them and they leaned on us. We were emphasizing all United Nations activities not just because of Libya's historical connection to the UN but world-wide. Living in town, Josephine had to chauffeur Gregory to and from school in Fueihat and with his tonsils acting up, to the doctor, at the Seventh Day Adventist Hospital. With our three boys we always kept good relations with the Adventists because they worked on Sunday. Years later in the States Adventist doctors and dentists were life savers.

Colonel Hannah, within days of departure, was focused on his next post and approaching retirement. His successor, Lt. Colonel Warren Phillips, had long been his deputy and at this time had been or soon would be promoted to full ("bird") colonel. He was one of our pigeon hunters who loved to accidentally, of course, spray me with buckshot. We celebrated his promotion with pigeons I had killed placed on each shoulder. For ambitious lieutenant colonels any "bird" will do.

On the day at the end of 1964 Colonel and Mrs. Hannah departed I was not informed until after they had left for the airport. I grabbed Josephine and with our Libyan driver at the wheel made it on to the airport tarmac as the last passengers were boarding the Misrair plane. We bounded up the rickety boarding steps and while I sought him and Mrs. Hannah, Josephine stayed at the door, one foot inside the plane, the other on the boarding ladder. I found the Hannahs and launched into my farewell speech. I kept talking longer than I thought. Finally the plane captain came back and asked if I would leave and take my wife out of the door so he could take off. I did and he did.

We saw the Hannahs years later in Washington after he had retired. They kindly took us to dinner at Ft. Belvoir, but it was an empty gesture, none of us could think of anything polite to say.

November 1964 was a busy month for public appearances. On the eighth I laid a wreath at the British War Cemetery. This is a pretty place and much smaller than their huge cemetery in El Alamein. The British regiment was turned out in full regalia. The Colonel was very sentimental about the "Last Post," the British equivalent to "Taps." Our M.A.A.G. chief, Colonel Warren Phillips, also laid a wreath.

On the sixteenth I presented the White House Collection of books to the University of Libya's library. I have forgotten what the titles were and in which language they were printed. I doubt it was Arabic. On the twenty-second I read the lesson at the church and followed it with the president's Thanksgiving Day Proclamation. We went to the Church of England at the Wavell Barracks.

In the church, there is a pew with an "American Consul" brass plaque. It is behind the pew for "Her Britannic Majesty's Consul General." One Sunday morning a gazelle came trotting, clickety-clack, down the marble paving of the center aisle during the sermon. Fortunately, our political officer was absent or he might have shot it in order to claim he had hunted gazelle in Libya.

December was a busy social month with two formal, sit-down dinners and a birthday party for Gregory on December 14. He was seven and gregarious Gregory really enjoyed this, his first birthday party. With the children of our American employees and local employees we had eighty children.

Clayton and David flew in to Tripoli on December 17 and I drove our new consulate Chevrolet over, about 1300 miles round trip, to meet them. I spent time "consulting" with my colleagues at the Embassy which made it official business. We got home to Benghazi just before our December 20 children's party. Clay and David immediately pitched in and helped serve.

On the return from Tripoli we spent a night at our Coast Guard Loran "G" Station near Sirte, at Matratiin. The Coast Guard had hundreds of these, Long Range Aid to Navigation (LORAN), stations worldwide which provided a precise navigational grid. These stations worked in pairs, a "Master" station broadcasting a low frequency radio signal, the other, "Slave" station receiving. At the intersection of two signals crossing at angles to each other, navigators could determine their location. The Commanding Officer was Lieutenant (Junior Grade), Michael Schiro, from my home town, Tampa, where his parents ran a fruit stand. I didn't know him but he married the younger sister of a girl I had dated in high school. I think the Schiros were married in Tripoli. Later, out of the Coast Guard, he was elected mayor of Tampa.

Michael was hospitable but said they were inundated by a stream of Americans who think the Coast Guard has nothing to do but provide them a rest stop. I never spent another night there but kept going. Nearby Sirte, later to be known as Qaddafi's hometown, had a hotel. Oil company employees and contractors had access to the Esso complex at the port of Mersa Bregah, near the western most outpost of Cyrenaica. Mersa Bregah had been the site of Italian death camps for thousands of Libyans.

On December 24, Libyan Independence Day (also Christmas Eve) we hosted a large brunch, and in keeping with the ecumenical nature of life in Benghazi, on the 26th we hosted a German style Wassail Bowl. That brought us to the end of the month and of the year, December 31, 1964. That night we were premiering at our house, *Years of Lightening, Day of Drums*, the John F. Kennedy documentary movie, with refreshments afterward, for ninety people..

Ambassador E. Allan Lightner maintained close relations

with King Idris and visited him often in Tobruk. This Christmas Ambassador Lightner had his parents over for a visit and took them to meet the King. King Idris and his wife met with them and other Embassy wives, not Josephine and me.

The year 1965 started well with the Moslem month of Ramadan taking most of January. Good Moslems fast and others pretend to do so. Many Moslems take vacations at this time. After a month of daytime fasting, they celebrate the end of Ramadan with the holiday *Id al-Fitr* (Breaking the Fast), when they exchange gifts and little girls especially get bright, sparkly new dresses. I went to the Royal Diwan and made calls on the Crown Prince and signed the "book" for the King who stayed in Tobruk. I called on the Governor and Mayor of Cyrenaica and Benghazi respectively. The British garrison held a memorial service for Churchill, who had just died, and I signed the "book" at the consulate general. Air Chief Marshall Sir Charles Elworthy, now head of the RAF, who was Commander in Chief of the British Forces in Aden in our time, was one of the four Service Chiefs guarding Churchill's coffin in Westminster.

In February 1965 we made an area familiarization trip as far east as Tobruk but, of course, only the ambassador consorted with the King. In WWII, Tobruk sitting astride the main east-west route between Benghazi and Egypt held out for a crucial year in 1940-41. The Australian garrison withstood everything Rommel threw at them. British officers were in command and by the end of the siege British troops had replaced the Australians. The Australians still got most of the credit for holding Tobruk and deserved it.

A British Army chaplain we knew named Haydon Parry, who later became a Canon of the Anglican Cathedral in Cairo stayed in Tobruk throughout the siege. One Sunday the Germans penetrated the thirty-mile outer perimeter of Tobruk's defenses. Parry had completed morning services in one of the breached trenches when, still in his vestments and carrying his portable altar and religious supplies, he was confronted by a German officer. The German shot him point blank in the chest. The German was killed, but Parry survived. He ended the story saying that the first thing he would do in the hereafter would be to ask the German why he had shot him. We liked Cannon Parry and his wife Margaret. Gregory was impressed by the solemn dignity of Canon Parry celebrating Communion.

In early 1965 Tobruk was an interesting ruin although the sunken Italian warships had been removed from the harbor. We visited the caves the garrison had lived in during the siege. The one hotel was so awful Josephine told the boys that if they dropped anything on the floor to leave it there. Due south of Tobruk is the village of Mekhili, a World War II desert British strong point we visited on a later trip.

Going and coming along the beautiful Via Della Vittoria we passed through Derna, the site of the 1804 battle between William Eaton, the American Consul in Tunis who mustered a small army in Egypt, and the forces of the Ottoman Bey of Tripoli. Five American Marines out of seven with Eaton were killed, buried there and are the source of the reference to Tripoli in the Marine Hymn. The five were subsequently moved to a small cemetery for infidels near the Palace of the Crown Prince, east of Tripoli. In a Veterans' Day speech I described the Marines' burial site this way:

A small, tidy cemetery, not on any American Battle Monuments Commission list, nestles, hot and dusty on the North African shore of the Mediterranean. Treeless, barren as the desert, nevertheless, it is to my mind a memorial garden. A high, plain mud brick wall encloses a dozen or so graves of foreigners, mostly seamen. The caretaker, a wizened, ancient Arab in a straw hat, shapeless clothes and homemade leather sandals, will unlock the hand wrought iron gate for visitors he deems suitable. He lumps together Europeans and Americans as infidels. Inside we stop by one large, neat, chest-high, stone-covered tomb, the clean white sand around it swept clean with artistic care. That old Arab has the best job in the world, caretaker in a cemetery where American heroes lie and takes his job seriously. The silence is palpable except familiar notes from a distant bugle seem to echo the Marine Hymn, "...to the shores of Tripoli," but it's only the desert wind. In this tomb are the remains of the five U.S. Marines killed while fighting the Barbary Pirates at Derna. Two other Marines lived to fight another day. The pirates were eventually taught not to bother us.

* * *

West from Derna we climbed to highest level of the Green Mountain at Baida close by the ruins of Cyrene. Adjacent to the ruins in a grove of magnificently tall cedars, are workshops and residences built by archeologists over the years especially, the Italians. An American archeologist, Herbert DeCou, was murdered here by Arab religious fanatics about 1900. His simple headstone is incongruous in the middle of the ancient Greek necropolis. The house known as the "Director's" house, now a summer residence for our ambassador, is large and comfortable. Although in WWII the Germans and Italians on the one side and the British Empire troops on the other passed through Cyrene several times they left it unscathed. Even the furniture is as it was before the war. At this altitude it gets cold here in winter. Other quarters, used for guests, although not so large, are warm and comfortable. A museum houses beautiful Greek statuary and mosaics representative of the inhabitants of two and a half millennia ago, which lie around helter-skelter in stages of repair halted by World War II. Founded in the eighth century B.C. by a prince and his followers from Athens, Cyrene flourished for a thousand years. Its location centers on a wonderful freshwater source, the spring of Apollo. Many foreigners, especially Americans, including yours truly, collect the water in bottles to take home. It is great for coffee. Repairs have been attempted by foreigners but Libyans are not interested in the works or history of infidels, who are fit only to be killed.

An honorary Turkish consul has a consulate a few miles from Cyrene. He must be the sole remnant of four hundred years of Ottoman hegemony in Cyrenaica. His combined office/residence has a charming site on the fertile rolling Green Mountain. On the road from Cyrene I was caught in a hailstorm, which filled the gullies with so much hail it looked like snow.

Ancient Cyrene must have been a wonderful place to live, not only because of its lofty, incomparable site but also because its society, which included a Jewish colony, was a cultural, artistic and religious center. Simon, an artisan, who helped Christ is a good example. From almost any viewpoint the Mediterranean, three thousand feet down and ten miles away, with an occasional coastal steamer or schooner passing by, is clearly visible. All in all I would love to live there, even today. We know that at least three of the inhabitants, models for the Eighth Century B.C. statue of the Three Graces, were lovely young nubile women. The city must have been full of them and their equally handsome brothers.

It is exciting to drive down the escarpment on the hairpin curves of an Italian road masterpiece to the ruins of ancient Apollonia, now Susa. One can swim in the clear water among columns standing along a Roman thoroughfare lined with the remains of shops drowned when the land sank beneath them. The 20th Century intrudes in the form of oil puddles and gummy balls staining rocks and sand along the shore.

The guest quarters in Cyrene were full of Embassy people so we stayed in the hotel. Like Shahat, the present day village, the hotel was unscathed by WWII. We were given Room 21, the best room in the hotel reserved for "VIPs, reserved then for Marshal Rodolfo "Butcher" Graziani, governor of Italian Libya, the Libyans blame him for deaths by starvation of tens of thousands of Libyans at Mersa Bregah.

On his one visit to Libya the room was used by Mussolini himself. We all, IL Duce and the Tinnys, slept in the same bed, at different times, and they changed the sheets. Holding all five Tinnys together it was the biggest bed I have ever slept in. It was bigger even than Lillian Trasher's bed in Assiyut. The bathroom had a German "geyser" hot water heater which produces boiling water instantly. Josephine badly scalded one leg in the shower. The hotel, run by Tunisians, was comfortable and the cuisine with all fresh ingredients, reflecting a love-hate relationship with colonial Italy, was delicious.

From Cyrene we continued westward on a mountain road to Tolmeta. A recent rain brought out fields of yellow flowers. In ancient times this was Ptolmetia, with Greek origins and control by the Greek Ptolemys, heirs to Alexander. They ruled Egypt from Alexander to Cleopatra, the last Ptolemy. North Africa had a brief revival under the Roman Emperor Justinian in the sixth century defined by shrunken city sizes, useless walls and tiny Roman (Byzantine) Christian churches with mosaic floors. Savage Arab hordes of the seventh and eighth centuries flying the green flag of

Mohammed easily obliterated the remnants of emasculated Greek and Roman culture and urban civilized life in North Africa for the next thousand years.

From Tolmeta we continued west to Tocra where we rejoined the Via Della Vittorio. Tocra has a picturesque little fort, which resembles a medieval castle. This fort commands a long straight stretch of the Via which goes directly into Benghazi. It is indicative of the tenuous hold the Italians had on Libya that they had to live in and move from one fortified place to another. The Italians tried policing Libya with policemen and soldiers recruited in Somalia and *vice versa,* but it didn't work. Their hold on the Somalis, who are even more mean-spirited than the Libyans was no better than their hold on the Libyans.

To begin this next episode let me say I started shaving regularly about the time of Pearl Harbor, and for the next twenty-four years any after-shave lotion was fine. Starting after March 27, 1965, and ever since I have used only Original Skin Bracer by Mennen. It is a fine lotion, a deep rich green, astringent, and it smells good. However, the real reason I use it is this:

In early 1965 tension and rhetoric between the Arabs and Israelis was at a seasonal peak, which was to lead in a year or so to the Six-Day War. On March 27, 1965, Egypt's President Nasser asserted on the radio *Soat al Arab* (Voice of the Arabs) that the United States was arming Israel through West Germany. Nasser ordered his *fedayeen* commandos active on the Egyptian-Israeli border to attack American and other Western interests everywhere in the Arab world, "tonight!" As luck would have it, a West German freighter, SS *Koenigsburg,* was then in Benghazi. It carried cargo for the Libyan Army, but the stevedores had refused to unload it. While I was on a trip to the port area, they threw rocks at my car, the still fairly new Chevrolet, but most missed. The situation was ready made for the *fedayeen.*

To worsen the debacle, a destroyer, USS *DuPont,* arrived that day, despite my attempt to stop its long-scheduled "Friendship Visit." They told me our relations with Libya were sound. The king and our ambassador are "buddies." I wasn't the only one blind to fanatical Arab revolutionary nationalism.

With an Egyptian consulate general across the street from me, by looking out the window Egyptian intelligence was good. Minutes after *DuPont's* arrival, *Soat al Arab* broadcast that an American warship had come into Benghazi to protect a West German freighter in an Arab port, "proof" of Nasser's assertion of U.S. arms for Israel. The harbormaster maliciously docked the *DuPont* behind the freighter. I demanded the ship move out of the harbor and remain at anchor until the *Koenigsburg* departed. After conciliatory gestures by Germany and Libyan Army goading the stevedores unloaded the ship and it left.

Out of the early morning mists the USS *DuPont* hove to off the harbor entrance. The captain and the squadron commodore wanted in. They and other officers came ashore in the captain's gig. I took them to call on the crown prince, governor, mayor and army commander. All seemed quiet, so a first liberty party was brought ashore. On the second day after the *Koenigsburg* departed the *DuPont* came into the fuel dock on the far side of the harbor. Local officials called on the ship and public visiting commenced.

Too late, the *fedayeen* and their Libyan cohorts had set in motion a series of bomb attacks, beginning with my residence. This night a reception at the political officer's residence, less formal than the official greeting the night before at my residence, was bright with the gowns and jewels of the ladies, the sparkling white and gold braid of the Navy, the khaki and gold of the American, British, and Libyan armies. Some of the Libyans wore their traditional native costume.

The bomb's blast blew in the eight-foot-tall heavy wooden double doors at the entrance, split the marble and stone sill, scattered furniture, and shattered the nearside of my car, parked in front. Lamps on either side of the door had been blown away. They were replaced but were slightly askew thereafter.

The *fedayeen* then blasted the hallway apartment entrance to the nearby West German Consulate General. The Germans, more experienced than I, were better prepared and always kept an iron safe behind one half of their double doors. The *fedayeen* placed their bomb on that side so the blast reflected outward. The Germans sustained damage to one door and no injuries. The bombers were unscathed, but must have gotten a good scare. The doors of the apartment across the hall were blown off their hinges.

The *fedayeen* destroyed two Land Rovers and the garage at the British consulate general. Consul General Robert Dundas was at our party. The attacks on the Germans and British came while the authorities were at my residence. The *fedayeen* attacked through the rear and hurt no one.

The *fedayeen* set one tank afire at the Esso tank farm at Mersa Brega. Returning to Egypt across the Western Desert they damaged six producing oil wells jointly operated by British Petroleum and Texas oilman, Nelson Bunker Hunt. The manager for "Bunker," as he was known, in Libya was George Williamson, a young Texan. Williamson and I had a close relationship and we worked together on the ramifications of the various bombings. Later on Williamson proved to be a very good friend indeed. His voluntary intercession on my behalf a few years later saved my life.

In all twelve bombs had been detonated with obvious care to insure no Libyan was injured.

Josephine and I learned of the bombing in a telephone call from our son, Clayton, a mature twelve. He and his brother, David, ten, had arrived the day before from their English public school. Our youngest, Gregory, eight, lived with us.

Clayton said on the phone, "They have bombed our house and I have taken charge at the scene. Oh, yes, the Embassy in Tripoli called and I told them we were all right and that you would call them." Bravo Clayton!!

He carefully reassured us that neither he nor his brothers, nor anyone else was injured. He said our Libyan maid and Libyan Army guards had vanished before the bomb exploded. The Egyptians wanted no Libyans injured and blood feuds incurred. Now, CyDef troopers in battle dress, a mixture of paratrooper and Texas Ranger uniforms, ringed the Residence and consulate office.

Led by Clay, the three boys had done well, as we saw when we arrived after a fast drive across town by our expert Libyan driver, Yunice. The mayor of Benghazi, the governor of Cyrenaica, police and Army officers were comfortable in the sitting room drinking Coca Cola, American style, with lots of ice.

At the time of the attack, the boys had been in that room, located right above the entrance. Glass French doors opened onto a small, Mussolini balcony. Had the bombers targeted the balcony instead of the door below they could have injured, or—and I cannot contemplate the thought—killed all three of my sons.

The captain of the *DuPont* refused my request he said that night, citing his orders. He did recall the crew and cancel further liberty; so much for "Friendship Visits." Strong, vociferous Libyan public and private sentiment favored the Egyptians. I made certain new "orders," had the *DuPont* underway bright and early the next morning. Clay, David, Gregory and I, helped them cast off and waved, "Good bye."

The only State Department acknowledgement of the bombing was a belated cablegram from Assistant Secretary for Africa G. Mennen Williams, called "Soapy," ex-governor of Michigan and scion of the Mennen cosmetics family. He expressed outrage at the incident and his personal concern for the safety and well being of my family and me.

For this reason, I use only Original Skin Bracer by Mennen, to say "Thank you, Soapy."

At the end of March an article in the *Tampa Tribune*, datelined Bonn, Germany, wrongly reported bomb attacks had been made on the German and American consulates in Tripoli, not Benghazi and by Libyans, not Egyptians. The report added, correctly, that the German consulates in Yemen and Syria had been attacked and that the German Consul in Aden, who we knew well, had lost an arm to a hand grenade. The International Edition of the *New York Herald Tribune* also had a small squib on the bombings in Benghazi. Two weeks later another article appeared in the local *Key West Citizen*, which got it right. My cousin, Leslie Salisbury, the U. S. Customs Inspector there, sent me a clipping. Efficient Leslie later had the *Citizen* publish a subsequent letter I had written to him on the incident. Department of State efforts to squash reports of the incident were to no avail, at least, in Key West.

On April 12 the *ad hoc* or, preliminary inspectors, moved in to give us a practice run before the official Inspection. They stayed with us so we had them twenty-four hours a day. Our sons were very well behaved during this period. Our cook deserted us at this inopportune time. So, Clay started getting up bright and early and making coffee for everybody. It was the best coffee I have ever had.

The inspectors liked it too because I do not remember any adverse findings in their report.

Clay and David had an exciting holiday. I thought the bombing a high point, but they may have favored the visit and tour of the Wheelus Air Base near Tripoli. We visited the five Marines' graves. Clay went on one of our pigeon-hunting safaris and relished the pigeons his mother roasted. He banged away at pigeons with my ancient twelve-gauge, double-barreled shotgun and missed but vowed to try again.

Clay and David flew to England via an East African Airways "school" flight loaded with British schoolboys from east Africa, with its last stop in Benghazi. The boys offloaded here and while waiting to reboard congregated in the lounge. All were sitting in groups except for one boy sitting alone. Clay and David decided to see why he seemed to be ostracized and went over to speak to him. When they returned Clay said, "He's the luckiest boy on the plane. His father is the pilot and he gets to ride in the cockpit."

During our hot summer weather, a tramp freighter with a deceased seaman who had requested to be buried at sea put into Benghazi. Familiar with the port, I easily located a tug with a crew not violently averse to helping a Christian burial. The chaplain with the British regiment, admitting it was his first burial at sea, agreed to officiate. We chugged due west out of the harbor until the captain of the tug said we were in deep water. The tug had no fathomer and I didn't have a chart so, I took his word for it. With the tug rolling, the chaplain consigned the body to "the deep." We came about and headed for home.

During the summer we had a string of houseguests, starting with Barney May (Mrs. James A., wife of the embassy political officer who had given me such a hard time on the day I arrived in Benghazi) and their teenage son. After Ambassador Lightner departed, Hermann Eilts became chargé d'affaires, *ad interim*, pending the arrival of Ambassador Newsom, and spent a month or so in Baida. Of course, he and wife Helen must come to Benghazi, where he stays with us. Conversely we go to Baida but stay in the guest quarters or hotel. (I did stay with the Eiltses one night in Tripoli.) Nicholas Lakas, the commercial attaché in Tripoli, language student friend from Beirut, wife Eleanor, and their two sons tagged along with the

Eiltses. John Billings, a political officer in Tripoli, and family also stayed with us. Ambassador Newsom arrived in mid September and spent a night with us. He and his wife Jean were pleasant and good company. They did reciprocate when we were in Tripoli.

To help us keep track of the time it was soon once again British Memorial Day, Sunday, November 14, and time to place another wreath at their cemetery. I have about eleven months left in a normal two-year tour. Meanwhile life goes on outside my national and international diplomatic responsibilities, such as four days of nonstop affairs for hundreds of guests to meet our new ambassador and his wife.

Getting Clayton and David to and from their school in England usually required a two day trip to Tripoli. Problems with clothes and other items kept Josephine busy. For short school breaks we found "holiday homes" in England, sort of a recommended bed and breakfast usually with a retired couple, satisfactory. In Benghazi Gregory wanted a pet. First we got him a rabbit. Something went wrong with its ears and it died. Next we tried a "pi" dog puppy but it got lost. When George McCurry, my Administrative Officer, was transferred they gave us Inca their half-Siamese kitten. Inca had fleas. Friends, self styled experts on Siamese cats, told us Siamese have tender skins and cannot tolerate fleas. We tried special shampoos with only temporary effect. We ordered cat flea powder, vitamins and other medicine. Inca bit a little girl, Beth Stevenson, daughter of an American contract basketball coach here on a USIA grant, and Josephine. They both took the series of anti-rabies vaccinations. They survived, Inca died. We did finally get a Siamese cat, Barney (no relation to Barney May) but it was Josephine's pet, not Gregory's. We inherited Barney from the Esso Libya, General Manager, Hugh Goerner. Barney was large, twenty-five pounds, and awakened us every morning with a high-flying leap from the bedroom door, which he could open, onto our bellies or heads, his choice. Barney was well traveled and on Esso planes got the copilot's seat. We wanted to keep him but a subsequent Esso General Manager declared Barney Esso property so we took him to Esso in Mersa Bregah. Not for forty years did we find another cat as vicious and tyrannical as Barney, but he was not as big and had no flight training.

My Corvair was a continuous source of irritation. It was no surprise that with such poor representation American car manufacturers had an invisible share of overseas car markets. Finding headlights—real necessities in the pitch black, narrow byways of Benghazi—windshield wiper blades, and other bits and pieces was time consuming. Charging the air-conditioner with Freon was another challenge.   Let me explain: I got a can of Freon through the mail. The hose valve that punctured the can and controlled the flow of gas went on the compressor too easily. I turned on the car engine, turned on the compressor, opened the valve, and nothing happened. The sight glass should have been clear but showed a sickly yellowish liquid or gas. The weather was cool so I abandoned my repairs on the air-conditioner. Maybe by next summer the Egyptian *fedayeen* will have put my Corvair and me out of our misery.

On December 8, 1965, a "friend" paid me a surprise visit that ruined my life. The memory of that day keeps me awake at nights, grinding my teeth in frustration, with no end in sight. The fatal blow was delivered by that "friend," Colonel Warren Phillips, G.S., Chief, Army Section, Military Assistance and Advisory Group in Libya, and Chief of the M.A.A.G. in Benghazi. In a December 9, 1965, letter to the Chief of M.A.A.G. on the subject, "Non Cooperation, Diplomatic Representative Benghazi Branch Embassy." The first two sentences of Col. Phillips' letter read: "I approached Mr. Tinny with a request to contact the police on the behalf of the Williams family. He refused to act."

The story is that an American boy named Dunn, who lived in Belawn Farms, a British enclave, was raped by Libyan boys. A neighbor boy, the son of M/Sgt. Williams, was forced to witness the incident and told if he reported it he would be killed. The Williams boy did report the incident to the school principal, Mr. Davis, the police, and his parents. Later, he reported seeing one of the Libyans involved at the school. I had been informed of the incident and had discussed the matter with Mr. Dunn and turned the matter over to the police. All of the Libyan boys had been arrested but only the principal culprit was still confined.

Mrs. Williams, not the Dunns, demanded a police guard from Phillips, who had to act. His complaint went up the ladder to the top. Phillips says he telephoned to say that he was coming, but, if so, I never got the message. Harriet failed me this time. I was, unfortunately, "busy," when Col. Phillips walked into my office. Phillips wanted a policeman stationed in Belawn Farms. There are differing reports of our conversation, and eventually, at my suggestion, Phillips went to the police. My mistake! I should have gone. None of these details change the main thrust of Phillips's complaint that I was uncooperative. I have no defense. Phillips's charge is true and damning. To use Hume's comment on his ruin, "My goose was cooked." Not only was my goose burned to a crisp, I had done the cooking.

A highlight of our stay in Benghazi, oblivious to impending doom, began in 1966 after the Fourteenth Libyan Independence Day, December 24, 1965. Five Tinnys piled into a four wheel drive Chevrolet carry-all and accompanied by Harriet Lovett, my secretary and Victor Maffei, Communications, Code Clerk, in a British Land Rover, took off on a two week "familiarization" safari into the desert.

The carryall was lent to me by the USIS office in Benghazi, courtesy of George Naffei, the new public affairs officer. Equipped for off-road travel it had four wheel drive and two extra large gas tanks. To even the load, on the front bumper I hung a British Army wall tent with a double roof and canvas floor and the cots and blankets necessary to comply with Josephine's request I keep her and the children beyond the reach of snakes and scorpions. That load was topped off by five-gallon German, "jerry cans." Inside, we had the five Tinnys, liquid gas, one burner stove, and two weeks' supply of canned food and water. The roof rack held a bottomless wooden box with a toilet seat attached to the top, straw mats and a shovel.

In the Land Rover Vic and Harriet carried a kerosene prinus stove, more food and water and "jerry cans" of gas in outside racks. A couple of the latter were originals, twenty five year old veterans of Rommel's Afrika Korps, emblazoned with swastikas.

I had gathered an assortment of tools, tire repair kits, air pump and spare tires with inner tubes for each vehicle. We used it all. Everyone had extra clothes and personal items.

We made Tobruk, about 300 miles, the first night and camped south of town on the road to Jaghbub. The carryall was not running well. I dismantled the carburetor, cleaned out the sand and debris and put it back together. Surprise, not only did the engine run, it ran better. We topped off our gas tanks as we did every chance we had. Both cars are gas hogs.

Jaghbub, about 175 miles southeast of Tobruk is the principal shrine of the Libyan Sennussi Sect and the burial place of the Grand Sennussi, founder of the Sect. Except for the last fifty miles into Jaghbub the area had been mostly cleared of land mines. In the distance across flat desert plains towards Egypt and the Siwa Oasis, the remnants of Mussolini's 400-mile barbed wire fence were occasionally visible. Useless, the fence neither kept anyone in nor anyone out.

The tomb of the Grand Sennussi and his wife while not particularly impressive in size was beautifully decorated with tiled walls and marble columns from Egypt. More surprising were large lakes, which we came upon without warning. There was no beach. The edges dropped off like the sides of a swimming pool. The water was perfectly clear but we didn't trust it, there was always danger of *bilharzia*. The place seemed deserted although it wasn't.

The boys were well behaved and had jobs. Clay, as the biggest and oldest had the worst one. When we stopped he was to take the bottomless box with the toilet seat on top, the woven mats, the support poles and the shovel to a spot of his own choosing a few hundred feet downwind from the campsite. He was then to dig a hole as deep as he could easily, place the box over the hole. Dig smaller holes for the poles to hold the mat screens around the box and pile of sand. He left the shovel there and the toilet paper. He hated that job and David would not even consider it.

The job needed doing and in the end usually fell to me. Clay equated it with latrine duty and at his age it was too much like punishment he didn't deserve.

Our plan now was to head west across seventy-five miles of open desert until we struck the route of a proposed oil pipeline and then follow it north back to the coast. We would cover a big slice of desert without too much risk of getting lost or breaking down with no help in sight. I had discussed my plan with the general manager of the pipeline contractor and promised we would stay clear of his traffic, an occasional truck, but close enough to get help if we needed it.

This was hard, flat gravel plain, perfect for the tank battles and maneuvers of World War II when the British Eighth Army and the Afrika Korps tried to out flank each other by going south into the desert, away from the coast. There were patches of sand dunes that had to be detoured around without losing track of the pipeline and always keeping alert to marked minefields. Distances and directions in the desert can be deceptive. The terrain was hilly enough with dips and gulleys so that a vehicle would drop out of sight in an instant. We each kept track of the other vehicle. We had both magnetic and sun compasses.

Desert driving was always touch-and-go. Sometimes a soft spot would show vehicle tracks, which appeared and ended as mysteriously as they had begun. One thing that would have done us in was the *fesh-fesh*. This is more than just blown sand; it is like talcum powder but appears hard and has sharp edges where ridges break. Like quicksand, areas of *fesh-fesh* are, in effect, bottomless and to be avoided at all costs. Because of the dust clouds moving vehicles raised, I had mandated that when one of us approached the other, the overtaking vehicle should come up downwind. Vic and Harriet always followed me, but when they wanted something and overtook me, they came up on the windward side. Harriet was showing her displeasure at my remark that I was in charge of the expedition.

The idea for the trip had been Harriet's. Throughout the trip our relations had been harmonious and decisions were a matter of consensus. However, I felt that there might come a time when someone had to make a decision and that person should be me. To get her revenge she liked to bury me in clouds of dust especially when I was standing outside. She also appointed herself chief cook.

Desert travel was slower going than on the road south. Along in the second day, January 1, 1966, we came upon the 1942 WW II battleground of Bir Hakiim, Hakim's Well, the southern pillar of the British Gazala Line, composed of British "boxes." "Boxes" were based on the British square used at Waterloo in 1814, which shows how far British military thinking had advanced in 128 years. Theses boxes, or "forts" a mile square or more were ringed by minefields, contained fuel and supply depots, artillery and were intended to be strong points. There in a patch of desert which became the huge battlefield known as the "Cauldron" was a large "box" dubbed, "Knightsbridge. " A British Guards Regiment held the north and on the south, Bir Hakiim, was held by General Pierre Koenig's 4,000 man Free French Brigade.

The French forces now called themselves the Fighting French, *La France Combattante*, and this brigade had come up from Fort Lamy, Chad. According to Alan Moorehead these men were a mixed bag and had come from as far away as Indo-China, the jungles of West Africa and as close as the French held parts of North Africa. Most were French soldiers but many, neither French nor soldiers, included Poles, Czechs and Americans. Many of the troopers were ethnic Germans of the French Foreign Legion who, reportedly, fought well. The brigade had been armed and supplied by the British and during Rommel's all out attack in early June 1942 twice were re-supplied. Bir Hakiim was not a suicide stand but it was critical and might have been the key had not the whole Gazala Line crumbled.

The French held off the Afrika Korps for ten days of fierce fighting. If Bir Hakiim fell Rommel could claim the entire desert south of Tobruk and make the British position untenable. At the end 2,000 of the French managed to fight their way out. Koenig and his two female drivers, were the last to leave as Rommel's *panzers* crashed through en route to Tobruk and El Alamein. The Afrika Korps would be hours away from Cairo and the Canal. German motor-cycle outriders roamed the streets of Alexandria.

The French had been well dug in and mine fields protected the fort's perimeter. When we were there the center was a cemetery enclosed by a low stone parapet. The extensive minefields were marked by strands of wire strung between wooden stakes. I had to continually caution the boys not to step over any wires. In this dry desert mines in British and German "mine marshes" stayed alive for years so many still lived. Mine disposal teams from Bulgaria and Hungary had dug up millions of mines but not all.

I know Americans had fought at Bir Hakiim because three graves grouped together and set apart were identified as, "Americans." I like to think that one of them had been "Rick," Richard Blaine, known to us as the proprietor of Rick's Cafe Américain in Casablanca. (We know Blaine was a fictional character, or do we?) If one is Rick, who, I wonder, are the other two? The Frenchman, Louis Renault, Casablanca's Prefect of Police, maybe buried with his compatriots or maybe he escaped. As he once said, he blew with the wind; he was a survivor. Someone had to survive and come back to tell the tale.

From Bir Hakiim we continued north for a while then planned to turn west, just south of the major airfield at El Adem, a World War II airfield and now a major British RAF base. We wanted to stay in the open desert but travel parallel to the coast. We stopped short when a tire on the Land Rover blew out.

The damage to the tire was beyond the capacity of my repair kit and somehow the Land Rover's spare tire had been "misplaced." We agreed to leave Vic and Harriet with their vehicle and take the tire in the Carryall to Tobruk for repair. It was about midday and they had plenty of food and water if we were delayed. In Tobruk we were lucky and quickly got the tire and tube patched and inflated. The trick was to find Vic and Harriet in the trackless desert. Actually, the desert was covered with tracks.

I had exactly measured the mileage, noted the compass directions and we all had picked out favorite landmarks along the way. In the gathering dusk everything looked different. The terrain was undulating enough so that when we got to where we thought the Land Rover should be, there was nothing. I thought they had stopped on a high point, but maybe not or had they moved? With our bright lights on, using the horn intermittently and with Clay as a lookout clinging precariously on the roof rack, I cautiously began to circle in the moonless dark.

The best thing in the world is not brains, physical beauty or personal charm but just to be lucky. Whether it was their luck or ours as we drove up a low mound down into a gully, there sat Vic and Harriet nonchalantly enjoying coffee and a cigarette. Vic said they had moved to get out of the wind. We were glad to see each other and camped right there, "out of the wind."

We were now headed for the town of Mechilli, a crossroads of ancient Bedouin caravan routes, sometimes called "the heart of Cyrenaica," and another World War II hot spot.

As a focal point of battles for two armies, the Afrika Korps advancing triumphantly east before retreating west and the British Eighth Army doing just the opposite, there was not much left standing of the towers of Beau Geste–style Fort Mechilli. The scattered, straggly village and battered date palms bore vivid scars of war. Their mere survival attested to the hardiness of these trees.

In a clear area beyond the few tumble down mud houses of the town a group of boys were playing soccer, their ball a bundle of rags. Clay, David and Gregory took this pitiful sight under advisement and in unanimous agreement gave the boys their brand new black and white soccer ball. Bravo boys!

We headed west from Mechilli, on the long southern slopes of the *Jebel Akhdar*, Green Mountain. Mostly hard gravel plain, we had to cross wide, north-south, dry river beds which carried the runoff from the downpours in the mountains. This was dangerous country because this was still monsoon season and an unsuspected flash flood could be upon us without warning. We were warned when we came upon a flood in full spate. Perhaps a quarter mile or wider but only a few inches deep in places there was no getting across it. Going south would put us in soft going as the water soaked into the sand and going north would put us into rougher, rockier, hilly terrain. We were exploring along the eastern bank of this "instant" flash flood river when another horn blast from Vic brought us to a stop. We circled around to the Land Rover and this time it was not a flat tire, he had lost a wheel. Sure enough the lug nuts had come loose and the wheel collapsed. Our three boys scampered along Vic's track and did find one or two nuts. We had jacks and wrenches to do the job and got the wheel back on, easier said than done. I cannibalized a lug nut from each of the other three wheels. Vic and I checked all the wheels.

These repairs were time consuming and we decided to camp where we sat. We had been traversing a rather steep slope when the wheel came off. Farther down towards a dry river bed was flat ground more interesting and comfortable for camping with clean white sand, almost a beach. I vetoed any idea of moving down. One thunder burst in the mountains miles away could drown us all.

In the Yemen, while we were in Aden just a year or so ago, a party like ours was lost exploring close to Ta'izz. The leader was the British chief pilot for Yemen Airways, a World War II veteran of the desert war who should have been knowledgeable on flash floods. They had been in a ravine, traveling in the dry stream bed which made comfortable driving. With little warning, at least, not enough, a distant rain burst caught up with them. With no way out they tried to outrun the water. They failed and all five drowned.

West of Mechilli we were in great sand dune areas. Several times we found large piles of unused Italian artillery ammunition. Much to the boys chagrin I had to warn them off because if only one round had been live it would have been one too many, sorry boys.

We spent fourteen days in the desert and covered 1300 miles, almost 100 miles a day circling sand dunes and dodging minefields. We got international notoriety on the trip after the BBC correspondent in Libya learned of it and interviewed Clayton and David on their world news program in February. Clay was reserved and reticent but David talked a blue streak and our safari lost nothing in the telling.

Seven years later while we lived in the Persian Gulf emirate of Umm al Qaywayn, Clay hosted a radio music and talk show in Dubai he called Fly-By-Night Music, Inc. He was not afraid to talk on the radio and offered descriptive music lore and commentary. Some of the music was composed by him. In November 1979, having survived bombings, blinding sand storms, jungle and desert safaris, Clay was killed driving home in the wee morning hours of Veterans' Day when in a *petit mal* seizure he smashed headlong into an unforgiving oak tree.

In Tripoli James J. Blake had replaced Herman Eilts as deputy chief of mission. Blake later turned out to be a good friend. Paul Geren was the new counselor for economic affairs. With Ambassador Newsom leading, all three commute back and forth between Benghazi, Baida, and Tripoli. The Sixth Fleet scheduled another "Friendship" visit by a destroyer. This visit went off all right.

Nick Lakas, the commercial attaché in Tripoli brought in a C-130 Hercules cargo plane with a Lockheed salesman as a passenger.

They planned to sell ten of these to the Libyan government.

In our local diplomatic corps, British Consul General Robert Dundas was replaced by Peter Wakefield. There was also a flurry of weddings among the staff at the Seventh Day Adventist Hospital. This staff, headed by Dr. Ludington, is where we get our medical care.

Throughout the spring an early summer the consular corps in Benghazi and the expatriate community were determinedly active with cocktail parties and dinners. Even Hume and Nancy Horan in their mountain redoubt of Baida and Cyrene were not immune. At the end of June Hume's replacement, Sam Keiter, arrived with wife Betsey.

I met Sam Keiter and family at the airport and got them off to Baida. Subsequently, I introduced Sam to the consular corps and started them on the social whirl. The Keiters had a tough act to follow after the Horans but did well despite a minor calamity. Their two children had brought a beloved cat from Tunis, their last post, carried it through Washington consultation and home leave and safely to the airport at Benghazi. In the excitement and jostling at the airport, the cat escaped from his cage. Sam and I and anyone we could enlist made a diligent search but the cat was gone. Settle for what you can get and like it. The young Keiters had to settle for a Libyan cat.

Josephine and Gregory flew out of Benghazi on June 23 on East African Airways for London where they will rendezvous with my mother. Clay and David were in school in Eastbourne. With inadequate understanding of where to meet they almost missed each other but, with the luck God gives to amateurs they met on the escalator going in opposite directions at Heathrow Airport. They will look at other schools for Clayton, get David resettled and Gregory introduced to St. Bede's. After a few days in Eastbourne giving Mother her first look at England via Booth's Commercial Hotel, now owned by the Oldfields, with Josephine driving they were off in a rented car

The personal recommendations that happily had led us to St. Bede's three years earlier were missing, except for one not taken, this time Josephine's unfamiliarity with the schools led us to put Clay in first, one poor choice, Hurn Court, and again in a second poor choice, Christchurch. Later on we did find a much better school on a personal recommendation for Gregory in Bishop's Stortford College, south of the fen country north of London.

June 1966 was the last completely satisfactory month of my life. On July 2 while entertaining Ambassador Newsom and his party from Tripoli, Vic Maffie, handed me a letter, addressed to me, marked, **"To be opened by the Addressee only."** If I expected orders to a new post or anything good I was to be bitterly disappointed. In terse, unemotional, and unequivocal terms the letter announced my "retirement" from the Foreign Service. It was due to the, "exigencies of the service."

According to my daily diary, July, August, and September were busy with embassy people and departmental visitors coming and going one right after another; but to me that period is a blur. To house and feed them with Josephine gone and no Clayton to make the coffee was a real chore. They didn't get Josephine's high quality of care. Servants were of minimal help, and the other consulate and M.A.A.G. wives were not to be seen. I was on my own. My attempts to reverse the department's decision were useless to begin with. There was neither appeal nor amelioration. The deciding straw that broke the camel's back was my failure to act as Warren Phillips had asked, as described in his letter of December 9, 1965.

Before Phillips there were others who piled on equally heavy straws. These are some of those who are identifiable. Genial Walter Chapman in Cairo mistakenly believed I had deliberately asked to get out of Cairo and resented me for that. In Aden my alleged inhospitable treatment of Flinner, Richardson, and Vaughan had given heartburn to high levels of AID people. Adrian Middleton and John Wheelock with their own skins to protect had fed the flames. The CIA and rangy, redheaded Jones found me abrasive. All had their own agendas. Some rose to my defense. James J. Blake, who replaced Hermann Eilts, wrote a spirited helpful letter to the department. Of course, there were several things I would have handled differently had I been more thoughtful. George Williamson, Nelson Bunker Hunt's manager in Libya, was the only one who stood by me. Three years later he was the most helpful.

***

Italian nuns had been housed in the apartment we occupied and part had been a convent school. I was now living there alone. It was behind the consulate and across the street from the Egyptians. Sometime, either in the halcyon days of Italian hegemony or the brutal days during the war, but before all the Italians in Cyrenaica were unceremoniously shipped to Italy by the British, one of the nuns was murdered in these quarters. Whatever her crime was, if that was a motive for her death, the facts were unknown. Her killer was never identified. Worse from a religious point of view would be the possibility she committed suicide, the oft told story, more rumor than fact, was not precise on these details..

Her ghost had haunted the place for thirty years and had been heard hurrying up and down the long hallway connecting the bedrooms. In these days two years later at the tag end of my tour, after Josephine and Gregory had left for home, it was just me and the nun. The ghost was my steady companion.

Josephine and the three boys were touring southern England with my mother. They attended the public installation at Dover Castle of Sir Robert Menzies, former prime minister of Australia, who succeeded Winston Churchill as Lord Warden of the Cinque Ports. They would then catch the SS *United States* at Southampton for the crossing to New York.

Back in Benghazi during this period I did not give them the bad news and spoil their holiday. Late one night after having been invited out, and sitting alone in my bedroom I heard someone scurrying down the hallway outside my door. The story of the ghost was familiar but the sound was so clear I thought it could have been an intruder or someone with a message. I plainly heard the padding of rapidly approaching soft soled footsteps on the bare floor, the swish of clothing, along the wall, the clicking of something wooden or metallic. I grabbed my .45 Colt automatic kept handy since the terrorist attack last year, flung open the door and dropped to a crouch, ready for what? The uncarpeted shadowy passage, dimly lit by a light at the far end was barren and silent. My heart pounded, disappointed, and back in my room, I dropped into my chair. Had I heard the ghost of a murdered nun or what? After this introduction

she became my best and most steadfast companion. It was too bad
she hadn't been a cook.

A welcome interlude of a few days interrupted my busy final three
months. I called it murder but the evidence is circumstantial. The
unfortunate victim, a nodding acquaintance I will call Leroy, was a
tall American oil worker from Texas where everything is the tallest
and best. He was happy-go-lucky when things are going right,
his way. Like most of the oil field workers he worked hard but
when things were not going right he could turn mean and ornery.
He worked in the Esso concessions, for a contractor company,
headquartered in Mersa Bregah. He was unaccompanied by
family, and spent his free time in Benghazi, at the Palace Hotel, best
described as scruffy, boring but tolerable..
    On the day of his death he was alone, driving north on the
coastal highway from Mersa Bregah to Benghazi, about 120 miles.
Here Libya's coastal highway, the Via Bella Vittorio (Via Balbia),
north of Agedabia was straight and level for eighty five miles into
Benghazi.
    This area was the scene of the February 1941 battle Between the
British and main Italian army, south of Soluq, west of Beda Fomm.
The British killed and captured all of Graziano's 20,000 man strong
army. For the first time of five times in the war the British had tenuous control of Cyrenaica.
    Leroy was about thirty miles south of Benghazi's southern out-
skirts. This area had been crossed by the British, Germans, and Italians but the road itself used by both sides was not an actual target.
Forces on the road of the other, enemy side, were legitimate strafing
targets by the British or the Germans. The Germans desperately
planted mines alongside the road during their final 1943 retreat.
    The paving had been worn by heavy wartime traffic and repairs
were haphazard some good, some bad. Crumbled along the edges
and narrow by our standards it was basically a good road. Italians
built excellent roads, smooth and straight, but asphalt is not up to
ancient Roman levels of durability. Kilometer markers were frequent and there were the occasional abandoned, once defensible,
stone rest houses. The country here was coastal plain, there were

no shoulders on the verges of the road, nor ditches. Sparse under-brush, which once allowed Libyan marauders to ambush Italian convoys had been cleared but there were groves of tall and sturdy eucalyptus trees. This stretch of the Via, like many other stretches from the Egyptian border to Tunisia, was designed for speed, in fact it encouraged speed. Not only are Italian roads built for speed, the fearful, albeit motorized Italian colonists in Libya, had found that one of their best defenses against Libyan guerillas on horse-back was speed. On a hill east of the road and overlooking this long straight stretch of it was a picturesque but pitifully inadequate Ital-ian fort, also long abandoned.

With no traffic in sight in either direction, on a hot, dusty bor-ing stretch of road Leroy drove with windows down and gas pedal floored in his big two-door pickup. The report given me by an Arab (Palestinian) Esso employee at the site the same day went some-thing like this:

As the road entered a grove of trees, he crossed the highway to the west, went off the road, at great speed, passed between trees for a couple of hundred feet, then slammed sideways, on the driver's side, into a great eucalyptus. His bare head banged into the upper door jam and he was killed instantly. His hard hat, caps with the company logo, along with a small duffle bag were on the seat with him. The truck was only damaged on the lefthand front door where the door hit the tree and was drivable.

I saw the truck and the accident site. There were no skid marks. There was, in fact, nothing to see. I did not see Leroy. It was a hot, late summer day. In a manner not explained to me, nor in an ex-plicit time frame, news of his accident had reached Mersa Bregah. In a matter of hours his body was quickly taken there and put into refrigeration.

I don't believe this story as told to me. In my two years here this stretch had been the scene of other fatalities, although none Ameri-can. The area was popular for groups drinking bootleg whiskey, which led to many accidents. If the bottle didn't contain alcohol, it contained something even worse. I don't think Leroy had been drinking; the truck had no whiskey odor, just the stink of sweat and oil.

In other cases, a cause for curiosity, there were rutted tire tracks, marks on the tree. Recently a Fiat sedan with five Libyan youths had run off this stretch of road, smashed into a tree, and had broken into two very separate pieces, each going off on different sides of the tree. All five were killed. Telltale ruts and other signs on the ground of this latest accident were plain to see.

Was Leroy's truck traveling sideways? There was no evidence that it was—the ground here was firm with good traction. I believe Leroy was lured off the road by men who wanted him dead for reasons of their own. The dispatch with which Leroy was handled after the accident indicates the presence of others. I do not think he was killed by religious fanatics as was Herbert DeCou. Leroy was certainly not an Israeli sympathizer. He likely did engage in the crude but popular sport of Texas-style teasing and patronizing Arab "ragheads." Libyans are proud; they will not do servile work. They harbor grudges.

Once out of his truck Leroy was hit hard by a heavy bar, pipe, or long-handled wrench. Precious little hair and blood were stuck on the upper door jam under the roof. This was the wrong place and a telling piece of evidence. My first thought was that there was too little blood and a smear that had no hair and did not look right. Leroy was not a weakling or infant. A blow to kill a strong, healthy young man like him would need to be very severe. My second thought was, if the truck had been in motion when it struck the tree, why wasn't he thrown forward, onto the steering wheel or windshield. And why was he going sideways, and if he was, where were the gouges and skid marks in the dirt?

There was nothing for me to do. His employer quickly spirited Leroy's body out of Libya. I subsequently wondered why they bothered to tell me at all. No report of his death or the accident was made in Libya. Obviously, the police had never been involved or even informed, and I was not obligated to tell them their job. The Arab Esso employee who told me about the accident did know but, probably, had told no one else. My visit to Mersa Bregah was to no avail. The company was sorry for the man's death, of course, but, "pardon us, please," we have work to do. Leroy's personal effects for me to inventory, a familiar consular chore, had disappeared except for the duffle bag. My report on the death of an American citizen had blanks and no hint of foul play. "Cause of death," a one-man road accident. There was no point in making a fuss, involving others, and creating an incident that could have become bad news for the companies involved. In a welter of vague circumstantial evidence it was equally possible there was no "murderer" to be brought to justice. I did discuss the case with my new political officer, the successor to Paul Jones, and the resident "spook." He did not argue with my analysis but was noncommittal.

It was macabre that my Foreign Service career began and ended with two deaths that looked like murder to me. Leroy reminded me of day one in San Pedro Sula and the death of Jack Briscoe a decade ago. There, I had hoped to learn, but my forensic investigations then and now led me nowhere.

With Leroy's demise apart, my final departure preparations proceeded in earnest with my daily routine of business. Everything seemed to be as it should. After the departure of Harriet Lovett I had a procession of temporary secretaries who were strangers to me and to Benghazi. In the way of short timers, the routine of greeting friends, and enemies was a travesty of what had been some of the happiest days of my life. Thankfully, nothing lasts forever, and Friday, September 30, 1966, 4:00 pm, the end of my twenty-fifth month in Benghazi, was the sailing time for the Italian packet steamer, *Citta di Livorno*, on its regular run to Naples. I would be on it.

Here are the highpoints of my schedule on September 29, 1966, my last full day in Benghazi. At 6:00 am and already up, I was trying to organize what must be done today. Foremost was to write final performance reports and say goodbye to the staff, American and Libyan. At 9:40 am I was informed that the flamboyant, Black Prince, a powerful, maverick member of the Royal Family, was arriving at 10:00 am on a US Air Force plane from Wheelus and I must meet and take care of the group. He was bringing two U.S. Air Force doctors to tend to the broken leg of Prince Sadiiq Abiid, O.B.E. his brother and my friend. Sadiiq Abiid, an Officer of the Order of the British Empire, was opposite in character from the Black Prince and influential in his own right. A year or so later he visited me in Washington and I introduced him to strawberry shortcake.

With Yunice at the wheel I made two round trips to the airport. The first followed a long, princely lunch, the second, at 6:00 pm, was after the broken princely leg had been set and I had gotten the party boarded. I watched until the plane was safely, "out of sight," as I would have done for a courier. This was my last appearance as the American Consul in Benghazi and the final official act of my career as a Foreign Service officer.

My shipboard going away party was low key and perhaps for that reason, quite pleasant. Anthony Santiano, the egotistic but efficient consulate administrative officer came alone to the *Citta*. Tony was a decorated crewman in World War II on the noted Long Range Coast Guard Cutter *Spencer*. In the North Atlantic the *Spencer* had forced a German U-Boat to the surface and had captured it. Tony bid me farewell and left to meet Sigrid for yet another cocktail party hosted by one of the British Army officers.   All the British liked Tony. He was gregarious with a rehearsed, Buffalo Bill Cody persona. His attractive wife, Sigrid, was a German Valkyrie out of Wagner he had met during the occupation of Germany. With unaccented English, Sigrid was a perfect foil to Tony's outrageous Wild West image. Buffalo Bill had been popular in England and they could not get enough of Tony in that role.

Earlier I had talked to George Williamson who begged off coming down to the *Citta* to keep a family commitment. Subsequently, George and I corresponded to my great benefit but more later.

Major Ralph "Rafe" Nickson, a senior officer, and long time member of the British Military Mission (BMM) to Libya was also present to represent the Mission and its chief, Brigadier Lough, who was going to the same party as Tony. No Colonel Phillips, no one from our M.A.A.G. came.

Rafe belonged to the Black Watch Regiment, who, along with the Gordon Highlanders, in triumphant pursuit of Rommel led the way into the open city of Tripoli on January 23, 1943. This night Rafe's familiar, colorful Black Watch trews and bottle of Chivas Regal whisky served to brighten a colorless occasion. At the, "all ashore," as he was leaving, Rafe ceremoniously presented me a regimental BMM necktie with the dark red and green Libyan national colors. I don't know if he intended it for the American Consul or for me, but I still have it. British are adept at short farewells, they know how to leave.

Benghazi was not only anticlimactic in my life but not even good drama. Conversely, Hume Horan's life reminds me of Hugh Conway, the hero of James Hilton's 1933 novel, *Lost Horizon*, and a glorious jaunt on the Golden Road..

Hilton wrote in *Lost Horizon* that at Oxford, just before the Great War began in 1914, his protagonist, Conway was an outstanding student and scholar. He had a likeable, peculiar charm, a sort of winsomeness so that those who met him always remembered the occasion vividly. An Oxford don called his school record "glorious," so he became "Glory" Conway. This sounds like Hume Horan and his outstanding record at Harvard in his undergraduate and graduate years.

Both men had many talents and a surprising familiarity with a variety of subjects and did well at whatever they put their hands to. Both had an effervescent combination of mental and physical prowess. After four horrendous years on the battlefields of France, Conway joined the British Consular Service.

In the mid 1920s the American State Department combined its Consular and Diplomatic Services into one Foreign Service, but the British kept theirs separate. As an American Foreign Service officer Hume nevertheless held himself distant from consular work. His talents and driving ambition led him to move upward into the arcane, glamorous international policy and political assignments.

Conversely, in my own Foreign Service career, it came to me too late that I was more suited to consular work. These are the mundane, grubby jobs. That was clear in San Pedro Sula and Aden, but the siren song of political reporting clouded my judgment. Surely, life in the political section was the Golden Road to Samarkand. I wouldn't admit that the low road of consular work might have served me better.

Here we have three young men starting off on similar quests. Hume Horan and the fictional Hugh Conway are bright, talented, sophisticated young men with every advantage. Language proficiency, a touchstone for success in either facet of Foreign Service, came easily to these two. For me, the third man, trying to emulate those two was a fatal mistake.

In the meaningful but convoluted and artificial life Hume and I had chosen, the pangs of ambition drove us blithely onward. He was too good, and I was not good enough. Our transitory successes led us to disaster. When he was sworn in as Ambassador and Minister Plenipotentiary, A.E. & P., to that dark corner of black Africa, it must have been bittersweet

As for me, the titles American Consul in Benghazi and Senior American Representative for Cyrenaica were also bittersweet. Hume accepted his fate as did Conway with a "passionlessness" that was part disillusionment and part clarity of mind. Lacking that clarity, I was lost.

Hilton saw Conway as a wanderer between two worlds divided by his wartime combat experience, as was I, and we floundered in both. Hume had no wartime combat experience with that dividing line between personal worlds it creates. Perhaps it makes no difference, because in the end my wartime experience didn't help me. Instead, Hume had overwhelming self-confidence in his one world. He may have been superior to me, but in one respect I have been luckier—I have survived longer.

In the 1970s and 1980s while Hume was glorying in his first tour in Saudi and being "knighted" (his word) in darkest Africa, my fortunes also turned better thanks to a staunch friend, George Williamson. After two years in Washington assigned to the Department of Commerce, George, now an executive in Occidental, recommended me to Dr. Armand Hammer, chairman of Occidental Petroleum Corporation.

Dr. Hammer offered me a job in the Persian Gulf that was too good to turn down. After three years with Hammer, the Continental Oil Company (Conoco) offered me better prospects. For the next twenty-five years I was able to return to the desert and walk again on the tops of great sand dunes and roll down their sides. Josephine and I do not walk on a Golden Road to Samarkand, but these years were golden.

Sadly, in June 1982 George had an aneurysm in the left front temporal lobe of his brain, two and a half inches long. He lost most speech, vision, and comprehension. It was a slow death. Fortunately, between Nelson Bunker Hunt and Occidental, George had done very well financially. In October 2008, a caregiver wrote his last words to me, "I do not know you…" He had been a faithful friend and colleague since October 1964. He did as much for me as any man could when I most needed help.

Thanks to Dr. Armand Hammer, I lived on the southern littoral of the Persian Gulf, the Trucial Oman I had explored ten years earlier on my field trip. That was a joy and I am grateful. With Conoco I returned to Libya, for a time as acting president of Conoco Libya. I climbed again the immutable dunes of the Great Sand Sea.

From their crest I now had a clearer view of a familiar landscape of windswept dunes. As before, I let golden grains of sand run through my cupped fingers, eternity's hourglass, and disappear into the infinity from whence they came, as do human lives. The dirge of the sands stills the tumult raging in my head. True desert dwellers facing the unknowable submit. "*In sha 'Allah*," they say, "as God wills." Not a true desert dweller I did not submit. Not before and not now do I know the will of God.

In my mind's eye I see my first post, the God-forsaken San Pedro Sula. The words of the director general with his haunting, provocative question set the tone for my career and my life: "Just where is San Pedro Sula—Mr. Tinny?"

The golden but narrow and uneven road on which I saw life and death in fetid jungle and dry desert sands may have led to Samarkand, but it wasn't for the likes of me. I never found Samarkand.

I know where San Pedro Sula is, and I will give you a hint. It overlooks the spectacular grandeur of Mother of God Mountains. It is inhabited by philanderers, gun-toting *pistoleros*, fugitive Nazis, Afrika Korps generals, beautiful *Valkyries*, Josephine with her newborn, and, last but not least, Mrs. Williams.

You hold in your hand my fading memories, fragments of a life at once reflected in a mirror with only one surface but with two sides, now shattered. One side led to Samarkand, the other to San Pedro Sula. These fragments are fitted together to reflect a few of the events and passions on my quest. I never reached that goal with which Ruth teased me when she said, "You could be an ambassador."

The enviable Hume Horan was an ambassador four times over, but Ruth, I don't envy him. San Pedro Sula, prostrate under the shroud of Don Pedro, was the beginning of an exciting search for a road that in the end has led me, and now you, to this place. Sometimes the sunsets have a golden glow.

Sorry, Ruth, *ave atque vale.* Thank you, Josephine.

Notes

1 Summer 1956, First Post, First Week

1. Ruth was then secretary to the U.S. ambassador to Greece. Under the Truman Doctrine, we were helping the Greek government in its civil war and its guerrilla war against the Communist Yugoslavs. On a reserve cruise, we had delivered 300 fighter planes in a roundabout move to Yesilköy in Turkey. Ruth, true to the end, wrote that she still had faith in me.

2. A humorous parody of the written exam, entitled "Weeding out the Dummies," in the *Foreign Service Journal* of June 2008 had "sample" essay-type questions. Here are three: **Political Science:** Start World War III. Report its sociopolitical effects, if any. **Epistemology**: Take a position for or against truth. Prove the validity of your stand. **General knowledge:** Describe in detail everything you know. Be objective and specific.

2 The Visa Mill

3. Columbus still thought he had reached the East Indies. This tree was considered native to Asia.

4. In 1924 the Rogers Act combined the separate Diplomatic Consular Services into one Foreign Service. The "diplomats" dealt with" national policy" matters while consuls dealt with "commerce, seamen and the like." The Rogers Act equalized salaries and made members of both services career Foreign Service officers "subject to promotion based on merit." The president kept his Constitutional power (Art. II, Sec. 2.) to appoint ambassadors, ministers, and consuls with the advice and consent of the Senate, but he could not insert such appointees into the *career* service. In the way of all flesh, and diplomats, no one was going to go quietly, and some differences were preserved. For example, on June 14, 1956, I received three commissions, nominated and appointed by the president, by and with the consent of the Senate. One made me a "Vice Consul of Career," a second made me a "Secretary in the Diplomatic Service," And the third tied it together and made me a "Foreign Service Officer of Class Six." As

an "attaché," a diplomatic title, Smith could not sign a visa, but as "vice consul," he could.

5. During my dozen years in the Foreign Service, the number of those killed in the line of duty reached at least 150. They are listed on plaques in the department's Diplomatic Lobby, beginning with William Palfrey, lost at sea in 1780. Victims of tropical diseases are not listed. Victims of "lead poisoning"—a bullet in a vital organ, by mistake or not—are plentiful. Of those victims, I knew George Curt Moore in Khartoum, 1973; Roger P. Davies in Cyprus, 1974; and Malcolm H. Kerr in Beirut, 1984.

8 Aden

6. The current regiment, 1st Battalion, King's Own Scottish Borderers (KOSB), dates from 1689. For over three hundred years the KOSB was a revered regiment in the British Army, Lt. Col Alistair Thorburn now commanding. Amalgamated with another regiment, at this writing it is now the 1st Battalion Royal Regiment of Scotland. In World War II, a KOSB officer, John Tiltman, at the Government Code and Cypher School, broke the Nazi SS, police ciphers, and, just before D-Day, the German teleprinter code. Tiltman, one of the best of the code breakers, proudly worked in the purple and green tartan trews of the KOSB. Our first Sunday, all-day curry lunch was hosted by Col. Thorburn and the KOSB; it was the standard by which all others curry lunches were measured.

7. Johnson has published two books that I know of: *Full Circle* (Ballantine Books, 1964) gives a complete understanding of combat fighter plane tactics. These were developed in World War I through the Korean War, where he flew with the U.S. Air Force, and the Cold War to the mid-1960s. *Wing Leader* (Stoddart, 1956) is the record of a brilliantly successful fighting career in the air from the Battle of Britain to victory over Germany and beyond. He gives a modest, straightforward account of the life. (His life was one of "the few... to whom so much was owed by so many.")

8. In August a familiar ship, the USS *Bigelow*, DDL 942, remembered from La Ceiba five years before, came down from the Mediterranean to join the Third Fleet. Designed as a destroyer leader, *Bigelow* now flew the burgee as flagship of Destroyer Squadron Sixteen (DESRON16). Commander Bruce Flory had replaced Audley McCain as captain, and Captain James M. Palmer was squadron commander. Bob Pond brought his destroyer, USS *Perry*, through Aden on October 7 and on into the Indian Ocean.

9. I think that most of the crews of the ships coming in, leaving the delights of the Mediterranean and the excitement of being part of the huge

Sixth Fleet, with its carrier battle groups, regarded joining the tiny Third Fleet as some sort of penance. However, the Yemen's September *coup d'état* and the saber rattling by Egypt's Nasser and the Soviet's Khrushchev in defense of the fanatic and nationalistic Yemen Arab Republic (YAR), in defiance of the British, should have livened up life in the Third Fleet's domain, and it did. In October we had the destroyer USS *Meredith*, under the command of H. L. Smith Jr.; November brought the USS *Power*, under Robert S. Hayes, flying the flag of Commander Destroyer Division (COM-DESDIV) 142 Captain D. M. Carcher. For a change we had a submarine, USS *Sailfish*, SS572. In December we met the destroyer, USS *Lloyd Thomas*, C.O., Al Van Archer, on January 5, 1963. The USS *F. T. Berry* arrived on January 25, in company with the USS *Duxbury Bay*, under Captain John M. Nutler. The USS *Greenwich Bay*, with P.A.M. Griber, Third Fleet Chief of Staff, relief for the *Duxbury Bay*, came in February. In March, USS *Haynesworth*, C.O., R.C. Light, carrying Commander Destroyer Division 222, came in headed east. My notes fail me again as to the destroyers Semmes had with him. In the area were USS *Fisk*, C.O. Cyrus H. Butt; USS *J. K. Taussig*, C.O. Grant J. Walker, carrying Commander Destroyer Squadron 36, CDR Carol A. Turner; William L. Read brought in the USS *Van Voorhis*, a DE.; and R. J. Mallow brought in the *Hank*. In May the *Harlan R. Dickson* stopped by, and Fred Kelley brought in the USS *Forrest Sherman*, both en route to the Indian Ocean.

10. Lt. Colonel W. B. Thomas, D.S.O., M.C., called "Sandy," was likeable and gregarious. He possessed a remarkable ability to get on well with Arabs, especially his own troops, although he spoke little Arabic. I think he earned his D.S.O. (Distinguished Service Order) for his role in the escape of seventy-three RAF POWs from the German Stalag Luft III near Sagan in March 1944. The main story (minus details) was told in the movie *The Great Escape*, with Steve McQueen and many others. Thomas stayed in the Army and retired from Singapore as a major general. The D.S.O. ranks fourth below the Orders of the Garter, Thistle, Bath, and the St. Michael and St. George.

11. Wheelock entered the Language School in Beirut six months after I did. A Princeton graduate, he was six months older than I. He married Anne Hendy-Pooley, an Australian, and they had three sons. From 1943 to 1946, he was on active Navy duty. He joined the State Department in May 1950 and missed Korea. He served in Paris with the ECA. Other posts were Basel, Nouméa, the State Department, Aleppo, Jerusalem, and Doha. He took a huge 1960 Thunderbird convertible, referred to as the "Blunderbus," to Beirut and then shipped it to Aden. It was probably the only one in Arabia. I found in the 1950s and 1960s the Arabs favored Cadillacs, as they were dependable. Wheelock retired from the Foreign Service

about 1980 and, unfortunately, switched from Thunderbirds to compacts. In 1981, on Bradley Blvd. in Chevy Chase, he was broadsided by a heavier car and killed. Josephine and Anne have stayed in touch.

12. The Aden Women's Association, which Josephine had been asked to join by Lady Charles, wife of Sir Charles, speaker of the Legislative Council, who did many good works among the poor of Sheikh Othman and spent much time there. Josephine spoke of the "nappies" (diapers) and the sleeveless garments suitable for young boys and girls that they had made and distributed along with soap and other things. Josephine saved the clean scraps and later stuffed three full-sized quilts, each with a white nylon blanket.

13. Stookey belonged to an early class of Arabists. After language school in Beirut, he served as principal officer in Basra, political officer in Cairo, where I first met him, and now Ta'izz. After the October revolution in the Yemen, our Third Fleet spent a lot of time in the Red Sea. In classified radio traffic, Stookey was garbled into "Snookey," which the Navy took to be a code name and used it as such. Service in Ta'izz sounded a death knell for three Foreign Service wives: Louise Stookey, Orietta Scotes, and Catherine Sizer. Like Wheelock's Thunderbird, Stookey's Baldwin Grand was one of a kind in South Arabia.

14. Sizer is a capable officer, knowledgeable, likeable, and efficient, with an innate dignity. Harry and his wife Catherine were a sophisticated couple who always knew the best restaurants. He had two enviable posts at opportune times. In addition to Ta'izz, the long defunct consulate in the Sultanate of Muscat and Oman was reopened and upgraded to an embassy. Harry was deputy chief of mission, his last post. Now a widower, Harry and I have met and corresponded over the years.

15. First minted in 1751, the 23.4-gram coins are 1 5/8 inches in diameter and are dated 1780, the year of the death of the buxom empress, whose image is popular with Arabs and Africans. They have been used as a political weapon, and in World War II both sides furiously coined thalers At least 320 million had been minted at this count, and more are minted in Vienna at a rate of 3 million per year. While I was in Aden, Egypt confiscated 300,000 thalers at Suez and melted them down for the silver.

16. Actually Badr survived and joined royalist tribesmen in the mountains.

17. I never could discover whether or not any of these ships carried nuclear weapons.

18. In 1967 Aden and the Protectorates proclaimed themselves a Marxist state, the Peoples' Democratic Republic of Yemen, and a Soviet ally. Aided by the Saudis the royalists fought the Yemen Arab Republic, aided by Egypt, until 1970, at a reported but impossible cost of 150,000 lives. In

a three-cornered war the two Yemens and the royalists fought each other until united, May 21, 1990. Southern secessionist tribal entities rebelled in 1994 but were coerced into submission by northern forces. An amended constitution dates from September 28, 1994.

19. Thomas J. Abercrombie, 1930–2006, is remembered in a six-page obituary plus six full-page photographs in the *National Geographic Magazine*. He authored forty-three articles for the magazine. In 1965 he converted to Islam and made the *Haj*, the pilgrimage to Mecca. Tom's hallmark is that each article has a photo of an attractive woman.

20. Crouch was stationed at Dhala farther north along the frontier at a six- or seven-thousand-foot elevation. He and his wife, Lynette, were a handsome young couple whom I had met on a familiarization trip. They were both children of Kenya settlers but had emigrated during the Kikuyu uprising. Lynette was a pretty, petite blond who sunbathed in the nude, or so I was told. Her body, at least the small part I saw, was covered with a light peach fuzz. Michael, also blond, habitually wore a .38 caliber revolver. When I discovered that a rifle being demonstrated by a Dhala tribesman had the inscription "Property of the United States Government" engraved on the barrel, I mentioned it to Michael. That night at dinner, Michael showed me his pistol. It had the same engraving. We arm the tribesmen and their British overlords indiscriminately.

21. Sir Charles Johnston wrote *The View from Steamer Point* (Collins, 1964), which recounts his service in Aden and the Protectorates. After a brief interregnum, he was succeeded by Kennedy Trevaskis (later, Sir Kennedy). Trevaskis was considered the sire of the federation. Five months later, on December 10, 1963, as Sir Kennedy was departing to attend a conference on the Federation, he was the target of a hand grenade thrown from an upper window at Aden Airport. George Henderson, one of the most redoubtable of the political officers, saved Sir Kennedy from serious injury but in the process received a mortal wound and a bar on his George Medal, posthumously. I arrived late, but I believe that the grenade was thrown by Abdulla Asnag, leader of the opposition Trades Union, who was seen at an upstairs window.

22. Johnson came to Ponte Vedra in January 1992 on a book-signing tour. I have two of his books, *Wing Leader* and *Full Circle*. We reminisced about our time together in Aden.

23. About this time the KOSB (the King's Own Scottish Borderers), with whom I worked in Aden, in Benghazi, and finally in the Trucial Oman (later the United Arab Emirates) and considered good friends, were transferred. Their replacement battalion was from the Fifth Royal Inniskilling Dragoon Guards, otherwise known as the "Skins." They were good to have around, and we followed along together to Libya.

Index

www.ingramcontent.com/pod-product-compliance
Lightning Source LLC
Chambersburg PA
CBHW020656270326
41928CB00005B/148